Back to

HAUSFRAU AT

With friendly greetings

John Wendel

February 1997

THE AUTHOR

HAUSFRAU AT WAR

A GERMAN WOMAN'S ACCOUNT
OF LIFE IN HITLER'S REICH

by

ELSE WENDEL

in collaboration with
Eileen Winncroft

The Pentland Press Limited
Edinburgh • Cambridge • Durham

First published in 1957 by Odhams Press
This edition published in 1994 by
The Pentland Press Ltd.
1 Hutton Close
South Church
Bishop Auckland
Durham

ISBN 1 85821 209 X

Printed in Great Britain by Redwood Books,
Trowbridge, Wiltshire

CONTENTS

ILLUSTRATIONS

Foreword
by Hans-Peter Hoppe
Pastor of the Dietrich-Bonhoeffer Kirche, London

This is a book of 'Erinnerungen', the German word for 'remembrance'. This word 'Erinnerungen' incorporates the word 'inner', meaning that we keep something in the very inner part of ourselves.

With the word 'Erinnerungen' we express what goes on in those inner parts of us; images before our inner eye let things become contemporary that were long thought to be past.

For us younger people, it is important that such Erinnerungen are taken to the surface and talked about. Only in this way can we learn about them and from them. There is a huge difference between reading in a historical book about the figures of death that war has left behind, and coping with the names of 'Feldmarschällen' (Field Marshals) and 'Generälen' (Generals) who seem to have lead the war on their own, and someone telling us that it actually was women and children who did not lead the war, but suffered from it.

Else Wendel is meritorious in her factual account of her own experiences in wartime Berlin, to let us have a part in this dark chapter of our history. The avoidance of any dramatic exaggeration and the point of view from [down below] lets the report of this contemporary witness become even more impressive.

The book does not try subsequently to excuse German guilt for the tragedy of the Second World War. It shows, in the connection of historical events and personal experiences of a woman and mother, the point of view of an 'ordinary' human being during the Third Reich.

Fifty years after The War, we still talk about the necessary reconciliation. It can only happen when those inner images of us, beyond all barriers of language, become words and actions, and 'Herr und Frau Schmidt' and 'Mr and Mrs Smith' start to share their lives.

1

Waiting for Richard

"It's a boy," said the nurse softly. My eyes were closed. I was too exhausted to open them yet.

"Come along, wake up, wake up!" It was the doctor. "Aren't you happy to have a son? He's a lovely baby—heavy too—nine pounds . . . come along open your eyes and have a look at him."

Slowly, and with infinite effort I opened my eyes. Dr. Martin—tall, fair, blue-eyed, stood there in his operating robes, holding my son; my second son. He held the bundle towards me. "Perhaps you would rather have had a girl—this time?"

That question woke me up sharply. "No," I said quite loudly. "Even if I had five children, I want only boys." I was now quite conscious.

At last it was over and I was out of the operating room and being pushed slowly along the bright corridor to my own room. As I was trundled along I strained my eyes to try and catch a glimpse of my husband. I saw other men pacing up and down, holding big bunches of spring flowers in their hands. I did not see Richard.

"Has there been a 'phone call from my husband?" I asked the nurse.

"No, not yet."

"Has anyone 'phoned?"

"No, not so far as I know." She looked down at my face, and added quickly, "but I am sure your husband will come as soon as he can, perhaps tomorrow."

"Yes," I repeated after her, "tomorrow."

That night I could not sleep, tired as I was. I could think
only of Richard—would he come, would he 'phone, was he
thinking of me, or of our child? I lay quietly on my back
looking at the ceiling. Surely he would come? Richard did
not come. Nor was there a 'phone call. My parents were in
Italy, they had been there since the early spring, now it was
the end of April but they had not returned.

Uneasily I turned my head towards the window. Outside
in Berlin there was brilliant sunshine. The birds were singing and the excitement of spring was in the air. Now I had
two children whose father did not care whether they were
alive or dead. How would I be able to bring them up? If
only I had a flat, I thought. Richard had left me so cruelly
and suddenly that I had not been able to keep up the expensive house in which we lived. All I had been able to do had
been to leave the big house quickly, store the furniture, and
rent one small room for myself and Wolfgang, my first son,
who was two years old. But where could I go now that I had
two sons, and no husband or help of any kind?

There was a knock on the door. It must be Richard
coming to see me to say he was sorry, wanting to see his son
and asking to begin a new life with us, telling me he still
loved me. . . .

It *was* a father, but not Richard. A man, both arms full of
lovely roses, rushed into the room. He went quickly to the
bedside of the young woman next to me. He was so moved
and so happy he couldn't say a word to her. He kissed her
tenderly. I turned my head away quickly. No, I thought, I
won't cry. It's weak and stupid to cry. I began to pray that
the woman on my other side (there were three of us in this
room) would not receive a visitor. I couldn't bear that, but
the door opened again and a father, all smiles and loaded
with flowers and gifts, came in and embraced his wife.

I could only look up at the ceiling and cry.

The visiting hour seemed to last for ever. I became
feverish and restless. At last, a nurse came in and asked the

visitors to leave. The young mothers protested, for they could not believe that their time for visiting had passed so quickly.

The nurse took my temperature. "Don't you feel well?" she asked. "Your temperature has risen? Are you in pain?"

"No," I said. "I have no pain."

Dr. Martin arrived. "Where is your husband?" he asked.

"He is very busy," I said.

"I see," he said slowly, sitting down by my bed, "but is there nobody else we could inform about the birth of your son?"

"No, no one."

"Where are your parents?"

"In Italy."

"Have you brothers or sisters?"

"Yes."

"Do any of them live in Berlin?"

"Only my sister."

"Would you please give me her address and telephone number?"

It would make little difference to me, I knew, but still he insisted, and I gave him Hilde's address.

Weeks later I learned from Hilde that Dr. Martin had 'phoned and asked her to try and contact Richard, and in any circumstances to tell him that all was not well and that his presence was essential.

The night came again. I could not sleep. Bitter thoughts were rising in me now. Why was it that men had such advantages in life? They could produce children and yet take no responsibility for them. My lawyer had said that times had changed and nowadays no one made any fuss about a divorce. Why should two people be unhappy and chained to each other for life if they find they are not the right partners?

"But the children of the marriage," I said, "what happens to them?"

11

A contemptuous smile crossed my lawyer's face. "Every mother thinks she is indispensable. Have you never visited one of the marvellous new *Kinderheim* (Institutes for Children) of the State Welfare Department? I assure you no individual mother can ever take such care of her child as they do. Take your children there. If you can prove you have no money then everything will be completely free."

I thought over all my very practical lawyer had said. He had completely swallowed the idea of the *Muttertier* (mother-animal) which Hitler was so successfully planting in the minds of the German men and the idea that all a child needed was regular food, good housing and proper clothing. "Look here," he added, "you are intelligent and attractive. What's more you have plenty of sex-appeal. After the birth of the baby you can take both children to the *Kinderheim* and then begin to enjoy life again. Forget this marriage. Get over your troubles with a nice new adventure." My lawyer had chuckled at his joke as he made it.

I lay there in hospital going over this conversation again. As he had spoken the words I had felt the child move in my body. Joy and despair had run through me. No, I had determined, I will not take your advice. Somehow or other I will keep my children. I won't have them brought up to be like you. But that was several weeks ago. Now I had the hard facts to face, and I was tired and ill.

As the long hours of the night went on, I began to weaken. Wouldn't it be easy and nice to take the children to the *Kinderheim*? To step out of this hospital in ten days' time into a May morning, and just hand over my responsibilities, and then go off, get new clothes and be young again!

But my baby, and my little son Wolfgang? How would it affect them, a cold, institutional upbringing; would they not become just like my lawyer in the end? Cold, hard and unable to love any woman? Of course they would. I had got to find some other way out. Richard? I must win back Richard's love. Then in the hot night I saw the plain facts.

Richard had been living with a girl for months. He was only waiting for our son to be born to have his divorce and be free to marry her. I had promised I would not oppose a divorce. Everything had been ready for the divorce before I went into the hospital. I must be mad to dream he would ever return to me, want me, or love me.

All right then, he did not love me. He loved this new girl. But surely he would come and *see* his son? And if he came wouldn't he at least try to help me find a flat or see us sometimes so that the boys still had a father?

A flat? That was a real and desperate problem. There were so few flats in Berlin, none that I could afford. But Richard was a Party member and Party members could get flats. If he came, then I should beg him to find us a flat. It must be nearly four o'clock I thought. My thoughts had dropped lower and lower. All I worried about now was a flat. It was the last hope left in me.

"Don't marry him," my father had warned. "He'll never be a good husband or a good father. He's an artist."

Richard had laughed at this.

"It's not that he's bothering about, it's my being a member of the Party. Too risky, your father thinks . . . he's a typical business man, all he cares about is how much I've got in the bank. No ideals at all."

In the end I had married against my father's wish. He had refused to come to the wedding and had forbidden my mother to come. And here I was. I was as alone and forsaken as if my children were illegitimate—had no father. I nearly jumped out of my bed at this last thought. Why, that's what the hospital might be thinking, that my husband had refused to come—that my parents were away, simply because this was *not* his child. Richard *must* come. He could not shame me like this, or his son.

That night was one of the longest in my life. In the morning when the nurse came I was bathed in perspiration. She was in a hurry and did not lose much time in asking, "How

13

are you?" But after taking my temperature she stopped bustling and spent quite a few moments cross-examining me about my sleep, pains, and so on.

Soon Dr. Martin arrived. I was taken for a special examination. I had a high temperature and for seven days parts of my body were paralysed. I was given injections, a special room to myself although I was only a "third-class" patient. Sleeping tablets were permitted.

That afternoon my youngest sister Hilde came. Immediately I sensed that there was something wrong. She tried so hard to be cheerful—too hard. She asked a whole lot of questions about baby and about me. But Hilde did not deceive me. I knew her cheerfulness was forced.

At last I challenged her. "Have you seen the doctor?"

"Oh, yes, I happened to run into him." All said a bit too quickly.

"What did he say about me?"

"That you didn't sleep last night."

"What else?"

"That he was making an exception and letting baby stay with you all the time. He *is* a good little baby, isn't he?" She turned away to gaze at my son.

"Did he speak about Richard?" I asked outright.

Hilde hesitated.

"Please tell me the truth. What does he think? Does he think I have made a mistake . . . over the baby, I mean?"

Hilde explained, "Else, you must be mad. What on earth are you talking about? Why should he think such a thing?"

"Because Richard has refused to come to see me; he hasn't even 'phoned. They may know we are having a divorce . . ."

"Darling, don't be so silly. The doctor thinks the world of you. He said you were too brave, that was your trouble. If only you had screamed or given way at the birth, you might not be paralysed now."

My young sister looked so upset and indignant about my

14

crazy idea of an illegitimate baby I had to smile in the end. I imagined how amused Richard would have been. "What a bourgeois you are," he would have said. "Whatever difference does it make whether the baby is legitimate or not? Don't you realize we are at the beginning of a new era?"

"How will you name this new age?" I had once asked him. "The Brown Age?"

Richard had been annoyed. "It is the era of the Nordic superman. It is led by our Führer," he had told me angrily.

"And I have the honour to be married to one of them?" I had commented at the time.

"You certainly have," Richard said, taking my would-be joke quite seriously. "Look how the women run after me."

I can remember how astonished I had been at this remark. Up till then I had taken all the chatter about the Nordic superman as a joke. I did not dream that any intelligent man took it seriously. Too late I learned that flattery will mislead even the most educated of men—provided it is repeated often enough. And to look at, Richard was certainly the ideal of Nordic splendour. He was very tall. He often boasted that he was taller than one of Frederic the Great's bodyguard famous for their stature. He had fair hair, his eyes were blue and his shoulders very broad. He had a deep, velvet voice. A virile, strong and superior man to look at. When Richard stood conducting his orchestra, he had won the hearts of half the female audience before he even lifted his baton.

Did Hitler realize the danger of all this Nordic nonsense, I had wondered of late. And how could he believe in it himself when he cut so insignificant a figure? As for Goebbels —Richard himself had told me that secretly Goebbels was called the *Schrumpf-Germane* (the shrinking Teuton). All these thoughts were rushing through my mind again now.

"Why do they never talk of the super-woman?" I asked Hilde.

"Are you sure you feel all right?" Hilde quickly put a

cool small hand on my hot forehead. "Would you like me
to ring for the nurse?" She looked worried. Of course she
had not been following my thoughts at all.

"Answer my question," I insisted stubbornly. "Why don't
they ever talk about a Nordic super-woman?"

"I wish they would." Hilde tried to joke. "Then I should
certainly be one!" She picked up her mirror and looked at
herself.

"*You* wouldn't pass the test though, darling."

She was only too right. I was dark, and my eyes were not
a nice bright blue. Several times Richard had suggested I
dye my hair blonde as the others did. But I had refused.

"*I* will tell you why they never talk of a super-woman. It's
because they don't want one. She would compete with the
men. They want to reign alone in their glory. Women are
just to be creatures to make love to and bear the children.
That's all they are worth. Then the children are to be
handed over to the State Welfare Department to be brought
up. We are to be animals. . . ."

"You shouldn't take it so seriously just because
Richard . . ." Hilde halted. She looked nervous. Obviously
her tongue had slipped.

"Go on," I encouraged her. But Hilde was silent. "Because
Richard has left me in this degrading way. Is that what you
were going to say, Hilde? By the way, have you seen or
spoken to Richard?"

"No."

"But you wrote to him, didn't you?"

"Oh, yes," Hilde hastily replied. "Of course I informed
him. But I have been told he is not in Berlin at the moment."

It was a lie, I could see that. Hilde could never tell a lie
without giving herself away.

I turned my head aside and said nothing. There was
silence in the room. When I looked up again Hilde's blue
eyes were filled with tears. Now I knew there was no hope.
It was quite clear. Richard did not care in the least whether

I, or his sons, were dead or alive. He could not even bring himself to send flowers. Nothing. Just nothing. Worse perhaps. He would probably be greatly relieved to learn that I *had* died in childbirth. It would make things so much simpler for him and his new love. No divorce, no scandal, no nagging conscience. He would perhaps like me dead. And why not? Why not die? What was there to live for? I had a high fever already. It shouldn't be difficult to get a higher one. I hated being a mother-animal. I hated it.

"Else," came Hilde's gentle voice. "Please do try to pull through, for your children's sake. Don't leave them alone. The doctor says if you would only have the will to live even your paralysis would gradually disappear. Please, darling, don't give up."

So she had not just "run into" the doctor as she had made believe. But I did not tell her she had given herself away again. She was very moved, and she had tried to do her best. A nurse came in then to tell Hilde that I should try to sleep. When she kissed me good-bye I could feel the tears on her cheeks. She left after promising to bring me books in the morning. The nurse took my temperature, and the doctor came in again. This time he stayed quite a time.

"Relax," he said. "You cannot be a super-woman all the time." So he had been talking to Hilde on her way out?

"I am not a super-woman. I have not got fair hair, nor blue eyes. Besides I don't wish to be a super-woman," I replied.

"On the contrary," the doctor replied, "you have tried very hard to be a super-woman. Why didn't you scream at your pains as all other women do?"

"I can't bear that screaming. It sounds like animals. I can't bear to lose control of myself."

"You wanted to be super-brave perhaps?" asked the doctor.

"Yes," I agreed.

"You mark my words," he said slowly, "it's a mistake to

17

be super-human. You pay for it in the end. You are paying now. You should have screamed. It helps you to relax. So does crying."

"I'm afraid I was brought up differently," I told him. "My father trained me never to cry in front of anyone. If I ever broke down I was put in the corner to stand there till I could control myself."

"A Prussian upbringing," said the doctor. "I have a son in the *Hitlerjugend* (Hitler Youth) who has fallen for that line too. I don't like it. It's unnatural. We are human beings first. Still, I suppose it is better than being a weakling." The doctor stopped abruptly. Then he went on. "The trouble today is that one dare not talk openly to one's children. Even if I merely tell him to relax, he frowns at me. If I dare to question his heroic dreams, he becomes fanatical. He says my generation have failed Germany. We left her in poverty and despair. Hitler needed only one year to rid Berlin of its slums."

I lay there listening rather apathetically. But it was true what the doctor was saying. I had seen social conditions in the slums. I knew what it had been like in Berlin at the beginning of the 'thirties. I told him of my own experiences in welfare work. I had studied this work very thoroughly and was a welfare worker in the Wedding (one of the poorest districts in Berlin before Hitler came). The poverty was appalling.

"There you are," said Dr. Martin. "My son has us beaten. That's why I have brought the subject up tonight."

I looked at him with astonishment. "What on earth has Hitler or the political situation to do with me?"

"Not the political situation, but your attitude to life," he told me. "You've got to face facts. Your husband has left you. You have two sons. At first you rage against your husband. Now you are trying to blame Hitler and the Party idea of supermen. It's no good. It won't help you to hate. There are lots of women left for younger girls today. I know

18

it's part of the superman idea. But you must think of your-self. You were so brave during the birth . . . why collapse now? Can't you go on being brave? For your sons' sake?"

The doctor paused. I felt more desperate than ever. All right for Dr. Martin, I thought, he was a man. He had not lost the key to life. The close and tender protection of a husband. Why even to see Richard would give me strength at that moment. Men were so hard, so divided. They could put their hearts on one side as they donned their overcoats to go to work. Women couldn't. Women lived by their hearts.

"You are telling me to be a man as well as a woman," I said to him. "That was only physical pain I was brave about. What you are asking is a lifetime of mental pain, and alone. How can I do that? It's too soon, anyway. I'm not strong enough yet . . ." My voice trailed off.

"I know," said Dr. Martin, "but you mustn't be bitter. You mustn't blame anyone, or yourself or God," he added. "Don't make a martyr of yourself. We all get our bills to pay. After all, you never know what is in store for you tomorrow."

Poor Dr. Martin. He certainly did not know what was in store for him in the future. Perhaps I should tell the story now, as that hospital talk comes back so clearly. It was not until seven years later that I saw Dr. Martin again. It was in 1946 in the Heerstrasse, that wide, long road leading from the outskirts of West Berlin to the Brandenburger Gate.

I was walking along the Heerstrasse when I thought I heard a faint groan. I looked round, and saw on old man swaying in the rubble of a villa. I went to his help . . . to find that the old, poorly clad man in my arms was Dr. Martin!

"My God," I whispered, hardly able to speak aloud. "Can I help you? What are you doing here?"

He didn't recognize me. "Nobody can help me," he answered very slowly. I helped him to sit down. He was

19

trembling and very thin, as we all were. He seemed to look right through me, and did not take in anything of his surroundings.

"What are you doing here?" I repeated.

"I am looking for my son," he answered.

I realized then that he had gone slightly mad, so I adopted the attitude which one takes towards ill or insane persons. As calmly as possible I explained. "But you cannot find your son here. This is all burned down. Nobody is living here."

"Oh, you think I am mad, do you?" the doctor laughed in a shrill, unnatural voice. "How I wish I were! But don't be nervous, I am quite sane. The corpse of my young son is lying somewhere around here. I *must* find him and bury him decently."

"Dr. Martin," I said as gently as I could, "don't you recognize me? I was once a patient in the hospital in Charlottenburg. *I* was in despair then. You were so kind to me. You told me about your son who had just joined the *Hitlerjugend*. Now let *me* try and help you. Sit down and tell me everything that has happened."

He stared at me and I could see at last that recognition was coming. His twisted face relaxed.

"Let's sit down here," I urged, pointing to a big block of stone that was smooth and not blackened from the smoke of the fires. Without saying another word, Dr. Martin put down his shovel.

"I have two slices of bread and margarine. We can share them," I continued. At that time even an extra slice of bread was a treasure and not easily to be shared with anybody. We ate our bread in silence, both of us staring at the long row of ruins on either side of the Heerstrasse. It was spring again and the birds were singing exactly as they had done seven years ago when I lay in the hospital of Charlottenburg.

I wondered idly how they had managed to survive the

fierce battle raging on the Heerstrasse only a year before.
Burning houses, burning trees, bursting grenades; had they
flown outside Berlin? Were these all new birds, or had they
hidden for a while and returned to nest in ruins?

"Now I remember you." Dr. Martin broke the silence.
"You know," he said, "you are the first human being for ages
who has not made me feel that I am a criminal or an outcast."

I said nothing. It was best to let him take his time.

"When you knew me before it was all right with me. Now
I've lost everything, my son, my wife and my home, my
work even. I can't practise as a doctor any more, because I
was once a Party member. I have to sweep the streets, that's
my job over there . . ." he flung out a tattered arm. "My job
is to clear the rubble away from the houses here."

I dared not be sympathetic. I knew he would break down
completely if I were.

"How did it all happen?" I asked, instead.

"I was lucky during the war," Dr. Martin began slowly,
"though we were in Berlin the whole time. My house wasn't
bombed, we weren't too short of food as a friend in the
country helped us. But the crash came in 1945, all at once.
Hans, my son, was ordered with his group to defend the
bridge of the Heerstrasse against the Russians. 'To the last
man,' he told me . . ." He stopped talking for a moment and
stared in front at the ruins in the road.

"Hans was just eighteen. Some of the boys he was leading
were only sixteen, some even younger. Hans knew the job
was tough, even though he was still a fanatic about Hitler.
He was pale that night he came home to tell us. My wife
knew that there was something terribly wrong. She asked
him about the 'latest nonsense,' as she called it. 'It's my turn
now, Mummy,' Hans replied. 'I have to take my group to
defend the Heerstrassen Bridge against the Russians.' My
wife was just about to lay the table for our afternoon coffee.
She swayed on her feet when he told her, and the tray

21

with all the cups of coffee fell with a crash on the carpet.

"'Oh, no,' she said 'not you, Hans . . . you can't . . . you are only a boy.' I shall never forget the look on her face. 'You are all children . . . you can't do it.'

"Hans was leaning against the door of the lounge. He was as white as a sheet.

"'Children or not, Mummy, we have got to go. No more lip service to the Führer, we must give action now.'

"My wife began to cry. 'Children against the Russians,' she sobbed. 'My God, it's easy for the Führer. He has no children, he is not half-starved; he does not know what it is like in Berlin; he has no heart at all.'

"Hans stiffened. 'Don't talk like that about the Führer. He is fighting with us. He has not left Berlin like the others. He is staying with us till the end.'

"'Till the bitter end,' my wife repeated. Her voice was so bitter and so full of anguish that Hans ran to her and put his head in her lap.

"'Mummy; don't give up hope, please, Mummy. I've just been to a meeting. They read out a speech by Goebbels. There is definitely a secret weapon on the way, right at the last moment. It's going to come into action as the Russians approach Berlin. Hitler has been working day and night. Right at the very gates the Russians will be defeated. We have only got to hold them back till the weapon is ready.'

"My wife stopped crying at that. Her hands were running over the fair young head in her lap.

"'When are you going?' she whispered to him.

"'Tomorrow morning at six o'clock.'

"'Right then.' She got up suddenly. There was a fierce determination in her voice. 'Then we have no time to lose. We must go at once. I will pack what is necessary.'

"Hans and I stood and stared at her.

"'What do you mean?' I asked.

"'What do I mean?', my wife laughed hysterically. 'You don't know much about mothers, either of you. Do you really think I would sit here and do nothing, and let Hans run to his . . .' She paused a bit, refusing to use the word 'death' . . . 'to his ruin, with those other children? Do you think I believe those fairy tales about secret weapons?'

"We were both silent. 'We shall go tonight when it is dark. We can walk through the night to Uncle Willy in Oderbrueck. He will shelter us until the worst is over.'

"As she spoke I could see the hope rising in her. But Hans' face reddened with shame. 'I am not going to run away,' he said, 'I have given my word to the Führer. I shall never break it.' He spoke in a high, unnatural voice. He was near breaking point. The change in my wife's face was terrible. Due to all the rationing she had grown very thin, and her clothes hung on her loosely. I can see her standing there, her face ravaged with pain.

"I spoke quickly. 'It's too late, my dear, whatever Hans decides, it's too late to go now.'

"My wife said nothing. She turned now to look at me. 'Yes, it's too late,' I said again. 'You know Fritz Müller from the Hebelstrasse, don't you? Well, this morning they brought what remained of him to the hospital. It was my job to bandage him. I wouldn't have recognized him except from the card tied to the stretcher. He was just a mangled, twisted mass of bleeding flesh.'

Hans stepped back. His eyes widened in horror.

" 'They had beaten him up?'

" 'Yes, and made a pretty thorough job of it.'

" 'Father; will he die?'. Hans' question was almost a scream.

" 'Hard to tell.' I shrugged my shoulders. 'He was weak and undernourished to start with. He had lost a lot of blood before I saw him. Several bones are broken. He has definitely lost the use of one eye anyway. It all depends on the internal injuries now.'

"Hans had now recovered some of his dignity. 'But surely it wasn't the *Hitlerjugend* who had beaten him up?'

23

"'I didn't say so. Nobody says so. All we do know is that
Fritz got an order similar to yours last night and he did *not*
turn up. Whether he tried to escape or not is hard to say, but
what I do know is this.' I turned to my wife. 'The Heerstrasse is the only way out of Berlin not in Russian hands.
Do you imagine we should ever get through? Would they
allow one able-bodied man out of Berlin now? *You* might
escape, but do you think Hans or I could?'

"The howling of the sirens started at that moment, and I
had to return to the hospital. I grasped my son's hands and
wished him luck. I never saw him again. After that as you
know there was one alarm after another. I just went on
non-stop at the hospital as they carried in the victims. Every
moment I expected to see my own son among them. When
at last I was able to stumble home I found only German
soldiers in the house. No trace of my wife, nor of my son.
The soldiers were busily turning my home into a fortress.
I asked about my wife. They told me she had left a message
saying she was taking some food to Hans in the Heerstrasse.

"I found her a few days later. She lay on the side of the
road. A splinter from a heavy shell had gone into her head.
She must have died instantaneously. By the way, her
basket was empty," he smiled bitterly.

"Someone had relieved her of the food. That's all," he
said. "Oh, no," he corrected himself, "not quite all. Later
on I watched my house burnt down. The Russians were
furious at the fighting inside the barricades, so they
piled up furniture from the houses around, poured benzole
over the lot and set it alight. The heat was so intense, I am
sure the soldiers inside were roasted to death pretty quickly.
. . . But you must excuse me now, I must get on with my
digging. I have got to find my son's body."

That was Dr. Martin's story as I recalled it at his words;
"You never know what is in store for you tomorrow."

At that moment in the hospital in 1939, however, he sat

by my bed and urged me to try again, be brave and have hope in my future. Then he felt my pulse and asked the nurse to give me sleeping tablets. After he had left me, I repeated his words under my breath. "Try to make the best of it; never give up; go on trying; go on believing it will be all right in the end."

The next morning I was inundated with flowers and letters and telegrams. Dr. Martin looked as pleased as Punch. The drugged sleep had left me depressed. I had already glanced at the cards, letters, and flowers. There was nothing from Richard, so they didn't matter. The less interested I became in my post, the more fun did Dr. Martin take in reading out the names on the cards and examining the flowers.

"What's this?" he called out, as he bent over a basket of glorious roses. He took the card and read aloud. "*Reichsleitung der Deutschen Arbeitsfront, Abtlg. Bildende Kunst.* (Headquarters of the German Labour Front, Department of Art.) Well, I never. Here I am trying to explain party politics and defend myself for becoming a member, when all the time *you* have a boy friend in one of the highest positions of all. I hope you haven't been trying to trap me into indiscretions?'

He was laughing as he spoke, but I could see a suspicious gleam come into his eyes.

"He's not my boy friend," I said quickly.

"Sorry, sorry," Dr. Martin apologized. "Is he a relative?"

"He's my boss," I said briefly.

"Your boss?" There was astonishment in his voice. "*You* are employed in the Headquarters of the Labour Front? In other words you are a member of the Party yourself?" Dr. Martin sat down suddenly, still holding Mr. Gerhard Wolter's card in his hand.

"I'm not a member of the Party," I answered.

"Come, come," objected the doctor. "You can't tell me you are working there and not a member?"

I shrugged my shoulders. "Believe it or not, it's true."

"I'm sorry. It's a bit too much to swallow at one gulp," said the doctor, laughing.

"I suggest you ring up Mr. Wolter for yourself and check it." I was rather annoyed by now.

"I certainly will," said Dr. Martin briefly, and got up to go.

The rest of the day passed drearily enough. I had several treatments for my paralysis. My temperature refused to drop, and the awful thoughts about the future continued. If only I could think of somewhere to go with my children when I came out of the hospital. Suddenly Dr. Martin was standing by my bed. "Good news!" he called. "I 'phoned your boss, as you suggested and I find after all that they *do* allow non-members to work in the Headquarters of the Labour Front."

I did not know what to think of this. Was he really so inquisitive, or was he joking?

Dr. Martin guessed my thoughts. "You thought I was joking, didn't you. Oh, no, I wasn't. I spoke to Mr. Wolter in person. He explained that due to shortage of office staff they had been obliged to accept non-members. He told me that originally they planned to keep you only for a short time, until they found a Party member. But you proved so efficient they didn't like to let you go."

"Very kind, very kind of him indeed," I murmured, and wished Dr. Martin out of the room.

"What's more," Dr. Martin went on, apparently slightly amused by me. "What's more, he will help you to find a flat."

"What?" Like a flash I sat upright in my bed.

"Now, now, take it easy." Dr. Martin pushed me gently back on my pillows. "Tomorrow he will ring me to let me know the results of his efforts."

I began to cry, but with relief this time. A flat, a home for my children, somewhere to go to when I left hospital.

"How kind you are," I said to the doctor. "I didn't know you were helping like this. I'll try to get better now. I know I will."

"That's just what I want," said Dr. Martin.

That night I began to mend. And the next day the doctor got a message that a flat with one large living-room, a kitchen and bathroom was reserved for me; and would I please hurry up and get well as I was needed at the office. I laughed at this last bit. It was typical of my young boss, Mr. Wolter.

"I didn't know you *could* laugh," said Dr. Martin. "But since you can, tell me something about this job of yours. What on earth are you doing in the Art Department of the Labour Party?"

"We organize painting and sculpture exhibitions," I told him.

"Painting and sculpture on the Labour Front? That sounds more like Dr. Goebbels' department."

"The idea is to try and make the factory worker interested in art. It's Hitler's idea to bring the working man up to a higher cultural level, and give him the same chances as the professional man." I began to grow enthusiastic. I liked my work, and I thought the idea a brilliant one.

Dr. Martin was still a scoffer but he made me tell him more.

"You know there were quite a lot of people with these ideas long before Hitler. And surely the art exhibitions are open to all workers, and free on Sundays. If the working classes wanted art, they could always get it. But they don't want it. They stay away."

"That's just the point," I said eagerly, sitting straight up in bed. "You've put your finger right on it. Up till now they have stayed away, but our way we bring the art *to* the worker. We bring it right to the place where he is working all day. We organize exhibitions right in the factories."

"Isn't that rather difficult?" asked Dr. Martin.

"Of course. But we have found new ways. We have, for instance, movable exhibition walls which we can erect in any big room or canteen. And then we send an artist with the exhibition to explain the pictures or sculpture to the workers, and to show them how it is done."

"And do they take to it?" asked the doctor.

"Very well indeed. I could show you figures to prove the success of the exhibitions."

"I'd like to see one of them," said the doctor.

"When I'm back at the office I'll take you," I promised him.

From then on my recovery was quick. I would get my flat. Perhaps I could squeeze both children into it, provided I found someone reliable to look after them while I worked. I furnished that flat in my imagination a hundred times during the last days of my stay in the hospital. On the seventh day after my son's birth I heard at last from my husband. He congratulated me briefly and filled the next page telling me how busy he was. That was all. No question as to how our son was, or where I should take him to live. He did not mention money or offer to help with expenses over the baby. It hurt me bitterly.

After a fortnight I left the hospital and took my children to my cousin Karl and his wife while I furnished the flat. Many things were needed. I got the furniture out of store and there made the discovery that Richard had not even kept his bargain to pay for the storage. The new flat was in the south of Berlin in the district of Baumschulenweg. It was on the fourth floor of a huge new block. It had a tiny sunny balcony, and overlooked a park with many trees. If I had not felt so weak and exhausted, I should have been happy as I stood there for the first time.

My taste of happiness, however, was very brief. It came about just as Dr. Martin had warned. I did far too much in those early days. I would come home exhausted to take over the children and perhaps have a disturbed night with little Klaus, the baby, and then back early to work hard in the art department. Dr. Martin had told me not to overstrain myself at the beginning. Like an idiot I neglected his warning, and one day collapsed at the office. I went to the welfare officers, but they couldn't help me. I could find no one really reliable to take full charge of the children, day and night, at least not at a fee that I could pay. There was nothing else to do. If I was to keep my job and support the children I must have proper sleep and rest. I would therefore have to be parted from them, even the baby.

Now all my dreams and hopes had really gone. Many years have now passed, but I still remember that night on my tiny balcony in Baumschulenweg. It was in May 1939. A warm night, and I couldn't sleep. The mental pain was so terrible I felt like calling aloud into the rustling green of the trees below. I looked up to the sky. Huge wide beams of searchlights were chasing a plane and trying to catch it. It was a silent cat and mouse game. That was actually the first time that serious thoughts of war entered my mind. That very morning I had heard people complaining about the butter ration, and how difficult it was to get. My own problems had driven these thoughts right behind me. Now they came back in full force. To lose my children and be plunged into war. This would be more frightful than anything.

I stood on the balcony until the beams died away and the lights faded. Surely Hitler *must* know what he was doing. He had had success after success since 1933, and all of them peacefully. In the morning, a decision came to me. If I had to lose my children it should not be to the National Social Welfare Nursery. Instead I would send them to some private family, even though it would be far more expensive in the end. But even this bitter decision proved difficult. I just could not find a family ready to take both children together. So in the end I had to separate them. My cousin and his wife took Wolfgang, and the baby Klaus I sent to a nice home in Caputh near Potsdam.

The summer of 1939 was a hard time for me. Any holidays or recreation were out of the question. From my salary I should only just be able to pay for my two children. I had no one to live for any more. Exhausted with weeping alone in my small flat, I put away as many signs as I could of the children, and went back the next day to the art department of the Labour Front—the *"Kraft durch Freude"* (Strength through Joy).

2

Picture Propaganda

THE head office of the Labour Front, Section KDF—
"Strength through Joy", lay in two large, four-storied
houses in the Kaiserallee in West Berlin, centrally heated,
and with high, well-proportioned rooms. Five minutes away
by bus and I was in the most fashionable part of the city,
the Zoo-Viertel. My department was quite small, consist-
ing of my chief, Mr. Wolter, his artist-assistant, Mr. Hans
Eschenbach, and myself. The atmosphere of the office was
bright and pleasant and I enjoyed my work there very
much.

Strange as it may sound, there was more adverse criticism
of the National Socialist regime in this, the very heart of it,
than in the outside world. Mr. Wolter was not afraid of
anyone. When he thought a thing wrong, he said so, no
matter what the consequences. He was a member of the
Party, and he wore the Party badge but not the uniform.
Being an artist, he loathed uniforms, and I presume the
leader of the Strength through Joy movement (*Amsleiter
Pg. Scholz*) made special allowances for him on this score.

Every day Mr. Wolter would produce new jokes about
the Party leaders, about Hitler, Goebbels, Goering, etc. He
also liked to tease me. I remember a moment when I much
needed a rise in salary. I did my best to put my claims forward.

Mr. Wolter scowled and said sternly; "What? You dare
to ask for a rise in salary, and you aren't even a member of
the Party? I shall report you. We don't want your kind of
worker here!"

I went pale. I really thought he meant it. Then he roared with laughter. I just stood and stared at him, not knowing what to think now. Seeing my bewildered and worried expression he came forward and touched my shoulder.

"Honestly, my dear, I never thought you would take me seriously; don't you know me better than that? Don't you know by now how much I hate the Party attitude?"

Mr. Eschenbach's entrance suddenly cut short our conversation. He came storming in with a picture in his hand.

"Look at this," he said without wasting time on any preliminaries. He was furiously angry.

"An excellent picture," said Mr. Wolter, picking it up. "Original too. Quite a relief from the usual farming pictures. I like the daring colours, don't you?"

"I think it's the best thing we've ever had, but it's been rejected out of hand by the jury. The Propaganda Ministry doesn't think this kind of picture 'suitable'. They want the workers to get the old-fashioned stuff they're used to, they say. Did you ever hear anything to equal it? I'm utterly fed-up with the whole thing."

Poor 'Bachus' (Mr. Wolter's nickname for him) sat down and mopped his forehead.

"Now, now, calm down, 'Bachus'," said Mr. Wolter. "You know what to expect by now. It's not the first time we've had a show-down with the *Reichskammer*, is it? We should take a leaf out of our friend 'X's copybook in painting. I saw him last week. You know what he did, don't you? After one of his best pictures had been rejected by the judges of the Propaganda Ministry he got drunk . . . He then painted a satire and put in everything that Prop (one of Mr. Wolter's abbreviations for the Propaganda Ministry) ordered in their paintings, and more. He told me he painted just like a schoolboy and without any meaning or originality at all. Absolute nonsense the whole thing was, he said. He sent the picture to the *Reichskammer of Arts*, with a note saying nothing but, 'Heil Hitler, from "X"'. The very same day

32

Mrs. Wendel's sons Klaus (left) and Wolfgang from whom she was separated. Wolfgang stayed with her cousin and his wife who became so fond of him that they refused to give him up. Mr. and Mrs. Kroll, who had charge of Klaus, became equally possessive.

Below: The boys in the summer of 1942.

Christmas Eve is the heart of Christmas for every German; even in the dark days of the war it always brought, if only briefly, some warmth into life. Candles on the tree were lit and Santa Klaus came with his rod to hear the boys sing carols and to give them presents.

he got an official 'phone call from 'Prop' paying him compliments, asking the price and saying it was being sent at once to the art exhibition. Thus 'X' became famous. He is a rich man now. You, 'Bachus', must do the same . . . and become famous."

Mr. Wolter struck a ludicrous pose with one hand on his heart. 'Bachus' could not take it however. "He is a traitor to his work," he stormed. "'X' makes me sick. His pictures are frightful."

"I wouldn't put it as bluntly as that," said Mr. Wolter becoming grave and quiet. "Everyone has to live. 'X' has a family to support."

And that was that. Mr. Wolter made it quite clear that he did not want any further discussion on the subject. It was very clever of him, I thought at the time, but afterwards I found it was more than mere cleverness. One day we were talking about art critics, their views and importance in the scheme.

"We've got to have criticism, of course, but not criticism that endangers our work here. The factory exhibitions are a grand idea, in fact they are a very great ideal; am I getting too enthusiastic?" He stopped.

"Go on," I encouraged.

"You see," he explained, more slowly, "I felt just as frustrated as 'X' at the beginning. I paint too, but you'll never see my pictures, they are so modern that 'Prop' would faint if they saw them, and I should lose my job tomorrow. So they don't see them, they are stored away in my attic. Perhaps one day. . ."

"You mean you are never going to produce them; all these years of secret work?" I was dumbfounded.

"They don't matter. What matters is our work here. Our job is to educate the worker to appreciate art. He has got to go step by step, and we've *got* to have 'Prop's' support while we do it? Do you get me now?"

"I never knew you had such plans," I told him.

"I believe in the taste of the ordinary man in the street. The factory worker is the key-figure today. It is he who elected Hitler. He has a fine feeling for everything that is genuine, and he isn't handicapped by traditions.

"So you are painting for a time when the worker will be asking for your pictures, is that it?" I asked him.

"Yes," he smiled at me. "But it may not come in my own lifetime. Few men realize their dreams in this life. But if I can keep this department going I shall have taken the first step towards helping new artists to develop. One day they will be able to paint as they wish and feel."

"That's looking a long way ahead," I said, as I glanced at the picture dropped by Mr. Eschenbach on to the desk.

"It's the only thing to do. National Socialism is a revolution. There was no bloodshed, but it's a revolution all the same. In time our whole life will be changed. How can you expect that to happen without someone going to the wall? That's why I don't get excited about 'Prop's' blunders and blindness as poor old 'Bachus' does."

We both began to laugh then. There was a knock on the door and Mr. Frey the staff manager came in. He shook his head gravely at us. "May I suggest, Comrade Wolter, that you keep your jokes till the lunch-hour?" The twinkle in his eyes was becoming more obvious as we sat down and tried to control our mirth. "And may I furthermore draw your attention, both of you, to the fact that any jokes about distinguished Party-members are considered 'highly undesirable' as I think, the expression goes."

"If that's the way to get the latest joke out of me, you've failed," Mr. Wolter said.

"I don't need second-hand jokes, I have just got a good new one of my own," declared Mr. Frey quickly.

"Let's have it then," said Mr. Wolter.

And there we three sat, laughing our heads off at Party-members, National Socialism, the quirks and quibbles of our big organizations, and so on, right in the centre of the Strengh through Joy headquarters.

I remember one particularly funny incident. It happened over the Non-Aggression Pact with Russia.

I had got to the office in a hurry that morning and so had not yet read the newspapers. I rushed in with the mail and Mr. Wolter and Mr. Eschenbach jumped up. I automatically said my greeting of "Heil Hitler" to them. ("Heil Hitler" was, of course, our password to every single thing we did. Late in the evening, early in the morning, we all greeted each other with "Heil Hitler". When I went to a lavatory and greeted the toilet attendant, it was still "Heil Hitler" as I handed my pennies in.)

But to my greeting "Heil Hitler" on this morning, both my colleagues jumped to their feet, raised an arm with a clenched fist and shouted "Heil Moscow"! I was completely taken aback. I saw nothing funny when they both burst into laughter, sometimes men behaved like little children. I tried to smile indulgently.

"Didn't I tell you," Mr. Wolter roared, "she hasn't the remotest idea of what's going on? She goes home and just rocks the cradles of her children—that's all."

"May I share the joke?" I asked. How I wished that I *could* rock my children's cradles!

"We are laughing at *you*—not at our Heil Moscow," said Mr. Wolter through his bursts of mirth.

"Sorry, I don't understand." I put the mail on his bureau and went to the door.

"Stop!" called Mr. Wolter, and turned towards Mr. Eschenbach. "I told you she has no sense of humour. May I inform you comrade-assistant that last night the threat of a second world war has been banned and removed by our Führer. Hitler and Stalin have signed a Non-Aggression Treaty."

He spoke the last sentences very solemnly. This was no joke.

"But Russia," I stammered. "The Führer has just said that there is no bridge between Germany and Russia."

"As you see, the Führer can do everything. He has *built* a bridge between Russia and Germany overnight."

"It just shows you," Mr. Wolter added, "how little we all know of politics. While we are drinking our beer and talking about the imminent danger of war, the Führer *acts* and abolishes all our fears with a snap of his fingers.

"The only man I am sorry for," he went on, "is Dr. Goebbels. He must be very busy this morning burning all the leaflets and books in which he thundered against the Russians, and told us so carefully why and how they were such barbarians. This morning they are our blood-brothers."

We all laughed. At least that was a joke on Dr. Goebbels.

There was only one topic of conversation in the homes and cafés during those last days of August 1939, the Non-Aggression Treaty with Russia. It had come as a complete shock to all of us. Ever since the Reichstag fire in February 1933, Communism had been expelled from German political life. Members of the Communist Party had been bitterly pursued and put into prison. Russia was declared the arch-enemy. In February 1933 we had been told that Russia had prepared a revolution in Germany, and had it not been for Hitler we would all have been swallowed up in the Communist regime and now, after six years of hate campaigns, the Press suddenly declared unanimously that Russia had no wish to export her ideology to Germany. Nor did Germany wish to export National Socialism to Russia. The world, our Press said firmly, was wide enough for both ideologies to flourish side by side. What we did not know at that time, of course, was the contents of the secret agreement in the Non-Aggression Treaty. We had no idea that Hitler and Stalin had dealt with Poland between them.

Nor did we know that Hitler had given away the Baltic Sea harbours of Windau and Liebau to the Russians—in a telephone call. Our feelings now were a jumble of relief and astonishment at the quick change. Towards Hitler we had nothing but admiration and respect. A man who had the courage to step over the abyss between Germany and Russia to prevent war, was a man worthy of the highest praise.

Mr. Wolter told us all to read the writings of Machiavelli. "Get a copy of Machiavelli's book '*Il Principe*'," he told me. "Keep yourself up to date. Learn about politics, my dear comrade-assistant. The key is 'no morals'; forget the Salvation Army; be ruthless and have no remorse. No price is too high for peace for your home-country." He said all this in a stern voice with a half-twinkle in his eye. Then he became gentler and added : "You know in the long run this ruthlessness may be best. It's more merciful than a long 'decent, human' war, don't you agree?"

I agreed.

"In time you will get used to seeing the flag with the hammer and sickle flying in the Unter den Linden," said Mr. Wolter, ironically.

On 1 September, 1939, however, my personal views changed. The radio and newspapers announced the attack on Poland.

"You look like the Mater Dolorosa," Mr. Wolter said to me that morning. "You want your sons to live, don't you? Well, how can they live if Germany is to be cramped up— *ein Volk ohne Raum* (a people without living room)? Twenty years after the Treaty of Versailles and we are still separated from our own people by the Polish Corridor! Danzig is a German town. If the Poles won't give it back to us voluntarily, then, all right, we march in and take it."

He stood there completely jubilant. His strikingly blue eyes flashed as they always did when he was emotional. He was vain about his blue eyes. His wife encouraged him in this. I remember well the decorations of his office. He had decided to mix the distemper himself to a special blue "just to match my eyes," he had said triumphantly. Then he ordered a blue carpet, long blue curtains a shade deeper, and pleasant, dark oak furniture. Looking round at the finished décor, he had said: "This is perfect for me. I am here to work and this is exactly right." Many visitors complimented him on the room. It was certainly a very charming and artistic one.

He was very impressive to look at on that morning in September. Flashing blue eyes, tall, slim figure against the lighter blue walls.

"It's all trash when they accuse Germany of being responsible for the First World War, and say we must be punished. They talk of freedom to us, but where is freedom when a big town like Danzig can't come back into its Fatherland? Do you seriously think we would have got the Rhineland back if we hadn't marched into it?; or Austria?; or Czechoslovakia?; and our Army?; and our rivers; we weren't even masters of our own rivers till Hitler came! Now we have got our Army and no more foreign restrictions in our country." He looked at me with a certain pity. "But, of course, you women just don't understand politics. You have to be hard and strong to grasp such things. Women have the brains of babies over politics. My wife is just the same."

Somehow I just had to answer back. "But up till now Hitler has done everything peacefully. I *do* admire his foresight and diplomacy, as long as it means peace. But this is war!"

Mr. Wólter commented: "No need to worry at all. You take my word for it, this war against Poland will be just a *Blitzkrieg*. It will be over in a flash. By the way, that reminds me, we shall have to write a lot of letters altering our instructions, because of the war."

He now plunged energetically into his work. He ended each of the letters. "Heil Hitler and good-bye till after the war!" He laughed heartily as he said this. All over Berlin the enthusiasm grew wilder. Young men rushed off to try to join up and middle-aged men too. Hitler had freed us from

the Versailles Treaty, given us back our Army; our belief
in ourselves, the men thought, but not perhaps the women.

"Come in and help me," said Mr. Wolter to his assistant
one day. "At home it's my wife. Here it's my secretary. I
never knew German women had so little faith. My wife has
gone mad, she is rushing all over Berlin trying to get soap.
I keep on telling her the war will be over in a matter of
weeks."

That first September of the war nothing could go wrong
with us. The *Blitzkrieg* was soon over and Warsaw burned
to the ground. Berlin looked like a forest of flags. I went one
Sunday to visit my parents in Charlottenburg. They lived
in a big four-storied corner house in the Berlinerstrasse, a
wide street with space for three lines of cars on either side.
The town hall of Charlottenburg, a magnificent building,
towered majestically over the long row of beautiful houses.

At the moment, however, my mother had her own problems even in this pleasant setting.

"What on earth am I to do about blacking out these huge
windows?" she asked me. "Where can I get proper material?
Paper is no use, is it, for windows of this size? Do you
honestly think we need bother, Else?"

My sister Hilde was there that Sunday with us. "Of course
you must do the windows properly, mother," she interrupted. "The war may not be over as soon as we think."

"Nonsense," said my mother. "Of course it will be over.
Surely our Führer knows what he is talking about?"

I can see my mother now in that large room. She was a
tall and still slender woman despite her five children. But
the strain of the First World War and the long and terrible
years afterwards, had marked her beautiful face with deep
lines and turned her black hair almost white. She was, my
mother, the kindest and gentlest woman I have ever known.

. . . Mr. Wolter was right. The Polish campaign was a
Blitzkrieg. In one month everything was over. Russia
marched into East Poland, and on 17 September 1939 the

country fighting madly on two fronts was forced to her knees. Poland now no longer existed. Germany and Russia split most of it up between them. This quick and brilliant victory added much to Hitler's glory. It made it much easier, too, for Dr. Goebbels to dwell on Hitler as the man, "sent by Providence to us". The fact that England and France had declared war on us on 3 September did not damp our enthusiasm. Nothing had happened to prevent the Polish victory, had it?

Mr. Wolter was now busier than ever. He had been instructed to develop plans for a peaceful penetration of the newly won territory and to send "General Government of Poland" picture exhibitions of our usual style. It meant more staff, more travelling, and more exhibition walls. It was not easy, especially the question of who should be in charge of the new Polish factory exhibitions. The language difficulties also had to be overcome. It gave him a lot of work and many headaches. I, too, had my personal headaches. In all the glory and general flag-wagging after Poland's capitulation I was busy not with victory, but with my greatest defeat, my divorce.

Throughout September we had had wonderful weather, the so-called "Führer-weather" which was miraculously provided for so many of Hitler's campaigns. Now the first frost had come, and as I went by underground to the Alexanderplatz to petition for my divorce from Richard, there was no sunshine. The colossal statue of Berolina looked down sternly on me from a grey sky. I felt utterly alone and forsaken. This was the end of a life that had begun with such warmth and love.

I had no winter coat. I wondered indeed if I would ever have the money now to afford one, let alone the clothing coupons. The children needed everything I had. I shivered as I came out and stood in front of the huge grey building, the Court of Justice. My dark red suit with its brown fur trimming was by no means warm.

I enquired for "Divorces" from the doorkeeper. "Third floor, please," he said in a bored voice. .

Looking back now I realize of course there was nothing unusual or particularly depressing in the place, only in my own feelings. I was told to sit on a bench and wait with other people in a long corridor. Were all these people waiting for divorces then? I was shocked and somehow disgusted.

"Oh, there you are! I have been looking for you all over the place!" A well-known, deep voice sounded in my ears.

It was Richard! I got up and stood staring at him as though hypnotised. I couldn't say a word.

"You look very attractive," he continued, looking me up and down as he always did when introduced to a possible "new woman".

His hand came out to shake mine. I decided to ignore it, but alas I couldn't. Against my will my own hand went out to meet his. He took it and held it longer than was necessary.

"I tried to get you on the 'phone yesterday, but you were out," he said casually.

"I was at the opening of an exhibition."

"Let's sit down." He pushed me gently on to one of the empty benches. "It's a long time since I saw you." Richard's blue eyes were gazing at me intensely. "I had forgotten how charming and attractive a wife I have."

I had to turn my head. My eyes were filling with tears. It was Richard all over. Had he no heart at all to talk of charm and attraction to a woman he was getting rid of.

"Now please don't get me wrong," said Richard, as though suddenly reading my thoughts. He put both hands over mine and used his softest voice to plead with me—the voice that he knew I loved so much. "I really mean it. I really *am* sorry to lose you. Look, Else . . . look, darling," he suddenly began to wax enthusiastic. "I'll make a proposition to you. Let's cancel our divorce. Come on, let's start again. Seeing you again has brought me up against facts. Let's walk out of here. You have got a nice flat. Let's go there and start our marriage all over again. I mean it, darling." His voice was urgent and full of emotion. "Else, I still love you, I find," he whispered.

I jumped up and stared at him. What would I have given to have heard those words a few months ago while I was lying so desperately ill and unhappy in the hospital at Charlottenburg. One tiny sign of affection then and I would have forgiven him anything, would have trusted him all over again. But in my agony he had not come. Indeed if it had not been for Dr. Martin I might have been dead by now. And now, I thought, five minutes before our divorce, a sudden emotional whim rises in him and he wants me to rush back into his arms, overwhelmed by his generosity.

I looked down at him still sitting there with that look of intense emotion on his face, and I burst out laughing! All the tension and pain of the last hour suddenly exploded inside me, not into tears or words, but into helpless and hysterical laughter. I simply could not stop it. People near us turned round and looked with the gravest disapproval. It was hardly a place in which to scream with mirth.

"For goodness sake, stop laughing," Richard whispered. "Everyone is looking at us." His face reddened in embarrassment. "Besides *I* can't see any joke." I could hear the rising anger in his voice.

This made me laugh even more, and to make it worse I suddenly remembered my two white handkerchiefs all ready in my handbag against any possible breakdown on my part, and here I was, pressing them against my mouth to stifle my laughter.

Richard got up and tried to put an arm round me. He was very cross by now. Then he pulled himself together. "You are hysterical, that's what it is. But I understand, it must be the strain of what you have gone through. Never mind, it's all over now . . . come along, darling."

42

I was the startled one now. Could he possibly know me so little? Didn't instinct tell him that when a woman laughs at love-making, there isn't the ghost of a chance for a man? No, apparently it didn't. He stood there, tall, arrogant and quite confident that he was the answer to any woman's prayer, certainly to his wife's. He was merely waiting till I had pulled myself together a little, and then we should take each other's arm and walk happily out of the building and go back to my flat to live together.

Suddenly the thought of Paula flashed through my mind, the girl for whom he had left me. I would not have been a woman if I had resisted a desire to have a little fun myself.

"What about Paula?" I objected.

"Oh, her? Don't worry about her. She's not a girl for marriage really. I see it now. She's too young. Apart from the fact that she can't cook, she keeps running back to her mother after every little disagreement we have. I'm not going to marry her mother as well.'

I was highly amused. "I hope she is not going to have a baby?"

"I shouldn't think so." He shrugged his shoulders. "But of course one never knows. I haven't asked her."

I felt colder and colder. My terrible fight in the hospital came back. What kind of man was this?

Richard grasped my arms. "Come on . . . quick. There are our lawyers; they are looking for us. Let's get down the stairs before they come."

I pulled myself violently away from him. "I'm not going with you."

"Why on earth not?" It was now Richard's turn to be startled, and how startled he was; he even forgot to close his mouth.

"I don't think it's fair to Paula," I said.

The effect of my words was remarkable. I don't think Richard could have looked more dumbfounded if the roof had fallen on him. But before he could recover and speak

43

to me our lawyers had arrived, and I received them with my sweetest smile.

"It's our turn now," my lawyer said, and stepped up beside me. I left Richard without a further glance.

Richard himself was strikingly honest and strangely humble. He admitted everything my lawyer accused him of. He agreed to pay everything, though afterwards he never actually paid a penny. He continually looked at me, nearly endangering the whole proceedings, as my lawyer said afterwards. "There is nothing that judges hate more than to feel a well-prepared play being enacted in front of them. Everybody could see with half an eye that your husband was still in love with you."

"He's not," I replied. "Like most men, Richard hasn't the slightest idea what love is. He loves only himself. Richard was just a bit puzzled by a little riddle I gave him shortly before we entered the court. That was all. He couldn't find the right answer."

I said no more. In ten minutes it was all over. I was now a divorced woman.

"Quite a straightforward case," said my lawyer.

The doors of the courtroom were opened for us, and we went out together. Richard did not leave my side.

"I can't understand why you didn't cry," he said. "After all this *is* the end of our marriage."

Richard never did and never could know what my heart felt. He was too vain a man. It didn't occur to him that all my tears over our dying love had been wept long ago, when he first left me; in the hospital, and since, when I had lost my children. Nor could he understand the moment of truth when I saw him as he was.

"Will you come and have lunch with me?" he asked. This time his voice, perhaps, was not quite so full of confidence.

"No, thank you. I am in rather a hurry," I said.

I turned from him quickly and went back to the office, leaving poor Richard to return to his Paula.

3

Divorce and Difficulties

SITTING in the underground on my way back to the office
from the divorce courts I closed my eyes and let the bitter
sweet memories flood over me. Those first years with
Richard? They had been good. Then the last year in Brandenburg, that had been anything but good.

Brandenburg, once a small town near Berlin, was now
an industrial city. Richard had been chosen to build up its
first city orchestra. It was a great feather in his cap and he
had worked hard to achieve success. For a time he had
rented a furnished room there while I stayed on in our
house in Berlin. Then came the blow. One day Richard
came to tell me that he had fallen in love with his violinist
in the orchestra, and that this time it was serious.

"It's not just a mild flirtation; she is not the kind of little
girl you just kiss and flirt with. I want her to be my wife,"
he announced.

"But you have a wife," I said, half-mocking and half-
angry. Richard had always an eye for other women. I was
pregnant at the time—my second baby was expected in the
spring and of course I had no idea that this flirtation was
going on, nor did I know that they were now living together
openly in Brandenburg.

We argued. I'm afraid it was not very pleasant. Then
Richard stormed back to Brandenburg, and I said: "We
can't do anything until after the baby comes. Surely you
can see that?" I hoped and prayed of course that the flirtation would end, as had his former ones, by the time my
child was born. But it did not end. On the contrary Richard

stopped providing any means of livelihood for myself and little Wolfgang. I had to give up our rented house, store the furniture and had to live in a very modest furnished room and get a job. That was how I started working in the Kraft durch Freude Department. The months went by—Richard in Brandenburg and visiting me now and then, and I staying in Berlin with my baby son Wolfgang. Early in the new year Richard had his first big city concert to conduct. It was to be the official début of the Brandenburg Orchestra and I must of course attend as his wife. I altered an evening dress as best I could to disguise my figure—it was not worth while buying one just for this single occasion. I had, of course, to sit in the front row with the local personalities.

I was terribly sad and anxious that night. Richard still persisted that he loved this girl and must have a divorce, and that the only thing was for me to set him free the moment our baby arrived. In the end, in my misery, I actually promised that I would. What use holding on to a man who didn't want me or love me?

Richard stood on the dais just beyond me. He looked magnificent in his evening suit. It showed his figure to advantage and his impressive face, now pale with excitement. His somewhat over-sharp features were softened with emotion, and the lights caught the sparkle in his blue eyes and the gleam of his fair hair. He looked a man any woman would be proud and happy to claim as her husband.

The applause grew as Richard bowed to the public. Wagner's overture from Tannhäuser sounded through the concert hall and rose to a crescendo of passion as Venus fights against the holy pilgrims and Elizabeth for Tannhäuser's soul. I began to cry. I could not stop the tears which ran freely down my face. Normally I can control my feelings very well, but music of this kind goes straight to the heart. During the interval I quickly powdered my face and looked nervously at Richard to see if he had noticed how much I had been affected by the music. He was surrounded by an adoring and congratulating crowd. He was beaming. I needn't have worried for he had noticed nothing.

A few days later I got a 'phone call from Richard. He was furiously angry. How dared I cry at the concert? Why hadn't I told him how unhappy I was? He could have made some excuse for my breakdown if I had warned him in time. Bit by bit I drew from him what had happened. Some of the women in the audience had seen me crying, they had, of course, also noticed my obvious pregnancy. They gossiped together and discovered more facts and then decided to take official action.

On the second morning after his concert Richard found the entrance to his house besieged by angry Party women. They stopped the milkman supplying him with milk; they prevented the baker's boy delivering the fresh, warm rolls which every German likes for his breakfast. The women would not go away. With the Party badges on their coats they looked quite formidable in a group below there. Richard said he stood behind the curtains in his dressing-gown watching them. Then an official from the Party Headquarters arrived, talked to them, and they at last left him in peace. A few hours later however the Party leader informed Richard that he must arrange his private affairs so that no further public scandal would arise.

"What are you going to do?" I asked rather stupidly.

"What do you think?" Richard raged at me. "I shall have to separate from Paula for the time being. We shan't be able to live together until after the divorce. Narrow-minded bourgeois that they are! They don't deserve to be Party members at all."

"I didn't know you were living together officially," I told him. "It was stupid of you—Brandenburg is not Berlin."

Richard had banged the receiver down.

All of this—the very words indeed—I went through on the underground journey. The pain and the final awful humiliation and rejection as his wife.

47

Then at last I reached my office in the Kaiserallee and
went slowly to my chief's room—a free woman. Though
free for what, heaven only knew. I was not in the mood to
imagine that it would ever again be human happiness.

*   *   *

We were now getting used to life under rationing and
blackouts. So far there had only been one air-raid alarm,
and that had proved to be a false one.

General Fieldmarshal Goering, to give him his full title,
had told us: "From Posen to Berlin is only forty minutes'
flying time, but has one Polish plane been able to reach us?
No, it has not. Little chance, then, of an Allied plane
coming from several hundreds of miles. As you will see, it
is not easy to drop bombs on Berlin!"

Goering's speeches were always clever. He admitted our
human weaknesses and then explained facts away. One
amusing example went like this: "The air-raid alarm of
last night? I got up, too, and went to my shelter, when
actually there wasn't a single enemy plane within a
hundred miles. What happened was simple. At the beginning of a war we are all a bit jittery. The men at their air-
raid posts are 'trigger happy', they hear perhaps a sudden
engine roar in the distance—it might be perhaps motor-
cyclists coming through the night—to be on the safe side,
they sound a siren, that starts the man in the next district off,
and soon all the sirens around are tooting."

It sounds absurd now, but at the time we swallowed it.
Goering ridiculed away this one "false alarm" on Berlin
quite cheerfully for us. No bomb had fallen, anyway.
Everyone was relieved and thought, if the man responsible
for our defence can take it so lightly, then why should we
worry? We laughed and cheered Goering and cracked jokes
about the false alarm. Goering had explained away the
rationing by saying he was a more provident man than
those in charge in the last war. This time he rationed us *in*

time while there was plenty. He assured us there would be no shortage of rationed food, even if the war should last for years!

This last phrase was said with a laugh. Goering always referred to the "World War" as though it were quite a different thing altogether. None of us dreamed then that we stood at the beginning of a Second World War.

He laughed about the meat ration, explaining that meat was a seasonal thing. One month we might get beef only, another it might be pork. He introduced all the grades of rationing to us with heavy jokes, such as the one against bachelors over the milk ration. . .

"Children will get extra milk, of course. Not the bachelors. Though of course the first thing the bachelors will want is to drink milk—even those who despised it most—that's just psychological. It will soon pass, and they will soon call for their '*Molle*' (Berlin slang for beer) again."

One restriction, however, was very clearly put. "It is forbidden to listen to enemy broadcasts," Goering told us. "We aren't frightened of their lies. There is nothing new about enemy lies. In the last war they stormed against the Kaiser. Now they storm against Hitler. They say: 'We have no wish to fight the German population.' But I say, if they drop bombs, who is hit? The civilians, of course. In any case I will take care that the enemy does not drop any bombs!"

I was never tempted to listen to the foreign broadcasts myself. I suppose I just wasn't interested. It never occurred to me during the five years of total war to find out what the English radio was saying. It wasn't fear of punishment. We Germans are a very obedient people, and we admire loyalty. Perhaps that was what really held me back.

Goering's bitter speeches against the Poles, and Mr. Chamberlain's admiration for them, had a very strong effect on me. "What have you to say, Mr. Chamberlain, about the massacre of Bromberg?", Goering stormed one night. "Your

49

chivalrous Polish allies, as you call them. Foreign journalists actually saw the smashed heads and the cut-out eyes and tongues of the German airmen who baled out at Bromberg! This is not German propaganda, *there are photos*! How do Germans behave on the other hand, Mr. Chamberlain? A few days ago a German pilot shot down an English airman on the Dogger Bank and saw him floating in the sea. He landed his plane by the Englishman's side, saved him, and flew him back to a German hospital. I have five officers in the broadcasting station with me tonight to confirm this."

Night after night we listened to this propaganda, just as you in other parts of the world were listening to propaganda against Germany.

"All we want is peace," Goering or Goebbels would thunder after those first great victories in Poland. "Peace with honour, Mr. Chamberlain. We do not want to fight the English people. Nor do we want one inch of France. It is the English who are inciting war. Remember, you Frenchmen, what England has said in the past: 'We will fight to the last Frenchman!' Not to the last Englishman, mark you."

All speeches ended with a fanfare of adoration for the Führer. "It is the Führer who gives us our strength. It is the Führer who has made Germany live again. England will never understand what our Führer means to us. For him we will suffer all things . . . face the greatest trials and sorrows. No one can divide us from our Führer."

Often the speeches took on a religious tone. Neither Hitler nor Goering failed to appeal to God and ask His blessings on the Germans. "My German people, I know that God the Almighty will bless us and will help us. Even if He asks the last sacrifice from us, we will give it with the words —'We die so that Germany may live.'" They died all right, but not that Germany might live.

After this last speech of Goering's many of us were greatly relieved, my mother particularly.

"There is still hope," she said. "We could not express our will for peace better than that. England hates us. She is jealous, that's all. It was just the same in the last war. We are beginning to get too powerful for her again."

But my sister Evelyn, who had come over from Dresden for the week-end, disagreed. "It's not as simple as all that, or have you forgotten Munich?" She helped herself to another portion of bread pudding.

"What were you saying about Munich?" my mother said.

"I was only pointing out that Hitler changes his tune from day to day," said Evelyn. "Once he did everything peacefully and without fighting as in Czechoslovakia for example, now it is all war."

"The Czechs had more brains than the Poles," interrupted my brother Rudolf.

"Perhaps," Evelyn admitted, "but have *we* got more brains? Is it so clever to use force? What about the morality of the thing?"

"Come off it," said Rudolf, and took his glasses from his eyes and wiped them with intense care, a thing he always did when he became impatient in an argument. "I'm sick and tired of hearing, 'but the Führer promised this and the Führer promised that.' What *about* the moral question? Of course the Führer promised. That doesn't mean a thing in politics. If a statesman thinks something is good for his country, he may *have* to break all promises, even if he has taken a solemn vow, signed a contract, or knelt down in front of the Pope. Don't mix morals and politics, Evelyn. There *are* no morals in politics."

"But," gasped my sister Hilde, "then everything is pure hypocrisy; nobody could trust anybody."

"Exactly." Rudolf put a tender arm round her shoulders. She had always been his favourite sister. "Hildemaus, you have hit the nail right on the head. In politics and in the outside world, nobody can trust anybody. That's why we have spies, to find out what the others are up to."

51

"And why the others have spies to find out what we really mean; a funny world." Hilde shook her head in disgust.

"It's a risky game," added Evelyn. "You never know where you are. That's my point, Rudolf. If we let others down and break promises, they might one day do the same to us. The wheel might turn full circle."

"I find the whole thing utter rubbish," I burst out at Rudolf. "Why is it manly to talk about no morals in politics? I think it's weakness. We pride ourselves on building up a great western culture, on Christianity mostly. Yet when it comes to politics we try to break all the rules and think we can get away with it, but we can't."

"Listen to the preacher," said Rudolf ironically. "Else will never learn that a new era is coming, and that we are inventing new ethics and producing a new generation with a totally different outlook on life."

"Don't forget the superman," I cried out. Rudolf had put his finger on a sore spot.

"Stop it. For God's sake stop talking politics," said my mother. " I wonder if there's any spot in Germany where you can have a cup of coffee without a row over politics? Is there no private life left at all?"

Rudolf put back his glasses, and Hilde got up and went to my mother. "All right, darling," she said gently. "All over with the politics. We can't do much about it, anyway."

"What about Christmas?" said my mother. "Which of you will be here over Christmas?"

"I'll come on Christmas Day," I promised. "I'll bring the children too."

"Are they both going to be with you over Christmas, then?" she asked.

"Of course," I told her happily. "I'm getting everything ready now."

"What about coal?" my mother wanted to know. "Have you got enough? You must keep them warm."

"I know." I was slightly hurt by my mother's remark. "I

am saving up all my coal now so that there will be some for the children at Christmas."

"Take care, then, not to catch cold yourself," said my mother. "This winter is pretty grim."

Yes, it was grim. Often I was tempted to light my tall tiled stove when I came back to the empty flat on those winter evenings. Instead, I would keep on my coat and day-dream while I ate what food I felt energetic enough to prepare for myself; daydream about Christmas, with the beautiful great stove (which reached nearly to the ceiling) sending out a great glow of heat. In front of it my two children are with me again, and we are all so happy.

The next Sunday I went to visit my cousin and his wife in Pankow, the cousin who had taken Wolfgang. They lived in a luxury flat with central heating, and of course double-windows, as have most of our houses in Germany. I was so happy as I set out. Work and war were both forgotten. For a few hours I should be a mother again, able to love and kiss my little son. I hummed to myself as I dressed and walked quickly to the underground. It was bitterly cold as I stepped into the streets again. Nearly twenty degrees of frost and with snow on the ground. I still had no winter overcoat, and I began to long to get inside the warm block of flats. Though the hall heating was not on, owing to the war, there was still a soothing atmosphere of luxury on the broad staircase with its rich red carpet.

I envied my cousin Karl for possessing this block of flats. He must make a lot of money out of this place, I thought. The rents from these flats must be pretty high. At any rate Wolfgang was growing up in an atmosphere of warmth and well-being.

I pressed the button of my cousin's flat. After a while the door opened. Kaethe, my cousin's wife, peered out. She was perhaps twenty-three, but very plump, which made her look years older than she was.

She looked at me coldly. "Oh, it's you. What do you

want? We are just going out." She did not ask me to come inside.

"For God's sake, shut that door, the cold is coming in," shouted Karl.

Kaethe beckoned me in, and at that moment the lounge door opened, and Wolfgang rushed out to greet me. He flung his arms round my neck and clung to me with all the joy and enthusiasm of a three-year-old boy.

"Oh, Mutti, Mutti," he stammered, "have you come to take me out for a walk? I would love to go outside and play in the snow."

"Mutti won't do anything of the kind, Wolfgang," Kaethe interrupted him in an icy voice. "I've just dressed you in your best suit. It would be awful if you spoilt it in the snow."

As I looked at Kaethe's face as she spoke, I could see jealousy written all over it.

I tried to comfort Wolfgang. "We'll play together some other time," I said, "but we can still have a nice walk in the snow, can't we?" And I looked at Kaethe inquiringly.

"Impossible!" Kaethe made an impatient gesture with her hands, which were sparkling with pretty rings. "I told you, we are going out."

Before I could speak again, she opened the door to their lounge which was decorated in a beautiful soft green velvet. "But you can have a chat in here with Wolfgang."

She closed the door behind us, and I could hear her go into the next room, Karl's study. After a short while she reappeared again. There was a triumphant smile on her face when she called me. "Karl would like to speak to you." With mixed feelings I followed her to my cousin's room.

Karl did not bother to get up when I entered. "Good afternoon, Else, sit down, please." He made a vague gesture towards the easy chairs.

Karl spoke quickly. "Kaethe told me that last time you were here you wanted to fix the dates with her about Wolfgang and Christmas?"

54

"Yes," I said, unable to say another word as it dawned on me what might follow.

"Well, we are sorry, but you can't have Wolfgang over Christmas. On Christmas Day we are invited out for the whole day, and on Boxing Day we have our friends here."

I was dumbfounded, but trying to save anything that could be saved, I said: "That means I can only have Wolfgang on Christmas Eve then?"

"Christmas Eve?"; both of them yelled it into my ears. Kaethe, plump as she was, jumped to her feet in a flash when I mentioned Christmas Eve.

The actual eve of Christmas is a most sacred holiday in Germany. The morning and afternoon of 24 December are normal and like any other day, but not the late afternoon and evening. People crowd into the churches, which are hardly large enough to hold them, and then go home afterwards, light the candles on the Christmas trees, sing Christmas carols, exchange gifts and spend a quiet but devoted family evening with each other under the tree. Christmas Eve is the heart of Christmas for every German. Christmas Day and Boxing Day are filled with visits and parties, much like other festive occasions. But Christmas Eve means for every German a mixture of religion and family life at its best.

"Don't dare mention Christmas Eve to us," Kaethe was nearly screaming. "How can you suggest taking Wolfgang away like that? This is his home now."

The blow went straight to my heart. Had they taken him so utterly from me?

"Don't you realize how close he has become to us—as close as a son of our own. And now you come along out of the blue and want to upset everyone. Have you no heart at all? We have got to love him very much, and all the time you keep upsetting things by coming and drawing him away from us."

"To put it bluntly," Karl interrupted, " we are tired of

your visits. We think you should cut them down to a minimum. Besides," he smiled ironically, "you definitely don't pay us a sum that entitles you to come so often, do you?"

This was too cruel. I was so terribly hurt that I couldn't speak.

"Therefore we decided," Karl's voice came back to me, "to fix dates when you *can* come to visit Wolfgang. We thought every second Sunday afternoon. You can come and take him out. But we do not wish you to stay here and play with him. We have lots of visitors and it would be a bit embarrassing."

In what way I could not think. My clothes perhaps? I looked shabby. Or were they pretending to new friends that Wolfgang was really their son?

"I hope you understand now that Christmas is definitely off," said Karl.

"After all, you have Klaus as well," Kaethe broke in. "You can spend a very happy Christmas with him, can't you?"

Slowly I got up. My dream of a lovely Christmas with my little sons had gone.

Kaethe, feeling that I had accepted defeat, rushed on to take advantage. "About the summer, by the way. We shall be going to the Baltic a lot. You won't be able to see much of Wolfgang then. It's best for you to know now."

I looked at her. "You are going to my uncle's villa, then?"

"Yes," said Kaethe. "It will be fine for Wolfgang's health."

She was right. It would be fine. The villa—one that my uncle had built for friends and relatives who visited them —was in a most lovely place on the Baltic. There were miles of smooth white sands, pine trees, and the deep blue sea. No doubt Kaethe would live there the whole summer with Wolfgang, and Karl would join them for week-ends— it was only three and a half motoring hours away.

But what could I do now? I mustn't have a scene. Rows would only make the situation worse. Besides Wolfgang might hear, and it would upset him even more. I couldn't take him away from them, could I? I rejected the idea as soon as it flashed into my mind. Where could I put him if I did? In another home? To yet another "Mother"? One thing was certain, after her manner, Kaethe loved Wolfgang. Perhaps as much as she would have loved a child of her own. She was proud of him. She had taught him to call her "Mummy". She would boast of his intelligence which she thought she had discovered. I remembered her smiling face one day because the grocer had passed a remark saying how exactly *her* little boy's eyes resembled her own. Kaethe had been overjoyed at the remark. No, it would not be a good idea to take Wolfgang away. For his sake I must endure this separation.

As if she could read all my thoughts, Kaethe said: "If you don't want it the way we suggest, then you have only to take Wolfgang away."

"I'll think it over," I forced myself to say. I prayed that I wouldn't cry in front of them.

"You have Klaus," I heard Kaethe say again.

"Yes," I repeated like a parrot. "I have Klaus. Will you please tell Wolfgang that I have a headache and can't play with him as I promised."

"Of course, of course." Kaethe smiled. "I'll tell him."

The entrance hall of that elegant house seemed to me now as cold as the ice-queen's palace in the fairy tale. My heart was even colder. I noticed that the frost had painted its pretty flower patterns on the window-panes of the big door. Nobody was about. I leaned against the dark oak-panelled wall and cried bitterly. Here was I, the mother of a lovely little boy, and separated only by a few staircases from him, yet I could not touch or play with him. Probably Kaethe was at that moment trying to distract his attention by playing with his trains, trying to help him overcome his disappointment that "Mutti" had disappeared and broken her promise to play with him. I wanted a miracle to happen so that I could have Wolfgang for just a little while longer. But no miracle happened. No door opened; no one called me back. Kaethe and Karl had Wolfgang, and they did not care about his mother in the least. Presently I went out into the icy streets. There was nothing else for me to do. This time I was glad of the black-out. I walked on almost enjoying the biting cold, it made my heart forget its pain for a moment. It was so dark that people had bought luminous badges which they pinned to their coats. Now and then I saw little pin-points of light coming towards me and passing. I could not see their faces. They could not see mine. I could keep my tears to myself.

The next Sunday I went to visit Mrs. Kroll in Caputh to see my baby Klaus. They were living, Mr. and Mrs. Kroll, in a lovely large country house in a village near Potsdam. The owner of the house had the top apartment, the Krolls the ground floor. The house stood on a hill and had a beautiful view over the village. Caputh is a popular holiday resort for Berliners, and it has many fruit plantations. Even in winter the village is charming. As I climbed the hill to the Kroll's house I turned back to enjoy it all. Caputh, half-covered by the snow, stood there at the bottom of the hill like a fairy tale village with snow glittering on every bush and tree. Mr. and Mrs Kroll received me very kindly as they always did.

"Why do you want a baby at your age?" I had asked them when we first met, for they were both over fifty at the time. Mrs. Kroll had been quite honest.

"Well, first of all we need the pocket-money. We try to live on my husband's investments but they keep going down in value. I adore children and I have always longed for children of my own. I wanted five, you know, when I married! Then it went down to four, and so on. Now, old as I am, I would fall down on my knees and thank God if he just allowed me one! You don't know how lucky you are." She had looked at me with tears in her eyes.

I had now been to the house many times. It was always spotlessly clean and had such a nice homely atmosphere. Mrs. Kroll was an excellent cook and pleasant to look at. Her fair hair, which showed a few white threads was braided and wound in two thick plaits round her head like a crown. She had great dignity and kindness and her deep blue eyes sparkled and flashed with vitality. But this time when I spoke about Christmas, her eyes went cold.

"But you can't take Klaus away during this terrible cold?" she said. You know how bad the trains are, and the waiting rooms at the station are not heated any longer. He will catch a cold. Besides what about his milk ration?" She apparently thought this insurmountable.

"That's quite easy. I have only to go to the local food office and get some travel ration cards for his milk."

"It's not fair to Klaus, nor to us," she added in a lower voice. "He has settled down here and is very happy. It would only upset him."

I just wasn't prepared for this. I had known that Kaethe was desperately attached to Wolfgang, but not Mrs. Kroll.

"You can have him any other time . . . but, please, not at Christmas," said Mrs. Kroll. "You have two sons and many friends, can't you spend Christmas with them . . . go to parties, anything? You are young, you have everything in front of you. But we are old. Klaus is all we have."

It was an appeal. I looked at her husband. He sat there, his white hair shining round his head like a halo. He did not say a word, but looked very troubled. Little Klaus was playing at our feet on the carpet with a small ball and his teddy bear. Just at that moment he was shouting with joy, and seizing his teddy bear he crawled to Mrs. Kroll and held up the teddy bear and talked baby language to her. Mrs. Kroll looked at him, and on a sudden impulse pressed him, teddy bear and all, against her breast. "What has teddy bear done to you? Was he naughty?" she teased him.

Instead of answering, my little Klaus flung his arms round

59

her neck as far as he could reach and pressed his face against her cheek. And that was that. Mrs. Kroll was over-joyed, she laughed and laughed. Even Mr. Kroll gave a short laugh of relief.

I knew I had lost the battle and said no more. Neverthe-less I was desperate. What should I do at Christmas now? I had already asked Mr. Wolter for a few days' leave. I did not wish to tell him now that I did not want it.

Where should I go? Sit alone in my tiny flat? I felt I should go mad all alone there. To my parents? No! The first Christmas after my divorce? I knew what my father thought. After all, he had been right about Richard. Father would remind me of his warnings. Then he would add that I had a right to have my children with me, because I was their mother, and also because I was paying for their keep. To see the human side of it, or the point of view of the foster-parents would be impossible for him. He was a hard man. He would also, I imagined, argue that Richard should be paying for the children, and that I should go to court and sue him for the money. Father would not understand what pride, and contempt for a man, could mean. He only knew about one thing—money.

In my despair I wrote to my aunt in Haynau in Silesia. She had invited me several times to come to her whenever I liked. Her answer came quickly. She invited me at once for Christmas, and said she was looking forward to seeing me. Aunt Felicia—I called her Fee which she liked very much —was a doctor's widow. She too had had no children. One baby was born to her, but only after a very complicated Caesarian operation. The child died soon after birth, and Fee lost her figure completely. Before the operation she had had the tiniest waist I have ever seen. Afterwards, she was so disfigured that she was utterly ashamed of her body. To make things worse she was forbidden to have any more children as they would endanger her life. This made her very bitter.

Fee's husband had died comparatively young. She was left quite alone. From the money point of view she had no worries. She owned a well-built three-storied house, a chauffeur-driven car, and enough money to travel where she liked if she became bored with Haynau.

Haynau was a small industrial town in busy Silesia. It took about one and a half hours to reach from Breslau, the capital. There was nothing interesting about Haynau, and Fee was often bored to death with the place. Therefore she was quite delighted about my coming for Christmas. However, when I arrived at the station she looked rather glum.

"What's the matter?" I asked her. " You don't look too well."

"Who can be well with this war going on?" she snapped back. "This awful, senseless war," she moaned, as we got into the car. "I can't sleep at all."

"But, Feechen, it will soon be over, and you have got a good home, haven't you?"

"That's what you think. You're just like all of them, can't see an inch in front of your nose."

I was tired after my journey, and I didn't want a political argument the moment we met, but Feechen could not stop.

"You are just as bad as all the rest. Don't you see what is happening. Your Hitler is leading Germany to her death."

"He's not *my* Hitler. And it's not a world war. Can't we have just a few days together happily at Christmas. I don't want to talk about the war."

But she went on. Danzig, the Poles, the pact with Russia, and so on and so forth.

We arrived at her flat. "It's lovely and warm in here," I said with relief. Feechen smiled for the first time, and then put her fingers on her lips. "I have my 'contacts'," she laughed. "Don't forget this is Silesia. Why should you Berliners have all our coal?"

"To have contacts" was a favourite Berlin expression in those days.

61

"I thought you were too old-fashioned for that sort of wangle," I laughed back.

"It depends what I am wangling," she told me.

Fee had everything; real bean coffee; a marvellous *Streuselkuchen* (a Silesian cake), and I could scarcely believe my eyes when she produced our lovely sweet whipped cream *"Schlagsahne"*, as we call it. I was thunderstruck, and jumped up and gave her a kiss. "You are being wonderful to me," I told her.

"You don't really deserve it," she said. "Not while you are such a baby politically. You should get only bread and water until you learn some sense."

I suppressed a sigh. If that was going to be the theme for the rest of Christmas I wasn't going to feel much better for it.

"I have another secret," she said suddenly. "But you must promise to keep as silent as the grave about it. Since you young people won't bother, we older ones have got to act ourselves."

"What on earth are you up to?" I asked her.

"I am listening in to the foreign broadcasts. I want to know what is coming, and get ready for it!"

"But you'll land in a concentration camp," I said quickly.

"Am I a child to be told what I can listen to and what I can't?" Feechen flashed back at me. "Don't you know that the English listen in to anything they like? And the French, and the rest of the world?" I looked at her in amazement.

"Did you know that the English even make a joke of our reports and have nicknamed one of our broadcasters 'Lord Haw-haw?'" I was astonished for a moment.

Feechen continued. "The moment Goering forbade us to listen to foreign broadcasts I got interested. I knew something was being hidden from us. Now I know the truth. We are right at the beginning of a Second World War, and a far worse one it is going to be than the First World War."

"Anyone would think you wanted us to be beaten again,

62

the way you talk just because you hate Hitler so much."

Suddenly Feechen became soft and gentle. Her flashing green-grey eyes became warm.

"Oh, no, my baby, it's not that. It's just my way of showing my real love for you all. I love Germany so much. I love her beautiful cities, her youth, her idealism. I love everything about her and in her. It is because I am older and wiser that I am so angry. This wicked man will lead Germany to her doom; destroy everything we have built up; all our ways of life." Feechen leaned back and closed her eyes.

"He may make mistakes, but you *can't* call Hitler wicked," I protested.

"Can't I?" she cried out. "And why not? Doesn't he break every solemn promise he makes? Doesn't he attack the weak and destroy the helpless?"

"Do you mean Munich?"

"Of course, and other things. When Hitler marched into Czechoslovakia in March 1939 he crossed his Rubicon as the English Ambassador Henderson warned us all. By that act Hitler lost all confidence abroad. From that time onwards England started to build up a European coalition against us, and she sent a solemn warning to Hitler that in future she would answer force with force."

Feechen paused, but soon went on again. "They say Hitler laughed at England's warning. He didn't take it seriously. He thought the English only cared about peace. He just hadn't read the history books, or learned from the last war. Only seven days after Czechoslavakia he attacked again. England had protested, France had protested. But Hitler went on—he didn't care."

"I don't follow," I was forced to say.

"I know you don't. You young people are so entangled with your broken marriages you don't see when your own roof is on fire." She paused, only to rush on. "Seven days after Czechoslovakia Hitler attacked Lithuania and demanded the Memel country back for Germany. Then he

demanded Danzig from the Poles. That's why England
became tough. She knew he would never stop now. That's
why they introduced conscription into England."

It was all so very gloomy. The warm flat, the lovely coffee,
the rich cake and cream, did little to counteract the warnings. I couldn't answer back. I honestly did not know the
answers. However I had to say something hopeful.

"We have at least a powerful ally in Russia," I suggested.

"Russia," my aunt said bitterly. "What good is Russia
except to bring in America against us?"

I put my beautiful Meissner china cup down with a
clatter.

"You mark my words, it won't be long before America is
in too . . . and not on our side."

"Never," I insisted. "They will stay neutral."

"That's what you think. Why don't you listen to the
foreign broadcasts and learn the truth? America is loathing
us more and more. All these broken promises. They keep
talking about Roosevelt's requests that Hitler and Mussolini
should join an international conference and stop these terri-
torial demands."

"When have they said all this?" I now asked.

"They have been saying it day after day for nearly a year
now. You should have known ages ago. You are supposed to
be an educated woman and you have two sons, why don't
you find these things out? You're hopeless. You are just as
childish as the rest of Germany. You have a leader, and
that is all you ask. Can't you ever take any individual responsibility at all?"

This didn't seem in the least fair, but Feechen went on,
while I sat back and took it. Then she began giving dates.
"The 14th of April 1939 . . ."

"Ah," I interrupted. "No wonder I wasn't interested at
that time. Klaus was overdue, and I was so terribly unhappy
about Richard. I was too ill to think of politics during those
days just before I went into hospital."

Right: Rudolf between his sisters Else (Mrs. Wendel, on the right) and Hilde.

Left: The author's brother Rudolf. He was in the troopship *Blücher* which was torpedoed off the Norwegian coast and later took part in fierce fighting on the Russian front. These experiences made deep impressions on him. Saddened and embittered, he became convinced that Germany would lose the war. Yet he insisted on returning to active service and was killed during the last stages of the Russian advance on Berlin.

Above: The author's mother-in-law photographed in the sitting-room of her son's home in Berlin-Kladow, where she came to live for a time after her own beautiful home in Hamburg had been destroyed by bombing.

Right: Else's younger sister Erna; after being a mistress at a kindergarten in Berlin she got a better job at a large children's nursery on the island of Norderney before getting a special scholarship to a youth welfare college in East Prussia where she helped to organize two hundred day nurseries.

"Yes, I know, my dear. I'm sorry." Feechen put her hand on my arm suddenly and softly. "You must forgive me. I get carried away. It's living here on my own and feeling so helpless at my age to change anything. But you know you aren't the only one who is blind, and sometimes it makes me boil over, this German characteristic of high intelligence and blind obedience mixed together is frightful. You are all so childish, and I was upset to find you no better than the others."

"I'm afraid I've always hated politics," I excused myself. "They are so dirty. People either get bad-tempered, or become fanatics. I simply haven't the energy to get to the bottom of it any more. I let them get excited and go their own way now."

"But," objected my aunt, "you used to be so different. The last time I talked to you, you told me you had signed up as a member of the Confessing Church, and you told me you had joined the Church to stand by Niemöller. You seemed full of spirit and ideas then."

"That was different," I told her. "That was religion. I feel very deeply about Niemöller and the Jewish question. I have great friends who are Jews, as you know."

"We won't talk any more tonight," said Feechen, and she got up to arrange the black-out curtains. "But I believe it is this Jewish question that will destroy Germany in the end; destroy all respect for her in the world. I tell you, anyway, it will be the Jewish question that will turn the scales in America against us—you wait and see."

Complete darkness fell on the room as my aunt moved about by the windows. I shivered in spite of the fact that the whole flat was centrally heated. I said nothing. I felt that in perhaps this one warning she might be right.

4

A Visit to Jewish Friends

ON Christmas Eve we were in church and listened to Christmas Vespers. The church was full.

We sang all the lovely Christmas songs like *"Stille Nacht, Heilige Nacht."* My heart was touched. There were many Christmas trees in the church. Suddenly I wondered, and looked at the windows. No peaceful sight there. The lovely stained glass was all blacked out with cheap curtaining. The war was in the church too.

At the end of the service we stood up to sing the Christmas message of the angels over the stable in Bethlehem:

> *"Ehre sei Gott in der Hoehe*
> Glory to God in the Highest
> *Und Frieden auf Erden*
> And on earth peace
> *Und den Menschen ein Wohlgefallen."*
> To men of goodwill.

There was a hush over the congregation. We all felt and knew at the same moment that there was no peace on earth and we were very far from goodwill. Could God be glorified by this war? I doubt if one man or woman in that church dared to think so at that moment. Certainly I did not nor did Feechen. I looked at my aunt and saw two tears rolling down her cheeks. I quickly looked away. She was a proud woman and would have resented my seeing her cry. I looked further round and discovered many people bowing their heads whilst singing "peace on earth," trying to hide their emotions.

When we left the church the stars sparkled in the dark sky. The bells were ringing, and Feechen and I walked home, arm in arm, in deep silence. I did not know that very soon I would curse them because they meant good weather and more air-raids from our enemies. The white, dry snow squeaked under our feet. Everything was so peaceful. Only the blacked-out houses reminded us of war. I missed the usual sight of Christmas trees in the windows.

At home I lit the candles of our own little Christmas tree, decorated only with silver-balls and lametta threads— nothing else. We like this kind of decoration in Germany. We do not have many colours on our trees. We think they look more serene when spun only in white and silver. Feechen got a bottle of wine and some home-made biscuits. I was thrilled about the Christmas present she gave me. It was a beautiful underwear set and blouse, both very valuable presents at that time. How she had managed to get such things I didn't ask. Here in Haynau they did not feel the iron grip of war as we did in Berlin.

We settled ourselves in easy chairs, and I exclaimed: "Oh, if only Wolfgang and Klaus were here with us at this moment."

"I know, my dear, but don't be bitter about it. Make sure this is the only Christmas that you ever have to spend apart from them. That's the only way to look at it."

"But what can I do? How shall I ever have them with me again? I tried hard enough this time, didn't I?"

"There's obviously only one thing to do. You can't make a home for them by yourself, nor is it good for them. You must marry again!"

I was utterly taken aback by her sudden proposal. I sat there, staring at her.

"Marry again? Just like that? There's no one I *want* to marry. You don't 'marry again' just like that."

"It's about time you grew up and faced facts," said my aunt quietly. "You must bury your dreams about falling in love and romance. You have two children, and they need a home and a mother and father. The best way to give them that is to find a good, kind man who needs a wife to look after him. You are still young and attractive, you have much to offer."

"It sounds just like a business deal. *He* needs a wife and housekeeper. *I* need a home and father for my children. And how do I transact this business deal?" I was very bitter and very upset at the coldness of the suggestion.

"Now don't go getting worked up, be sensible, my dear. It is your children we must think of first. If they are happy then you can be happy as well. Surely you realize that?"

"I would do anything for my children, you know that," I protested.

"All right then, why not re-marry?"

"But whom shall I marry? What are my chances as a divorced woman with two children?"

"It won't be easy, I admit that," Feechen stated. "But at least you can try."

"Am I to stand at the *Kurfuerstendamm* (the main luxury street of West Berlin) and wait for lovers?", I suggested ironically.

"Don't be so hasty," Feechen said and smiled a little. "If you have no friends to introduce people to you, you can only advertise, or go to a marriage agency."

I was speechless and could only stare at her. Feechen burst out laughing.

"Your face is a picture. You thought me completely Victorian and old-fashioned, didn't you? Yet, I'm the one to show you modern ways. You sit in your little flat and cry your beauty away and accuse God and Hitler, and it never occurs to you to do something about it yourself. But of course you must first of all drop these medieval ideas of a knight stepping up the stairs and falling on bended knee to you. The reality is quite different."

I remained quite silent, but Feechen went on.

"We no longer live in villages where we all know each other, and where you could meet a husband quite easily. I don't suppose you know a single family in your own block of flats, or anything about the tenants. So to stand on your little balcony in Berlin and wait for someone to ride up is quite futile, isn't it?"

"But," I said, and I felt myself change colour as I spoke, "isn't it very risky to put an advertisement in the paper?"

"Of course it is," Feechen agreed. "It is one of the risks that you have to take. But you are grown up and can form your own judgment about men. Don't be hasty. Don't get involved in any way. Take your time and watch. If you meet a prospective partner frequently you will find out what kind of man he really is. See him for weeks, months indeed, before you get involved even emotionally."

Feechen's suggestions partly confused and partly disgusted me. Yet how could I argue against them. Feechen shrugged her shoulders. "Life will teach you. At the moment you have lost your spirit and your hope. You mark my words, life is what you make it!"

Her words were still ringing in my ears as I sat in the train again on my return to Berlin after Christmas. It was a very quiet and a very cold journey. The other passengers were silent and engrossed in their own thoughts. It was the first Christmas of the war, and none of us yet knew what to expect. No move had come from the West. It seemed as though the whole of the world was waiting to see what would happen. Would the Allies ask for peace or would they launch a full-scale war on us? How had Hitler's words affected them by this time?

I know that we Germans are often regarded as boisterous and temperamental in other countries, but I can assure you that we are very quiet and disciplined sometimes. As the journey went on the silence in my compartment seemed to intensify. We sat without speaking a word, each of us sunk in his or her own thoughts, none of us wishing to express them. It was so utterly different from other Christmas journeys. Normally the people in the carriage would have been chattering by this time, perhaps having a snack together or a drink of coffee at the station halts, all bubbling over with Christmas gaiety.

Instead, we went along with blacked-out windows and in absolute silence. It oppressed me more and more. It seemed so unnatural and so unhealthy. Was it fear perhaps, fear of the future? I think it must have been. For years afterwards I met this same dreadful and unnatural silence among our German people again in Berlin 1944.

This time it was in the Berlin streets. I stood in the centre of Berlin, in the Friedrichstrasse, looking in a shop window for some things I had come up from Kladow to buy. The sirens suddenly screamed out over the city. Immediately there was a dead silence all round. Shops closed, business people and gossiping women stopped talking. Then they began to run through the street. Women with children in their arms, or pushing prams; young children quite alone; old people appeared from the houses with blankets and bags. All of them ran, and no one spoke at all. All had a look of blank fear on their faces. In a few moments the trams and buses were empty, and cars were left abandoned by the side of the street. In two or three minutes the whole life of a city seemed to have disappeared. I stood completely alone except for an air-warden I noticed in the porch of a house opposite. Like a scene in a film, it seemed. Then, very frightened myself, I went over to the warden.

"Where is the nearest shelter?", I asked quickly.

He replied by roaring with laughter. "Where do you come from?" I told him, from my house outside Berlin.

He nodded. " Don't you know the shelters are packed like sardines? Why, people queue up long before an alarm for they have a sort of instinct for trouble on the way. Mind you, it's well worth it. The shelters are quite bomb-proof— which is more than these cellars are." He jerked his head to indicate the mass of rubble on each side of him. "Not one soul was rescued from those cellars," he said morbidly. "Not one," the warden repeated. "So now you know why the public shelters will be full."

I began to get more and more frightened. "But where shall I go then?. Can I go into the cellar of this house behind you?"

"No," he said brusquely. "We are full too. The only thing you can do is to go back to the S-*bahn* (Metropolitan railway) and find shelter there in one of the underground tunnels."

"Isn't that about the most dangerous place in Berlin? Surely they always aim at the main railways?"

He shrugged his shoulders. "It's the only advice I can give you. Now, hurry and get off the streets. The Tommies will be here in no time. Heil Hitler!" He turned away.

I ran myself now, this time to the S-*bahn,* and into one of the underground tunnels. I shrank back as I tried to descend the stairs, the tunnel was packed completely full. People were standing on the long, wide platforms, tightly pressed against each other, *in silence.* A man in a brown Party uniform told me that there was no room left here, I must go to tunnel C. I pushed my way on—still that awful silence as I moved.

"Try and move forward as much as you can," the warden of tunnel C told me. "In a minute all the passengers of the last train will be diverted here, then it will be really crowded."

So I walked forward on to the platform as far as I could. The passengers of the last train came down the stairs, again in silence. Soon we were tightly jammed against each other. I suppose if I had looked in a mirror I would have seen the same expression of intense fear and seriousness on my face as I had noticed in the running crowds a few minutes ago. The bombing began. We heard the bombs falling. Some were very near. We could distinctly hear the crash of the

71

explosions and a rumbling noise of falling stones, then splintering glass—something like a gigantic cocktail-shaker.

I looked along the tunnel. The crowd stood motionless, listening. Nobody spoke. This silence! Like a vast crowd watching a funeral, it flashed through my mind. Or were we watching our own funeral? Until the air-raid ended nobody knew. Even the children amongst us did not stir. I was glad no child was near me. I could not bear the look on those tiny, pale faces. Suddenly there was a thundering bang right over our heads, or so it seemed to us. I felt as though the ground under my feet quivered for a second, then the lights went out and big clouds of smoke blew into our tunnel.

For the first time the crowd moved. They all surged forward towards the staircase to escape the smoke. None of us wished to be roasted alive by heat and smoke. If it was burning above our heads it was high time we got out. The lights came on again and a man in brown Party uniform stood at the top of the stairs and shouted: "Don't move. No one is permitted to leave the tunnel!"

The crowd obeyed automatically. We stood quite still in the thick smoke and waited. Children began to cry. The grown-ups near them took it in turns to pick them up and comfort them. Only one man spoke. He bent down and whispered in my ear: "If they manage to get a bomb in there," he indicated with his finger the wall opposite us, "where the Spree is flowing along, then it's good-night!"

I said nothing. I was too frightened to speak. To be drowned in that tunnel like a mouse in a bucket of water?

I went on standing motionless in silence like the hundreds round me, waiting . . . waiting . . . till at long last the all-clear sounded. Immediately Berlin became alive again. As if a spell had been lifted we began to talk and joke again.

"That was a pretty near thing," said the man next to me in quite a different tone of voice now.

That after Christmas journey to Berlin was longer than

72

usual because of this silence, but in a way it suited me. I leaned back on the hard wooden seat of my third-class compartment and went over and over all the things my aunt had said to me, the private advice and the political warnings. Her final outburst just as we left her home was about the German flag. I had made her laugh a little about that. In 1935 Hitler had abolished the traditional German flag with the black, white and red colours. Instead he had made the red Party flag with the Swastika the official flag of the German State. This had infuriated Feechen, who had loved and treasured her ancient flag.

"It's disgusting," she had said to me. "At every victory of our troops I have to hang out the Swastika. I loathe it."

I couldn't help smiling. "Come on, Feechen," I said, "tell the truth. I'll bet the Party flag isn't the only one you hang out, is it?" Then she had laughed. "Of course not. I hang out both of them. What's more I hang the big old flag out of the front window and a wretched tiny little Swastika out of the side window that no one sees."

"At any rate," I teased her, "it was the Reichstag (Parliament) which approved the change of flag you know."

"The Reichstag," she said, "the Reichstag is now a farce. Do you know what the Reichstag is today? Just a choral society, and the highest paid one in the world at that. The members have only to know how to sing *Deutschland über alles* (Germany over everything) and the *Horst-Wessel* song (the Party song) all day to get their big salaries, then they can go home."

I had laughed. I had heard that joke in Berlin too.

But there was no joke to be found in the story she had told me of the Commander-in-Chief of the German Army—von Fritsch.

"Do you realize why he died in the battle of Warsaw?" she had asked me, "or do you too think it was just bad luck?"

I told her I just hadn't thought much about it except to

c*   73

feel it was a tragedy that so great a general should be killed.

" 'Killed' is the word," said Feechen, "von Fritsch quarrelled with Hitler. He did it openly in conferences and in front of other high officials. Hitler never forgives anyone who disagrees with his wonderful judgments. Von Fritsch openly condemned the attack on Poland, and Hitler never forgave him for that. Surely you remember all the attacks in the Press on von Fritsch? How they tried to ferret out ugly things in his private life and could prove nothing against him. General von Blomberg suffered in the same way. Don't you see, my baby," she had said, "what your 'little corporal' is really like? I suppose to suffer a hero's death at the battle of Warsaw was the only thing General-oberst von Fritsch could do," she said.

"You mean it was suicide?"

"Who knows? I can't tell, nobody can, but he was a great soldier. Perhaps death was the easiest and most honourable way out . . ."

*   *   *

I was glad Christmas was over. It had been a gloomy time. I should now be back at work and able to forget some of my own sorrows. Talking about things didn't help. My job was to pull my weight in the Art Department and at least earn enough to make sure my sons had everything they needed. All the same, I did make one New Year resolution. I would go and visit the Treitels, my Jewish friends in Berlin—and try and cheer them up now that they had lost Gerda.

They lived in a large and beautiful house on the Heerstrasse. I chose a very dark evening in January to visit them. It was both unwise, and for me quite dangerous, to visit Jews, working as I did in a high Party organization. Gerda Treitel and I were of the same age. We had attended the same schools and had both passed examinations for the university at the same time. Gerda had decided to study.

chemistry, as her father possessed a pharmacy, and had built up a chemical factory as well. She was an only child, beloved and spoilt by her parents.

At first Gerda had studied in Berlin, then in Heidelberg, and in 1933 she had gone to study in Innsbrück. It was there that the first dark clouds descended on her. Fights and heated arguments were going on between students in Innsbrück about the new National Socialism. There was strong hostility to the Jews, and presently some of the more extreme students began shooting from the rooftops. Gerda decided to leave. She applied for entrance to several universities but was refused. Hitler had already introduced the famous *numerus clausus* which permitted only one per cent of Jews in each university. At last Gerda got an acceptance from Göttingen in North Germany.

Göttingen was a charming little university town, where she was still able to live an unmolested life as an undergraduate. But in 1935 came the "Nürnberger Law for the Protection of German Blood and German Honour". This made it impossible for her to finish her studies. Marriage with Jews was forbidden and every German had to prove his pure Aryan descent. I remember the turmoil this law caused. Not everyone possessed birth, marriage and death certificates belonging to his parents and grandparents, and apart from the difficulty of getting these documents, some of them brought tragedy when they were produced. One young undergraduate I knew had been a passionately loyal member of the Party up till 1935. He had hated the Jews like poison. Now, he found out that he himself had a Jewish grandfather. This young man shot himself.

For Gerda it meant leaving the university. She decided to go abroad. In Basle in Switzerland she managed to complete her studies. When, however, she wanted to return to Germany in 1938, she was told by the German Consulate that this was not possible. They printed the word Jew across her passport and threatened that if ever she attempted to

75

return to Germany she would be arrested immediately and taken to a concentration camp. She got herself a frontier passport which allowed her over the Swiss border for a few days within a certain area. She went to Freiburg in South Germany and 'phoned her parents, asking them to come to her immediately. They brought as many of her possessions as they could. Then they said good-bye. They never saw each other again.

In Switzerland Gerda's position became more and more desperate. No one wanted her and she had signed documents in Basle promising to leave after she had taken her degrees. At last an old friend invited her to England as a guest. All she dared take was a typewriter and two suitcases. In England, Gerda hoped for a miracle, but no miracle happened. The conditions in Germany against Jews became worse, not better. She put down her name for emigration to America, but was told she would have to wait at least five years. Slowly she sank into despair. Nobody wanted her. What it means to be without parents and without a country, only those will understand who have experienced these things. As the Chinese say: "to know what another man feels it is necessary to walk a mile in his shoes". Gerda was not permitted to obtain work in England as she had come only as a visitor. For a little while she managed to exist by selling her jewellery and doing private knitting; finally she married.

All this went through my mind as I groped my way to her parents' house. I had removed the luminous badge from my coat so that no one should notice me. I rang the bell at the Treitel's garden entrance. Slowly the door opened for it was important that no light should show in the garden. Mrs. Treitel hesitated as she came along the garden path.

"Quick, let me in!" I whispered, as soon as she came nearer. She rushed forward. "Oh, it's you! How nice! I thought you had forgotten us!"

There was very little reproach in her voice, only infinite

relief, but once inside her house she nearly burst into tears. She flung her arms round my neck and whispered: "For a moment I thought it was the Gestapo outside to fetch my husband."

Only then did I realize under what strain she must be living, when each time the door bell rang she thought it was the Gestapo. I took off my coat and hat, and was just going to hang them on one of the hooks near the big mirror in the entrance hall, but Mrs. Treitel stopped me.

"No, dear, please come upstairs. I will explain later," she added, while I followed her.

She led me into one of her guest rooms in which Mr. Treitel was sitting very quietly. He put the books aside and got up.

"Welcome to our new home!" he said ironically.

I shook hands with him, and said: "Oh, has it been redecorated then?" Mr. Treitel looked at his wife. "Didn't I tell you that they live on the moon. They have no idea what is really going on."

"Sit down, Else," Mrs. Treitel said, "and let me explain. We have sold our house to quite decent people, and they have allowed us to stay in part of it. That's why they got it so cheaply."

"Oh, I'm sorry," I stammered. "I'm so very sorry." I didn't know what else to say. This was dreadful. Of course I had heard that many Jews sold their property in these days, or rather, I should say, *had* to sell their property. They knew that if they didn't, then the State would soon grab it on some pretext or other. Mrs. Treitel saw my embarrassment and broke the silence. "I suppose we are lucky, really." She was interrupted by a grim short laugh from her husband. "No, Martin, you misunderstand me," she said quickly. "I meant lucky because we found a man who was not a Party member, and who has allowed us to stay in part of it."

"Which rooms have you kept?"

"Just our two guest rooms," she told me. "Luckily they

both have running water in them, so we can wash here and do not need the bathroom."

"Oh." That was all I could say.

"Mr. X told us this arrangement would be the best, so that none of his guests were likely to walk into us." Her voice broke off. Tears were welling into her eyes. She fought bravely for self-control. "We decided to have one really nice room to sit in. The other room is a combined bedroom and kitchen. In here we can pretend to be still elegant, and no smell of food cooking."

"There won't be too much to be cooked," Mr. Treitel interrupted sharply. "They are preparing special ration cards for Jews now."

"How do you like our new lounge?" Mrs. Treitel asked quickly.

I looked around and I thought it all looked fine.

*   *   *

Mr. Treitel had never recovered his old strength and spirit after his time in a concentration camp in 1938.

The fatal *Reichskrystallnacht* (State-Chrystal-Night) in November 1938 with its mad devastations of all Jewish property, and excesses against the Jews, had broken him. I remember the morning of the 10 November when after having left the railway station Berlin-Wilmersdorf I walked down the Kaiserallee and suddenly noticed a big luxury shop completely smashed. The big plate-glass windows had been broken and lay scattered in the street. This was a shop for lamps. The lamp-shades and stands had been seized and trampled down and no more lamps were hanging from the ceiling. The mess on the floor of the shop was indescribable. I stopped and looked in bewilderment at this wreckage. A man behind me stopped and shook his head.

"I wonder," I said to him, "that nobody around here heard this noise. It must have taken them quite a considerable time to achieve all this demolition. They could have been caught easily."

The man gave a short laugh and said: "This hooliganism has been carried out by the SA!" and he quickly walked away as if he was afraid of having said too much.

In the concentration camp Mr. Treitel had been subjected to every kind of insult and cruelty. He returned home a changed man. His wife had nursed him back to some kind of physical health but his spirit she could not restore. Once he had been a brilliant and witty conversationalist, now he sat silent. True, they had made many attempts at emigration before the war broke out, but every country had long waiting lists and they were no longer young. His factory, of course, he had to sell; now his home. Jews were not allowed to own factories or houses.

It was so difficult to talk to them. Everything I said only seemed to bring out their own plight more forcibly. I, at least, was free and honoured in my country. They, who had once lived so well were now sitting in terror in two rooms. Each morning Mr. Treitel had to rise at 6 a.m. and go out to wash bottles in a chemical factory. The owner of the factory, a former friend, had implored him not to miss a day's work or call attention to himself in any way. He swallowed all insults and all privations, but he became silent and morose. Only his large, dark brown eyes really showed his feelings now and they were infinitely sad. I didn't think he was attending to our conversation at all, but he was. Suddenly he broke into our talk.

"Don't you run away with any hopes of peace like that," he said. "There is no hope for peace. Hitler has gone too far. He has lost the trust of the whole world. He isn't as clever as he thinks, in fact he is a fool. He has lost every friend in the outside world. Hitler has isolated Germany, and we cannot survive in isolation. Roosevelt has clearly shown where American sympathies lie. They do not lie with dictators, either German or Russian."

"You mean America will come in against Russia, then?"
I interrupted. "That will mean a long war."

"Yes," said Mr. Treitel sadly, and then sank back into
his chair in silence again. I left soon after that. I felt I had
done very little good, but Mrs. Treitel was kind and affec-
tionate when I left.

"I'm so glad you managed to get him out of himself just
for a short time," she said. "Normally he won't speak to
anyone. Did you notice how thin he is?" Yes, I had noticed.

"He sits there as a rule not saying a word, just living in
solitary confinement. He used to love visitors but not many
people find their way to us now," she added slowly. "Sometimes he tries to convince me that he doesn't need people,
but he does, you know, only his pride won't allow him to
admit it. That's why I am so glad you came and made him
talk a little." I shook hands at the garden door and promised
her to come to visit them often.

5

My Sisters and Brother

I⒯ was the late spring of 1940. Nothing but victories had
come our way. Look at the list of them. The surrender of
Denmark without any fighting; the surrender of the Nether-
lands; the surrender of Belgium; the victory of Dunkirk;
the surrender of Norway; Italy declares war on France; the
armistice with France.

What stupendous successes! All my fears disappeared
for there was hope again. I loved that spring and summer,
and so did everybody in Berlin. Victory flags, victory music,
victory gaiety. Everything was all right in Germany.

I thought it a brilliant gesture when Hitler decided to
sign the armistice with France in the same railway carriage
in which the 1918 Peace Declaration was signed. The
delight of seeing photographs of Hitler sitting in the same
chair as Foch in 1918 was overwhelming. The French had
now had the tables turned on them, and the British too. Germany stood once again in her true place in Europe. A great
people who had proved themselves more than equal to the
rest of the world. France had asked for it and France had
got it. England had asked for it and she had got Dunkirk.

"What did I tell you?" Mr. Wolter asked me triumphantly
in our office. "Don't you admit now that our Führer is the
greatest man in the world?"

"Yes," I replied, "I do, and without reservations. As for
politics, I realize we women don't understand them at all."

Mr. Wolter laughed. "It took you long enough. Leave
politics to men, that's how it should be. By the way, can you
speak English?"

Oh, yes, I could speak English, had indeed studied it up to university standards.

"Very well, then, I will take you with me when we go to England. We intend to export the factory exhibitions to England, so one fine day we may find ourselves working in London!"

We both laughed.

Naturally we were all intoxicated by our victories. And if my personal life had not been sad, I too should have joined in the celebrations and victory parties. No doubt we now and then (at least the women amongst us) thought of our defeated enemies and were sorry for them, but the strongest feeling of all was our pride in Germany, showing the world that the Treaty of Versailles, with its bitter humiliations, had been broken. I was proud to be German. I was also proud of Hitler. Indeed all those who formerly had had doubts about Hitler were now carried away in respect and admiration. He had put Germany back as a great nation in the world.

Feverishly we waited for the invasion of England. Some of us were astonished that it did not at once follow the defeat of the British Army at Dunkirk. But this time I did not become sceptical. I had learnt my lesson that I really could not judge political or military situations at all. We must leave these things to Hitler and trust his judgment. The Press, too, assured us daily that the day was not far distant when we would land in England.

They were good and busy days for me. I got up early and went to the office to find everyone all smiles and confident. Soon we should invade England and then the war would be over. We didn't hate the English so much now, but just felt rather sorry for what was coming to them. Germany had proved herself to be the greatest nation in the world. England would no doubt turn out to be quite a valuable ally when she had swallowed her pride and acknowledged defeat. Only now and then did my spirits flag. When the day's work was over and I went for a lonely walk in the vast Tiergarten, a huge park similar to Hyde Park, full of trees and flowers and saw happy mothers playing with their children, then I began to feel very sorry for myself. Victories—a great future for Germany—what did they mean if I was never to see my sons, bring them up, and love them? In the evenings, too, I could not keep up victory feelings for long. I would shut the windows quickly so as not to hear children's voices and laughter.

I could see nothing for it but to stick it out. One moment I was buoyed up with hopes of a better job and a small home with my boys with me. The next I was in despair knowing I had failed once and should probably fail again. Usually these mental battles ended in a sleepless night. I got a fortnight's holiday and did not know what to do with it. Wolfgang had gone to Pommern on the Baltic, so I couldn't see him. And Klaus? The dream of having him with me had also gone. Klaus had become so attached to Mrs. Kroll that he was actually frightened of me when I went there. In the last months I had visited them this fact had clearly been brought home to me. I had arrived one afternoon when he was just waking up from his after-lunch nap, and had suggested I dress him while Mrs. Kroll prepared the coffee. I took one of his socks to put it on. To my surprise he drew back from me. Thinking he was playing, I took his ankle firmly and tried again. He started to cry loudly. I tried to soothe him, but the moment I came near he screamed as though I were going to murder him. Hastily the door had opened, and Mrs. Kroll had come to see what was going on. "Is he hurt?", she asked. The moment Klaus saw her he smiled all over his face and stretched out his arms to her.

"What happened?" Mrs. Kroll asked.

"I only tried to put his socks on," I explained.

After that I doubled my efforts to make friends with my little son, but it was all hopeless. He cried if I touched him, even while he was sitting on Mrs. Kroll's lap. I persevered for as long as I could but Klaus was terrified of me. So in the end I got up and said I would make the coffee.

"Next time you come you must try again. I expect it was just that he was upset after his nap, children often are touchy then," said Mrs. Kroll. I had tried again, many times, but it was always the same. Klaus was only interested in one person—Mrs. Kroll. I was not a welcome visitor. I daren't, therefore, suggest that I should spend my holidays with Klaus in my flat. Mrs. Kroll kindly invited me to spend my holidays in her house in order to be near Klaus and make him more accustomed to me. I accepted this gratefully.

But my mother suggested I should go there only for a week. "You couldn't," she said, "stand a fortnight of seeing another woman taking all his love; it would break your heart. Why not go and spend the second week with Evelyn in Aue?"

My sister Evelyn was engaged now. She had met and fallen in love with a young doctor of about her own age. They were to have their engagement party in July. His name was Manfred.

"That's a good idea. I should like to get to know the *fiancé*," I said.

So it was settled in the end. One week at Caputh with Klaus and one in Aue with Evelyn's future parents-in-law. It was lovely in Aue. Aue itself is a small town; its houses climb picturesquely up a rather steep slope from a valley. Manfred's home was situated on the top border of the valley, and had a lovely view over the whole countryside. You gazed down at the friendly little houses hanging like swallow's nests on the steep rocks. To-day, of course, Aue is a heavily guarded district of East Germany, undertunnelled as the Russians have found uranium there. It is now an industrial town and a forbidden area, but in 1940 the beauty and peacefulness of that valley touched the heart.

I liked Manfred from the very beginning. He was a very sympathetic young man and always ready for a joke.

84

Naturally he was full of forbidden jokes, as he called them, and I sometimes wondered if he really understood the bitter double meanings of some of the jokes he repeated so blithely. When he heard that I was working at the head office of the Strength through Joy movement, he asked whether I knew the picture by Padua with the title: "In the dentist's waiting-room".

I was rather embarrassed to admit that I did not know it. I tried to explain to him that I was rather busy, could not know everything.

He roared with laughter. "Perhaps I can help you," he exclaimed, "by giving you another title for the picture: 'The Leader (Führer) speaks!'"

Padua had painted a picture showing various persons respectively listening to a speech by Hitler.

He asked me how the "Mickey-Mouse" of Berlin was.

I had no idea what he meant.

"I mean 'Wotan's Mickey-Mouse'," Manfred added, trying to help me.

At last I got it. He meant Goebbels, the "Nordic shrinking German," as he called him, or Hitler's "Mickey-Mouse".

I was amazed. In Berlin I was used to the fact that anyone telling a joke usually looked round to make sure that the "air was pure," as Berliners said. But Manfred did not care whether the windows were open, or whether he was walking in the street; he said whatever he liked. He was so frank that I could not help calling him "Siegfried".

"Are you always like this, Siegfried?" I teased him.

"Always," he told me. He took Evelyn's arm, and my arm, and the three of us marched down the streets of Aue while he sang one light song after another. Passers-by stopped and laughed at us.

It was a lovely engagement party. All the relatives turned up, and each one had brought something. Evelyn was presented with dozens of clothing and textile coupons, so that she could choose new things for her trousseau. I thought she looked like a princess in a fairy tale that summer afternoon. She had on a charming pale blue silk dress with white embroidery on it, and her blue eyes and dark eyebrows were strikingly lovely.

"You'll always stay young and beautiful," I told her as I kissed her cheek. "You'll look twenty-five when you are fifty."

They all laughed at this, all except Evelyn. She took it seriously.

"Of course," she replied eagerly. "I know I shall, with Manfred by my side," and she gave him a long and tender look.

There seemed not a cloud anywhere, either outside or inside in the little family circle, not until Manfred suddenly asked Rudolf a question about his torpedo experiences in Norway that year. It was a tragedy really, but Manfred insisted.

"What was the water like? A bit colder than it is to-day, I imagine?"

"Icy-cold," said Rudolf abruptly. Rudolf had been on the big troopship *Blücher* which had been torpedoed off the Norwegian coast. Manfred was like a boy. He wanted to know full details then and there. Reluctantly Rudolf described how he was just standing on deck when suddenly a voice screamed: "We are torpedoed!"

"It made my heart stop for a moment," Rudolf said. "I was standing there stunned when orders came to abandon ship. We were told to jump clear immediately. Some hesitated, and some ran to the other side where the deck was lower, but it was the wrong side. Some men didn't move, they just went down with the ship."

I didn't grasp that bit. "If I had had the chance I should have taken it," I said. "Not stood there and gone down."

"You don't understand, Else. The ship had keeled over violently, and the deck was high above the water level. The water below was icy-cold too. It was a terrible risk. To me it seemed eternity before I came to the surface after I jumped."

"What was that about the wrong side of the ship?" Hilde asked.

"That was the side where the suction is, the side the boat is listing on. If you jump on that side you don't come up again," said Rudolf. "We had been warned before about this, but some of them were too scared at the height to jump and so ran to the wrong side. They went down in the suction and so did those who jumped badly on my side."

He went on to tell us all about the terrible swim to the shore. "It was so cold after a few strokes I couldn't feel my limbs at all; I just went on automatically. I didn't know if I was gaining on the tide or not, all I noticed was that the heads around me seemed to be growing fewer and fewer. The temptation to give up and sink, was very strong, but the waves seemed to play a cat and mouse game with me. The moment I had decided I couldn't stand any more, I was tossed up into the air. I came down again into the water and began to swim desperately.

"How I reached the shore, I don't know. One moment I was blindly struggling in the water, and the next I found myself stumbling up the shore to fall flat on the stones. There were others lying all round me. Sitting here with you in this sunny garden it's difficult to remember what I felt. But you wanted the details, Manfred, and you shall have them. You are a doctor, anyway, and you ought to know. We lay there more dead than alive. There were men screaming for help all round us, but I for one couldn't help, or didn't help—I had better be absolutely honest, I don't know which it actually was. Some men did, however, strip off their clothes and go back into the water to try and help their comrades. Often they failed, as the men in the water were too frozen to cling to anyone.

"Worst of all," Rudolf said, "was the screaming from the men in the water who were burning in the oil patches. The oil had caught fire suddenly. Those in them had only two choices, to sink and drown, or go on swimming and be burned to death. The sounds and sights were like hell, absolutely terrible.

"When I was a little boy I wanted to have an exact description of what hell was like. No one could give it to me. Today I can say I have seen hell. Many of those young soldiers called continuously for their mothers as they died. Their last screams were 'Mutti!' I'm afraid I can't forget. I can still see those heads going up and down on the grey-green water and hear those screams." He got up and left us abruptly and went for a walk by himself. We sat there completely silenced by his story. The birds went on singing. Evelyn twitched at her blue dress; Manfred forced a smile and took her hand, but none of us spoke.

Then at last Manfred's mother found the right words. "We can't get away from the war, you know. It's no use pretending. It's here right in the midst of our happiness. Perhaps it's just as well that Rudolf reminded us. It's useless to try to forget, and dance and be merry all the time. Let's face facts properly. We'll have another toast, darling," she said to Manfred. "We've toasted your happiness, now we'll have a toast for everyone's happiness." She lifted her glass, but before she could give the toast my mother jumped up and said: "To the end of all wars, and hope to all people".

We all stood and silently emptied our glasses. My mother and Manfred's mother had only met a few hours before, two mothers worrying for the safety of their sons.

"To the end of war," Manfred's mother repeated.

I travelled back to Berlin with my younger sister, Erna. She stayed with me for the night in my flat, and then we went out to Caputh to see little Klaus the next day. I hadn't seen Erna for two years. She had always been pale and thin as a girl, but now she looked frightfully ill.

"You look paler than ever," I told her that evening. "What is it? Is there something wrong?"

"I don't think so," she told me. "But I don't want to spoil this beautiful evening with my troubles," she replied.

It was indeed a lovely evening. We were sitting on my tiny balcony watching the light fade over the trees below. Berlin, peaceful for a moment, and without a light showing anywhere through the black-out, stretched out around us.

"Why should your troubles spoil my evening. Go on, talk them out of you, Erna," I suggested. "We meet so seldom."

She hesitated for a moment. It wasn't easy for her to talk to me. We were very different in temperament, and she was a shy person who hated to talk about herself. Even as children Erna and I had never got on too well. I had been the rebellious one in the family, always fighting my father; Erna had sided with him, perhaps for the sake of peace; so we had grown farther and farther apart.

I know, of course, she had passed her examinations and become an assistant kindergarten mistress in Anna von Gierke's college in Berlin. I knew she had done very well and been given two years' free tuition, but after that I heard very little about her. Now at last we were together again over Evelyn's engagement.

"Funny we should be like this," she began. "What a long time it seems. Do you really want to hear what has been happening to me?"

I nodded. " Of course I do."

"Well, all the work didn't amount to anything much in the end. There were too many assistant kindergarten mistresses. I got less than a servant to begin with and worse than a servant's treatment. Hitler's arrival didn't change things at all, you know. My salary still stayed at £2 5s. a month, with, of course, free board. I had to pay my fees at the college out of that while in a job. You can imagine that I haven't had a holiday for years, let alone proper clothes. Things were so bad at one time that I went out planting chrysanthemums in a nursery garden eight hours a day; they paid me twenty pfennig the day (4d.)."

"Why didn't you write for help?"

"What use?" she answered. "You all had your troubles in the family, and as father would have said I had insisted on this training, and it was nobody's fault but my own!" At last she got a better job as assistant in the Kaiserin-Friedrich Seehospiz on the island of Norderney. It was a huge nursery of eight hundred children run by a woman doctor from Siebenbürgen.

"The aim in that hospital was absolute perfection," Erna told me with a smile. "Physical perfection, that is," she added. "Thirty beds in one room was the average. We had to keep the beds in perfectly straight lines, indeed we actually used boards and string to fix them correctly, rather like a gardener clipping the edges of a lawn. The laundry in the children's cupboards had to be piled up to one pattern only, and to the millimetre of precision, otherwise—dismissal! The whole life of the nursery was run like a barracks." She smiled rather bitterly.

"Weight was the most important item. The children's weight *must* increase, whatever the cost. I actually saw small children putting stones into their mouths just before they were weighed. They knew quite well that if their weight hadn't increased that week then they would be made to undergo a 'rest-cure' and would have to lie down for long hours, mid-morning and mid-afternoon. Some of the children tried the trick of not going to the toilet for days so as to increase their weight."

"But how absurd, how cruel," I protested.

"I know. It depressed me horribly. It was completely against everything I had learned in my training. The whole place was like a farm for fattening up geese."

"Thank God, my children never had to go to such a place," I interrupted.

"I was just about to go, when in 1935 the Seehospiz was taken over by the NSV (National Social Welfare), and all kinds of changes took place. A trained youth welfare worker came and we were allowed to treat the children a little more like human beings.

"I can't tell you the relief when 'scales day' was just an ordinary routine, and not a torture for everyone. We all became enthusiastic again and thought out new games, new sports, and even new paint and decorations for the walls for the children. We didn't object at all to the brown uniforms we now had to wear, nor the swastika flag we had to hoist up each morning in a rather festive ceremony."

"Politics in the nursery, too, then," I teased.

"Of course," laughed Erna. "But at first they weren't too tiresome. We were asked to attend lectures by the Party leader on the island, but we got a lot of fun out of them. Have you noticed how pompous some men become when they start building new worlds?"

"It doesn't seem to take women quite the same way," I said.

"I remember one Party leader was being particularly pleased with himself and unintentionally funny at one of the meetings, and some of us started to giggle. I lost control of myself, and heads began to turn. You know how it is? An awful fit of giggling when everyone else is feeling solemn? I couldn't stop, and the tears began to roll down my cheeks. I grabbed my handkerchief and pressed it to my face—that finished it. A man came up to me and offered to escort me outside as I seemed so upset. I was shaking with laughter, but didn't dare to tell him, so I took his arm and accepted a drink of water, then fled to the cloakroom to finish my giggles."

She had, however, to leave Norderney in the end simply because they refused to raise her salary.

"I just couldn't keep body and soul together any longer. It was still only £2 5s. a month and more studies to pay for to qualify fully. I went off to take a course as a leader in the *Landjahr* (land year) scheme.

"I made an awful blunder though with my first shot. I'm

91

an idiot you know, Else. I never see the political side of things in time. There were about a hundred of us applying for the twenty-five jobs. I knew my subject thoroughly— the psychology, the sports, the handicrafts and the general health of young people. I had, however, to give a lecture on the value of the family. It must have been that speech that lost me the job. I began with Greek ideals of healthy mind in a healthy body, etc., etc., but I forgot to get up to Party politics, that omission must have signed my death warrant. All the members of the selecting board were high Party officials I found out afterwards, though not one of them knew anything about farming or about unemployed youth."

Eventually, Erna told me, the leader of the Norderney nursery helped her to get a special scholarship at a college for youth welfare work in Königsberg in East Prussia.

"The work there was very interesting, and there wasn't much Party pressure, only of course all the new history books and the new ideals of racial purity. Some of the activities were a bit boring (the folk dancing and national customs) but it was intended to inspire the farm workers. What I really wanted, of course, was to work with small children all the time. My chance came when they wanted a secretary to organize the day nurseries for the farm workers' children."

Erna was completely relaxed now. I looked at her, talking quickly and happily. It was an Erna I had honestly never seen before, even though she was so very pale and thin.

"You *do* love your work, don't you?" I said. "It means everything to you, I can see. I'm so glad."

"Yes," she told me. "I adore it. It was just the job I had been longing for. I worked like a Trojan, and in two years I had got two hundred nurseries ready for the seasonal rushes. I took them over from any source I could find, from the Red Cross, the Evangelic Church and from the Catholic Caritas League. In the end I decided to become a Party member so that I could really throw myself into the work."

92

She stopped for a moment and went on. "That's when the snags started. I found the Party were recruiting sillier and sillier men at the top. They were impossible to work with, I just couldn't see eye to eye with any of them. Only a few months ago, for instance, one of the new bosses called me in and told me that I must find ten new day nurseries in two months. Do you realize what he was asking? I had not only got to find the premises, but the staff as well! And the premises had to be bought and possibly entirely re-decorated and equipped. I told him it was impossible, and what do you think he said. He just shouted at me that I was being 'unco-operative'; that there was plenty of money to support me and that I should be proud and happy to get on with the job and not make all these silly excuses! He just hadn't a clue as to the work involved, none of the new men had. I don't know what is happening in the Party, only incompetent fools are getting to the top now."

By now it had become completely dark. The black trees down in the park below rustled gently and a half-moon helped to bring light to my sister's face. She looked more than worried; she looked terribly sad, I thought.

"Go on . . . what are you going to do now?" I urged her.

"I just don't know. It's hopeless really. There was just one man who understood. He's an Austrian, a quite out-standing person, with a lot of spiritual strength. He's the only one there who tackled the problems on their right plane. He's helped me a lot with the new Party chiefs, par-ticularly as he has enormous charm. I've been very lucky in having him as my immediate chief."

"And now?" I asked.

"And now he's gone," she said despondently.

"But why if he had the same ideals as yourself, and the work was going so well?"

"The Party fools from headquarters," said Erna. "And honestly it was all over a cigarette—that's what breaks my heart. A stupid thing like that, and all my work. . . ."

"Erna," I said, "it can't just die out like that," I protested.

"You just don't know, Else, about the insane things that happen today. . . ."

It seemed that a new Party leader was to be brought to East Prussia.

"It was all organized in the usual way. A huge reception at the Town Hall, flowers, music and crowds to applaud. We were ordered to attend an hour before the leader was due to arrive. On our way to the hall, my chief said: 'This will be about the most useless hour in my whole life.' I laughed as he said it. I found out afterwards I laughed a bit too soon.

"For a whole hour they drilled us. We were to greet the new Gauleiter with the words 'Heil Gauleiter' in a chorus. We were to rise, shout, and then the band was to play, and the flowers presented.

" 'What a circus!' my chief whispered in my ear. I burst into laughter. There were others round us also smiling a bit too broadly. It was a most ridiculous sight really. There we all stood—the whole town really—dressed in our best uniforms and dresses with flags and flowers everywhere. Carpets and the Hitler-Youth flanked both sides of the long alley from the exact spot on the pavement where the car would stop. The orchestra was poised at the ready.

" 'You will all shout 'Heil Gauleiter' three times as the new leader enters—once as he reaches the entrance, the second time as he reaches the bottom step . . . the third time . . . come on now . . . *eins* . . . *zwei* . . . *drei*.'

"Again and again we *'eined'*, *'zweid'* and *'dreid'*, all like good, well-drilled school children or soldiers. I dared not look at my chief any longer as we bawled and bawled our 'Heil Gauleiters' for that hour, and the poor exhausted orchestra practised and practised the opening bars of their *Deutschland über alles* and the *Horst Wessel* song.

"At last we were permitted to sit down and relax. 'Thank God for small mercies at any rate,' said my chief, and hastily plunged in his pocket for a cigarette. 'Another moment of that, and . . .' But just at that second the Gauleiter *did* arrive, so up we popped again and the chorus started, only this time in earnest.

"Everything went according to the book. The 'Heil Gauleiters', the songs, the flowers and the dreary speeches.

"Again we collapsed into our seats; the session was over and we could relax. 'Now for that cigarette,' said my chief. He found it, and began to puff away contentedly. Suddenly we heard his name shouted over the heads of the crowd.

"'Herr X, what on earth do you think you are doing?' A high Party official stepped up to us with all the air of an insulted god.

"'As you see, I am smoking,' came my chief's calm answer.

"'How dare you? But it's always the same,' the Party official shot his shoulders up in disgust. 'You Austrians are all the same. No sense of discipline at all. Stop smoking immediately, or take the consequences!'

"'I'll take the consequences, I think,' said my chief, and with a bland smile got up and left the hall, the cigarette in his hand." Erna stopped speaking rather abruptly.

"But that's not the end of the story, surely?" I asked. "Couldn't you put it right?"

"No," said my sister. "No one dared to try and bring the Party man to his senses. They all stood back and let him go around boasting he had ticked my boss off in public."

"But you, *you* will stay on?", I urged.

"No," said Erna, "I'm going too. I've thought it over a lot. It's useless to fight against them. Do you know what my chief said as he left? 'This is only the beginning of a very bad end. The top jobs are falling more and more to men who know less and less, the very scum indeed. All you have to do today is kneel down and worship Hitler—you don't want any other qualifications for your job of work at all.'"

"If it's really like that, then the whole thing will crash," I said.

"All I hope is they are just having the measles in the Party," said Erna. "I suppose the Party organisation has grown too quickly and hence all the trouble. All we get today is either favourites of the Party from Berlin and Munich or freshmen from *élite* German youth exported from Ordensburgen (training school for selected German youth for future high Party rôles). There's no room anywhere for the real craftsman."

"You're very bitter, Erna," I told her.

"I'm not so much bitter, as terribly sad. You don't know how I've worked at this job. I've put my whole heart and soul into it; and it's not that I'm losing faith in the Führer's ideals. I'm not. But it's the men he is choosing around him. . ."

"What will you do, then?"

"I shall try to find a quiet job in South Germany, somewhere a little farther from Berlin, somewhere much smaller, where the officials don't interfere so much."

The next morning we walked along the Havel to Caputh. It was such a clear and warm summer morning, and it was good to have Erna with me. We wandered along, through the small paths in the woods by the river banks. Serious problems did not fit in with our mood as we just chatted about little Klaus.

"Why, you didn't tell me how friendly and charming he was," said Erna, as Klaus showed his teddy bear to her. "He's the sweetest little boy. How terrible it must be to be parted from him."

She turned and looked at me with a lovely smile. "We've never understood each other before, have we? How glad I am I came back with you, I don't feel so bad now."

This photograph was taken shortly after Else's marriage to Heiner in 1942 and her re-union with Klaus and Wolfgang.

Left: The author's mother, a photograph taken in 1939. Of very gentle and kindly disposition, she was deeply affected by the First World War; the terrible years of the Second marked her beautiful face with deep lines and turned her black hair white.

Below: The villa near the Baltic Sea in which the author's mother lived and where, when the Russians overran the district, she committed suicide.

6

Advertising for a Husband

JUST before Christmas 1940 Karl and Kaethe put the thumbscrews on again. They had been more and more difficult all that autumn, happening "just to be out" when I called to see Wolfgang on even the alternate Sundays. But this time when I arrived they were both in, and asked me at once to come into the study. Without any preliminaries at all, they went straight to the point.

"We have decided we would like to adopt Wolfgang legally," they said. "Or," said Karl. . .

"Or what?", I asked in a whisper.

"Or you can take him back with you, here and now," he explained.

I sank down into a chair, for in their excitement they had forgotten to offer me one. Kaethe ran into the kitchen to bring me a glass of water, and Karl started to paint Wolfgang's future with them in the brightest possible colours.

"Think of the advantages," he said quickly. "If Wolfgang were my son he could have the finest education, some capital to start life with, and every advantage in the world. Look at the property there is, all that would come to Wolfgang."

I drank the glass of water.

Karl went on. "What have you honestly got to offer Wolfgang yourself and with another son to bring up as well?"

I said nothing. There was nothing I could say about material prospects for Wolfgang.

"Does Richard help at all?" Karl asked.

"No. He has never sent a penny," I said.

D

"I thought not. There you are."

It was now Kaethe's turn. "If you really loved Wolfgang you would think of him first," she told me. "You know that I love him as if he were my own son."

"I don't think you realize how much it costs to bring a boy up," said Karl. "The money you give us in no way covers the cost of his living here. To mention a small matter, he needs at the moment a new and larger bed, he has grown out of the one you sent. Have you the money to buy him a new bed?"

"Not a new one," I told them. "But I could find the money for a second-hand one perhaps."

"That's out of the question," Kaethe called out quickly. "I'm not having any second-hand furniture in *my* home."

They were quite pitiless. First Karl and then Kaethe put up their arguments, and always it was from Wolfgang's angle; what was best for him. Finally they agreed that I could not decide then and there. I might be permitted to think it over during the winter months.

In the circumstances I just hadn't the courage to ask for Wolfgang for Christmas. Instead, I left them at once and spent the saddest Christmas of my life, alone in my little flat. My mother urged me to come and spend at least Christmas Day with them, as Hilde and Rudolf would both be there, but I could not face anyone at all. So I invented an invitation from friends, and my mother accepted it as the truth.

It wasn't cold that Christmas Eve in my flat, as I had saved many sacks of coal towards the holiday, thinking that at least Wolfgang might be with me. I sat there, though, as cold as ice. I had not bothered to buy even the branch of a Christmas tree, nor any candles; what was the point? Anything reminding me of the day would only have brought tears. I wanted above all things not to cry. I *must* be calm and try to come to some decision about my future. I thought of last Christmas, and Feechen saying to me: "I have no

98

patience with people who sit down and cry instead of trying to tackle their problems. Life will teach you," she had added.

Life seemed to be teaching me. But what? Was I to give up both my sons to other women and forget all about them? Was that what was best? Wolfgang loved Kaethe—called her his 'Mami', and she was good to him. She certainly gave him all the love she was capable of. Besides there was a war on, I argued. Rations were getting smaller and smaller. Kaethe and Karl could afford the extras for Wolfgang that I could not. And supposing I took Wolfgang from them and put him with another woman in order not to have him adopted, what then? He might be treated badly. One could really trust nobody in this life.

Through the thin walls of my flat the voices of the neighbours' children began to come. They were singing Christmas carols. This was too much. I couldn't stay calm and collected any longer. I sank down on my knees and buried my face in the cushions to shut out the sound. But it was too clear. I rushed into my kitchen and decided to make coffee. The singing followed me. Then into the bathroom to plunge my face in cold water to try and gain some kind of control. It was useless. Everywhere the children's voices reached me, singing of this happiest of all nights in the year. In desperation I took a coat and went out into the night. There wasn't a soul on the streets. On Christmas Eve nobody goes out to walk about alone. They stay close at home with those nearest and dearest to them.

Berlin looked like a forsaken city. Certainly there was music and laughter coming into the air, but no lights, no candles and no Christmas trees showed through the carefully blacked-out windows. By now I had begun to run towards the park. I felt I must get away from the songs and the laughter. I ran on and stumbled over the root of a tree and fell down. I picked myself up and leaned against the cold bark. In the madness of misery I flung my arms round it as if it were something alive and warm. I even found myself talking to it. "What have I done to be punished like this?", I said aloud.

Then I dropped my arms. How stupid to talk to a tree. It had no heart. It was dead. By now my eyes had grown used to the darkness, and I could see other great trees all round me lifting their leafless branches to the sky. A queer thought came into my head. "They are as alone and poor as I am. All their life and beauty have gone, too, with their leaves. But they don't cry out and complain and behave like a madwoman. They just stand and suffer in absolute silence." A light wind moved their branches so that a little shower of snow fell down on my upturned face.

Slowly, as I stood there watching the snow floating down, some kind of peace came to me. I had to accept suffering and try to use it in some way, patiently, like the trees did. Another argument also came into my mind. God had given me children. He didn't then mean me to give them up. He meant me somehow to go on being their mother. I was responsible for them. I must think of some way of keeping my children. I must fight.

It was nearly midnight when I returned to my flat. All was quiet now in the neighbouring rooms.

I sat close to my warm stove and made my plans. I would do as Feechen advised. I would try to marry again. It was clear to me that a marriage planned in cold blood for my own advantage stood little chance of romance, but if I could find the right partner, our marriage could at least develop into a true comradeship, possibly without the golden edge of love, but still a happy one.

But where to find a partner? There was only one way, I must go to a marriage agency. I went. I chose one of the best and most expensive in Berlin. It was situated in the *Kurfürstendamm*. My heart was thumping painfully as I went up the wide marble staircase. I was terrified that I might meet someone who would recognize me.

100

The interview was very discouraging. First of all it would cost a great deal of money. Secondly the manageress did not hold out much hope for me.

"Two boys?" she said. "That's very bad. And what are your possessions?"

"Possessions?" I flushed.

"Yes . . . capital, shares, houses, etc.?"

"I am sorry, I have no possessions," I murmured.

She raised her eyebrows. "And what do you expect?" she asked.

"All I want," I said hastily, "is to stay at home with my boys and not have to go out to work."

She shook her head. "It won't be easy," she said. "The only value you have, is yourself."

"Yes," I said quietly.

The manageress was right. It was not easy. All the men shrank back as soon as they heard I had two children. They might have put up with my lack of material assets, but not two children. Many times I went up the marble steps to be introduced. Many times I came down rejected.

Spring drew near. I became nervous and anxious. Not one of the men had even suggested we should meet again. I felt utterly humiliated. I looked into my mirror. So far as I could discover there was nothing wrong with me. My clothes? Well, there was a war going on, and I was not fashionably dressed, but I always looked well-groomed, and I had quite good taste, I knew.

One morning I had a 'phone call from Kaethe. Wolfgang was ill, very ill. The doctor wished to send him to hospital, but I, being his mother, had to give permission.

Kaethe was so upset that she was crying over the 'phone. Wolfgang had pneumonia. He had already been ill for a week. I realized there was not a moment to lose. No time to ask for more details.

Mr. Wolter gave me leave, and said I could stay with Wolfgang and need not worry to 'phone the office.

I rushed off to Pankow. The underground train moved so slowly. I shut my eyes. Dear God, I prayed, I promise I will do anything on earth, if only Wolfgang lives.

Kaethe opened the door even before I rang the bell. Her face was pale and drawn. I went at once to his bedside. He had a high fever. When he saw me, he stretched out his little arms: "Oh, Mutti, Mutti, take me, I am so hot!" he cried.

Kaethe put his arms under the bedclothes, and told him he must lie quietly. She meant well, of course, but the effect was that Wolfgang started to sob, and then to cough —a coughing fit that seemed endless.

"The coughing makes him so weak." Kaethe whispered. "If only he could lie quietly and let the lungs get some rest. But he is moving all the time, all night long." She sounded desperate.

I was desperate too. On the spur of the moment I bent down to Wolfgang, wrapped him in his bedclothes, and picked him up in my arms. Immediately he stopped coughing. Without saying a word, I began to walk up and down the room humming a little cradle song. Quite suddenly Wolfgang heaved a little sigh, and then fell asleep.

I sat down very quietly, the child still in my arms, and let Kaethe take off my hat and coat. The boy stirred and he smiled as I pressed him closer.

"He mustn't go to hospital," I whispered to Kaethe. "I will stay here and nurse him."

"But the doctor said it would be the only way to save his life." Kaethe looked frightened.

"The doctor is wrong. He needs his mother," I said, quite firmly. "Will you help me nurse him here?"

Kaethe's usual arrogance had gone. She loved Wolfgang in her heart, and she realized now how wrong she had been not to send for me earlier.

"I will do everything I can," she said, quite humbly.

The doctor came. I had to sign a paper taking full

responsibility for what I was doing. But he was an old and experienced doctor and he knew that in final battles mothers are sometimes more successful than all the doctors and hospitals in the world. That night was long. The hours crept so slowly. Hundreds of times Kaethe and I paced up and down the bedroom with the moaning child in our arms. Wolfgang seemed to become worse. His temperature went higher and higher. Doubts came to me. Suppose I had made a terrible mistake? Perhaps the doctor was right? Perhaps the hospital would have been better for him? He hardly seemed to recognize us any longer. But he did not cry.

Up and down I walked. Kaethe came in.

"You should lie down now," she urged.

"I can't."

"Nor can I," Kaethe nodded.

She was very brave and kind that night. She took turns with me in carrying Wolfgang. When morning dawned Wolfgang became very quiet.

"He's dying," Kaethe called, and rushed to the 'phone.

The doctor came immediately. His medical examination seemed an eternity to us. At last he turned round. "Your son will live," he said. "You have pulled him through. He is utterly exhausted, but the crisis is over. But he mustn't be left alone for a moment. I would suggest," the doctor turned to me, "that you lie down with him in your arms. If he awakes he will still feel that you are near him, and will fall asleep again."

In that terrible night I had not only prayed for Wolfgang, I had made a vow to myself. Not only would I continue in my humiliating efforts with the marriage agency, I would also advertise for a husband in the matrimonial papers. Never would I be away from my little son again.

I returned home to my flat and my work a week later. In utter sadness I wrote my advertisement, and answered others that I thought might have some chance of success.

One day I wrote to Heiner, my future husband. He was a

widower and without children. He had always longed for
children, and so had decided to re-marry. He was looking
for a woman with children, he said.

We met at once. He was very thin, tall and with a rather
pleasant and dry sense of humour. He greeted me quite
naturally, cheerfully, at that first interview. He told me he
had had hundreds of letters in answer to his advertisement!
In fact he had a laundry basket full of them.

"Most of them are from war widows," he told me.

I said nothing.

But Heiner went on. "Some of them are so very young,
not even twenty and left with a child. Often the father has
not even seen the child. I have been very touched by the
tragedies in some of these girls' lives."

We were in a big and fashionable restaurant where we
had walked from our meeting place. Heiner was stirring
his cup of coffee rather vigorously and disturbing the blob
of mock cream on the top.

"If I were you I wouldn't stir too long," I warned him. "It
looks appetizing as it is, but all the stirring in the world
won't make it taste like cream, or indeed bring up any sugar
from the bottom!"

He laughed. "I know. I only hoped there might be a bit
of saccharine there."

I noticed at that moment how very blue his eyes were. I
had always had a weakness for blue eyes. Slowly and carefully I ate my little floating blob of mock cream. He
watched me. "I see you like *Schlagsahne* as much as I do."

"I love sweet things," I told him.

"All right," he said, and took out his wallet and began to
look for his food coupons. "I'll order some of the best cake."

I opened my own bag quickly. "Take my coupon, too," I
told him.

"Not this time," he smiled.

"But it's not fair," I protested.

"I shan't miss it," he told me.

"But you are so thin, you look as though you need every ounce of sugar you can get," I protested.

A shadow came over his face. "My looks are due more to my wife's death, than to any lack of food," he told me slowly. "I loved her very much; her sudden death has been a terrible shock to me." There was a silence which I didn't quite know how to break, as he was so complete a stranger to me. But after a moment he went on talking. "Are you optimistic about the war? I don't think it will really last very much longer, that is, unless the Americans come into the picture. I hear they are sending immense supplies of war material to the British. That might postpone our victory for quite a while."

The waitress came. She took out her scissors and snipped off Heiner's coupons. He spoke very charmingly to her. "I'll bring the best we have, sir," she smiled back.

"You *are* a very optimistic person," I told him.

"Why not? I've always been that way. What's the use of taking a gloomy view of everything? I was so optimistic at first that I planned to delay marrying again until after the war. But now that the Americans are being so difficult, I gave it another thought!"

His eyes were sparkling, and I couldn't help laughing. He was as confident and cheerful as a boy, and yet his face was deeply lined and bore all the signs of trouble and sorrow in his life. Smiling at him, I leaned over the balustrade and began to enjoy the luxury and peace of "The Traube". In the middle of the ground floor stood a fountain and a small pool of water in which tropical fish were swimming in light blue water. The spray of falling water from the fountain wove a pretty blue mist above the pool. There were tropical plants, palm trees and exotic flowers grouped around. Even parrots were perched on some of the plants.

"I wonder they don't fly away," I pointed to the parrots.

"They would if they could, no doubt, but they are chained down," he explained.

D*   105

"How stupid of me." I felt myself blushing. "I've not been here before."

"I don't suppose you go out very much, with two children, do you?"

"It's not that so much, but I just don't feel in the mood. This place looks like Paradise to me, with the lovely green of the plants, and the flowers and the parrots."

"Well, I hope they have real cream in Paradise, and not this *Ersatz-Schlagsahne*," he added dryly, and suddenly we both laughed together.

"Yes," I said, "and not quite so many military uniforms either." I pointed to a group of officers just coming in.

"They do look smart," said Heiner.

They did indeed. Most of the men were wearing the Iron Cross on their tunics. They looked young and healthy. Heroes of a victorious army, and confident of themselves, and so did their girl friends.

"Do you see the girl on the right. I'll bet that blue silk suit comes from Paris," I said enviously.

"And the silver fox fur round her shoulders from Norway, perhaps," added Heiner.

"And her shoes from Italy."

The laughing group had now reached our table and passed on.

"And the perfume?" Heiner asked. "Where might that have come from. From Greece, perhaps?"

It might, I told him. Berlin that spring and summer of 1941 was crammed with well-dressed young women. The returning soldiers on short leave were laden with gifts for their friends and relatives. There was a joke going around that the really clever girls were those who changed their escorts as we conquered each country. A smart girl could easily get all the luxuries she needed from Norway, Holland, Belgium, France, and now on to Greece and Italy.

As if he were reading my thoughts, my partner suddenly said: "I can't offer you things like that, you know,

106

unfortunately. I shall probably stay in Berlin all through the war, and never be in the Forces."

What luck, I thought. "You're lucky, most women would far rather have their men at home than have all the fur coats and jewellery in the world!"

"I'm not so sure, looking at those girls," he answered.

"I thought you were an optimist, and now you are judging all women from those girls! I've caught you out," I said.

"And I've caught you out. You live alone in your little flat, like the English do on their island, and you don't see what the rest of the world is doing or thinking at all."

"Does it matter?"

He didn't reply. "What about another cup of substitute coffee and substitute cream?" he suggested.

I liked this café. It was a lovely change from my little flat and the evenings alone. There were two bands, a dance band on the first floor and a concert orchestra on the ground. They played in turns. When the orchestra played famous melodies from the operas I could sit back and forget the war and my unhappiness, and look down on the fountain of pale blue water and day-dream. Suddenly Heiner leant towards me. "Can you day-dream to this tune as well?" he asked ironically. I came back to earth and listened properly. The dance band was playing "*Denn wir fahren, denn wir fahren gegen Engelland.*" (We are going, we are going, towards Angelland.) It was neither charming nor banal, but just a German victory tune. At several tables the officers were singing now. When the music stopped there was loud applause.

I didn't answer Heiner. "Won't you ever be a soldier?" I said instead. "Have you got a 'gold' party number, then?"

"Nothing of the kind," came his answer. "I am an engineer and have specialized in X-rays. My work is mostly in hospitals and clinics. There aren't many of us in my branch, and there is such a demand for X-ray work now that I shall never be freed to fight."

107

"That's marvellous news," I told him.

He shrugged his shoulders. "I don't know. My brother is in the Luftwaffe. He's ten years younger than I, and he's already seen more of the world than I am ever likely to. He gets a lot of fun out of life and has very few responsibilities." There was envy in his voice.

"Would you rather go to war than work in the hospitals?"

"I would if I didn't hate war so much."

"That's a bit complicated," I suggested, and we both laughed.

We separated soon afterwards.

"May we meet again?" he asked.

"Why, yes," I told him. "I've enjoyed the afternoon very much."

"All right. I'll give you a ring in a few days."

A week passed, but there was no telephone call. By now I knew that I was not in the running. Useless now, I felt, to sit always by the telephone and rush back into the room in case I should miss any call. Again and again I thought how nice and natural he had been. I went over every word of our conversation together. Perhaps I had made some mistakes, should not have said this thing, or done that. I remembered for instance that he had said I apparently had luxurious tastes . . . had this put him off? And then my stupid remark about the parrots.

I decided by the end of the week that I had no chance when he had a laundry basket full of letters from beautiful young widows? It had been on my lips once or twice to ask why he bothered to meet me at all if he could have much younger women?

The 'phone call came, on the tenth day after we had met. He apologized for having taken so long, but said he had been terribly busy. Very much later he admitted to me that he had been busy sorting out the laundry basket! I was completely jubilant over the 'phone, but very careful not to let him know it. I suggested a date in four days' time.

"Why so far ahead?" he asked impatiently.

"Because I'm so busy," I snapped back.

The unexpected happened. He roared with laughter. "Very well, then," he said. "I'll get tickets for the Scala for that evening if you like the idea?"

Oh, yes, I would like it very much, I told him. I was so excited and happy that I could have danced with joy that afternoon. But why had he laughed so loudly? I couldn't see why he found me so funny?

I left my office at the normal time and rushed along to queue up for my bus. Suddenly I heard somebody calling me. Like lightning I turned round. There stood Heiner with a brief case under his arm. He was smiling from ear to ear. I thought how attractive and smart he looked in his long grey overcoat. He wore no hat.

"You are so very busy, aren't you?" he laughed.

I went a little red and pulled my hand away, but he quickly took it again, and said gently. "Don't be cross with me, I was only teasing. I came along to try and see you to ask if you could spare me an hour or two this evening?"

Before I could answer, he went on quickly. "I've found a very good restaurant, quite near. It's small, but the food is excellent. We could get a big *Königsberger Klops* (minced meat ball) there. Please come with me."

I'm afraid I was so happy that I only put up a very brief resistance. This time it was rather late when we said good-bye. He told me a lot about his life; that he had been born in Hamburg, that his father was dead, but his mother still lived there. The biggest blow of his life had been the discovery that they couldn't have children. This had thrown a deep shadow over his marriage. I was surprised when he told me he was only thirty-five years old. He looked and seemed much older.

Heiner was completely open about his first marriage. His wife had been ill for years, he told me, although her death came as a terrible shock at the end. He had nursed her

109

patiently, but it had been a terrible strain on him. After her death he broke down entirely, and a doctor advised him to marry again as soon as possible.

"No wonder you look so thin and restless," I said.

"Restless?", he asked.

"Yes, I noticed how nervously you move your hands and feet," I told him. "I thought you must be living under some great strain."

"You're a very observant person," he told me.

"I'm terribly sorry about your wife," I added. "I can imagine what it must have been like, nursing her all those years and longing for the ordinary happinesses of life."

He put out his hand and took mine. "That was a very nice thing to say. You seem to understand so well."

There was a long silence between us. Then he looked up.

"I think we must get to know each other better."

After that we met quite frequently. We didn't go to the Scala as it happened, as every seat was sold out for weeks in advance.

"Berlin is certainly very gay nowadays," Heiner said. And so were we. We went to cinemas, theatres and concerts. We danced and dined in little restaurants. We talked late into the nights. I saw in those months with Heiner more than I had ever seen of Berlin in my life. Gradually Heiner —he had asked me to call him that from the start—became quieter and more settled. We had become firm friends, and he wanted to meet my children.

After every air-raid we 'phoned each other, just to make sure all was well, and the air-raids were now becoming quite a problem. Originally we had planned only to go out at night when we had a full moon. Now we had to alter that. The R.A.F. preferred to come out at moonlight as well, so the darkest nights now became the best ones for our meetings.

Heiner was luckier than I was during the raids. He lived

on the outskirts of West Berlin in a villa in Kladow. The raiders did not often reach him. But I lived in East Berlin, and near the industrialised part of the city, and anyway I wasn't allowed to stay in my bed during an alarm. The air-warden of our flats was a very conscientious man and went to each and every door to make sure we had gone down to the cellars. There was a heavy fine for anyone who refused to obey his orders.

The worst part of the raids for me, however, was being separated from my children. Were they all right; and if I were killed what would happen to them? I did not tell Heiner of these anxieties. Perhaps I should have done but I felt it was a personal matter. We often talked about the war and the bombing of England and how long they would last out.

"Do you think they can stand much more?" I asked him one night referring to the bombing of Coventry. "Much of the town has gone and there were heavy casualties. I should die if I thought that Wolfgang and Klaus would ever have to go through the things those English children must have suffered."

"If you start thinking that way in a war you will end up by committing suicide," he told me. "You've got to be hard, and think: 'It's the enemy or me and the sooner they give in the better!'"

"That's a frightful creed," I protested.

"War is a frightful thing, and it's no use thinking about it too much when you are in the midst of one. I'm glad for that reason that I shall never be called up. I might start thinking when I was in a plane and be too paralyzed to drop the bombs."

"But surely we needn't bomb civilians as we did at Coventry."

"It's easier said than done. Targets are close together sometimes. Bombs fall where they are not meant to."

I was silent.

"Coventry was a reprisal raid anyway. For the bombing of our towns," he added.

"I wonder who started first?" I wanted to know.

"I'll tell you after the war. No one knows the truth while it is going on," he told me.

"But will you know the truth even after the war?"

· "Oh, yes," laughed Heiner. "We'll know then. The man who starts a war is the one who loses it!"

"Which means England will be blamed for starting the air-raids on civilians?" I asked.

"Don't forget Hitler's speech in September when he threatened : 'If they attack our cities we will destroy theirs.' I'm afraid these air-raids are now such a mix-up of attack and counter-attack that one can never fix the blame fairly and squarely. This is now a total war, and woe to the one who loses it. It will be total destruction."

It was such a relief to talk openly to Heiner in those days. Especially when in March Berlin had its real taste of bombing. Ten thousand incendiary bombs were dropped on us. I was completely terrified. So too were Karl and Kaethe. She rang me up and said she had decided to leave Berlin immediately and take Wolfgang with her to stay on the Baltic. I went to say good-bye to my little son that morning, as they were leaving at once. He clung to me, but fortunately did not see how terribly unhappy I was. Kaethe was hard again (she had forgotten that night when we saved Wolfgang's life) she wanted only her own way again.

"Don't forget," she said coldly, "we shall want your decision about adoption by the end of the summer, you know."

It so happened that I could not let Heiner meet Wolfgang when he expressed a wish to know my children that spring. But one day he came to Caputh to visit Klaus. On our way I explained how shy Klaus was, and that he usually cried if anyone went to touch him. In this case I was completely wrong. Mr. and Mrs. Kroll were sitting on their terrace overlooking the white and pink blossoming fruit trees of the village when we arrived. Klaus sat at their feet, busy with his teddy bear. He took no notice of me whatsoever when I bent down to kiss him. But when Heiner stepped up behind me, he stared for a moment, and then got up in a flash and ran to greet him. Heiner picked him up in his arms and laughed. The three of us, Mr. and Mrs. Kroll and I, stood speechless at first.

"It's incredible," said Mrs. Kroll. "Why, he never goes to anyone."

Heiner beamed. At that moment Klaus remembered his teddy bear. Heiner seemed to understand the baby language, and picked it up for him. Klaus now sat there, high on Heiner's shoulders, and grinned down at us confidently. Even today I do not know why he so suddenly stopped being shy. Was it some sudden instinct? Whatever it was, these two were friends from the start. They played together for hours quite happily. For my part, my emotions were a bit mixed. I was delighted they had made friends, but I was still bitterly hurt that Klaus would never come to me.

Mr. Kroll was quite talkative that day. "Have you seen about the capitulation of Greece?", he said. "We are so used to victories now, that you can hardly turn on the radio at lunch-time without hearing of a new victory."

At lunch-time Heiner and I went down to the village to eat. We didn't want to take the Krolls' rations from them. Heiner was sure in his optimism that in a country place like this we should get a jolly good meal. He was wrong. The meal was just as poor as any we might find in Berlin, and it cost just as many coupons.

"What do you think would happen if we gave big meals here and took no coupons for them?", the waitress asked. "Our rations are the same as yours, you know. In fact, worse, because we have to send all our cattle and pigs to the towns around."

113

"But you get fruit and vegetables down here?", I asked.

"Well, yes," she conceded. "But our worst problem is butter. We don't get any more than you do, nor do the farmers who make it."

She was only kind over one thing. She refused to take Heiner's sugar coupon. "You look as though you need every coupon you can get," she told him.

"You know," said Heiner, as we walked back. "The butter situation makes me wonder sometimes if Hitler hadn't got this war planned out years ago. England certainly wasn't ready for war. They were completely unprepared. Perhaps that's a worse crime in the end, to have your country completely unprepared.'

"England had her fleet always," I said.

"A fleet's not much good today. Islands don't exist any longer. We're right at England's front door, and it's probably only a matter of months before we are inside."

"Yes, they say we shall invade in June," I added.

"I think Hitler's waited until the secret weapons were ready," said Heiner.

"Darling, it's a grand idea," said Heiner, flinging his arms round my shoulders. "A guided missile, which doesn't cost the life of a single soldier. Why, before the invasion starts they will be sent all over England day and night in such vast numbers that they can't offer any resistance to our troops at all. Hitler will save thousands of our soldiers' lives that way. It's the plan of a genius."

"It certainly is," I said, and tried to catch a butterfly, which poised for a moment on some white fruit blossom. I was lucky, and managed to catch it. Triumphantly I showed it to Heiner. "It's a *Pfauenauge* (Peacock), isn't it beautiful?"

But Heiner, who a second before had been exulting over the wonderful V1 and V2 weapons which would reduce England to a rubble heap, now became angry.

"Have you hurt it?" he said quickly.

"Of course not," I said, very surprised at his angry tone.

"Then let it go," he commanded. "Why do you want to keep it?"

"I wanted to show it to Klaus," I explained.

"The butterfly would die long before we reached home. It's not kind. It's such a beautiful day, let the poor thing go."

Reluctantly I opened my hand and let the butterfly go. We both watched how it spread its wings and sailed away into the blue sky.

"You *are* a contradictory person," I sighed. "One minute you say the Führer is a genius, with his secret weapons, and the next you worry about a butterfly."

"And you're a typical woman and don't understand the difference between private life and war." He laughed. "But let's make a vow—no more talk of war for today. I'm looking forward to playing with Klaus again. I wonder if I shall get the same reception as I did this morning?"

When I entered the house and stepped on to the terrace, I found Heiner lying full length on the lawn with little Klaus climbing all over him and chattering away. It was a happy and beautiful day for all of us.

7

I Find the Ideal Man

SLOWLY during that spring and summer of 1941 my life changed for the better. I had been so used to unhappiness that I actually didn't realize the turn of the tide at first. Heiner and I were seeing each other almost every day, and the more I saw of him the more I loved his ways and his character. He was so thoughtful and gentle towards me, so completely different from Richard.

I won't put my love for Heiner into words, everyone who has ever loved will know quite well how I felt. From an ordinary and very prosaic beginning he had now become the centre of my whole life. I thought of him continually, and I was almost sure by now that the same thing was happening to Heiner. So, despite the air-raids which were getting more and more serious, I was blissfully happy that summer. Happier perhaps than I had ever been in my life.

I was not the only one, however, who was changing in outlook. Mr. Wolter at the office was looking at life differently, but his view was for the worse, not the better. Mr. Wolter was becoming nervous. "Have you heard?" he asked one morning, "they are dropping bombs on West Berlin now on a bigger scale. It's serious. I had a real taste of it last night," he added. "They dropped bombs on the block of flats in the Bayerischer Platz. It smashed all our windows and shook the whole house. We were in the cellar, of course. The women and children didn't take it too well. The noise and screaming was frightful." He looked up for sympathy.

"Yes," I agreed. "It's bad for the women and children."

"It was bad enough for me," added Mr. Wolter with a wry smile. "I had enough, I can tell you. I couldn't sit down there scared to death with people screaming all round me. I had to go out and do something. I went along to the Bayerischer Platz. It was the most frightful sight."

He had got up now and was pacing about on his blue carpet. I had never seen him moved in this way before. Enthusiastic, optimistic, bitter and confident, I had seen all that in my boss, but not this pity and horror.

"It's easy to say, it was just a rubble heap, and leave it at that. But to me, and I passed the place every day, you know, it was the end of the most sumptuous and beautiful block of flats in Berlin. When I went there in the middle of last night it was still burning."

"And the tenants?" I interrupted.

"Dead! Practically all of them, I should say. They can't have lived through that heat. We worked like niggers for the rest of the night trying to dig an entrance to the cellars, but when I left to come to the office this morning they still hadn't got through. They now have tractors and cranes on the job. When they do reach the cellars they will only find burned bodies, I think."

He was still walking nervously up and down. It took him some time to get down to work that morning. This was the first time he had seen bombing in his part of the town. It changed him in a night.

At lunch-time I went along to the Bayerischer Platz to see for myself. There were hundreds of sightseers, all people who, like me, had come to make sure that the British had really got to the heart of luxury Berlin with their bombs.

"Now we can call him 'Meyer'," said a man's voice beside me. He referred, of course, to Goering's boasts in 1939 that Berlin should never be bombed while he was in charge, if it was we could call him 'Meyer' A woman next to the man plucked at his sleeve and pulled him away. It was an unwise thing to say aloud in a crowd.

117

Suddenly the cranes stopped working. A murmur went through the crowd. "They've cleared the entrance . . . they are going in now . . ." We stood on tiptoe, staring in horror and fascination. There was something moving, I could see at the entrance of the luxury block, something being brought out. A woman screamed sharply three times. It was the same awful scream that I heard from women later on when the Russians came.

"What's happening? What has she seen?", the people round kept asking. We surged forward to look. Police appeared and pressed us back. "Move on now," they said. "This is no sight to stare at. You'll read about it soon enough in the papers."

Actually we didn't read the truth in the papers. What had happened in the flats was too terrible to be printed. The tenants had not been burned but scalded to death. The water pipes of the central-heating system had burst, and boiling water had poured into the air-raid cellar. They found women with their arms stretched out holding their children above their heads as they died. They found people crouched on the top of piles of chairs and tables as they clambered to escape the rising, boiling water. No wonder they didn't print these facts at the time. There were hundreds of other flats similarly constructed in Berlin. Few people would have sought shelter in those cellars had they known what might happen.

"If ever that happened to my wife and children I think I should go mad," Mr. Wolter said. "I think I shall send my family to East Germany at once. I can't risk many more raids like that."

He left the office in the early afternoon, telling me to answer telephone calls and deal with the rest of the letters.

"We should not have bombed Coventry," he said. "Women and children should be left out of war, it's inhuman."

Heiner too was very worried that day, but mostly over

his brother Hermann who was in the German Air Force, and with the parachute divisions now in Crete.

"We haven't heard anything from him since they landed. I tried every way of contacting him, but it is useless."

"But, darling, there must be thousands doing the same. How can you hear at present?" I tried to console him.

"I know, but the point is we must cheer my mother up in some way on Sunday. I want you to pretend that everything *must* be all right. Will you do that?" he asked very seriously.

"Of course I will," I promised. "I'll do everything I can to reassure her."

"Hermann is the youngest of us. He is very close to her, and has always written regularly. That's why she is in such a panic. She is sure something has happened. I keep ringing and enquiring, but I just can't get any news of the parachuters at all."

This was to be my first visit to Heiner's home. It was the first Sunday in June, and I was very excited and happy. The villa itself lay on the outskirts of Berlin near the aerodrome of Gatow. It was high on a small hill overlooking the wide River Havel. The view on the far side was very lovely and peaceful, nothing but the wide river, the blue sky, the many small sailing boats, and a long green fringe of trees on the banks. Heiner's home was very beautifully furnished, and his garden had a smooth lawn, silver birch trees, and a small pond in it.

His mother was a very tiny woman, and looked far younger than she actually was. She was as lively and gay as a girl of sixteen. As I walked towards her I was full of embarrassment, and nerves, but the moment our hands touched and I heard her happy voice I knew it was all right. We were friends at once. She was so happy that day as early in the morning she had at last heard from Hermann saying that the attack on Crete had been strenuous, but he was safe and healthy. How she talked and bubbled over with relief at lunch. It couldn't have been a better first meeting for us.

After lunch she went to her room to rest while Heiner and I went for a walk. We strolled along the crest of the hill. The sound of accordion music came floating up to us. Heiner pointed to the island of Pfaueninsel. "That's supposed to be the loveliest spot around Berlin," he said.

"I learnt that at school," I said. "The summer residence of William III and Queen Luise, and the Kaiser until 1918. I wonder who owns it now?"

"Hard to say," said Heiner. "Either Goebbels or the German State. All I know is that Goebbels once gave a fantastic party there in 1936 Olympics year.

"Many distinguished people from several countries, including England were invited and attended. Every tree was covered with lights made in the shapes of butterflies. There were three thousand guests in addition to all the Olympic Games competitors. Rich and varied food and almost every kind of liquor were provided. Many of the guests indulged themselves too freely. There were disgraceful scenes and many of the distinguished guests were obliged to leave the party. Goebbels was wild with rage, and his wife felt herself humiliated.

"The following night Goering gave a successful party (a personal retaliation) but of a very different kind, at which only beer and sausages were provided for his guests."

We walked back to Heiner's home. He put his arm round my shoulder. The lovely feeling of protection and peace that it brought, crept into my heart. I would like to have stayed like that for ever. On that little hill, and with that warm, strong arm so gently on my shoulders. I didn't want to talk it was complete bliss but out of the blue Heiner spoke. He asked me then and there to marry him at once. I leaned against one of the silver birch trees and stared at him in surprise. It was the last thing I had expected just at that moment.

"No, darling," I said, just as suddenly.

Heiner gasped, and took a step back to look at my face. "But why not? What's the matter?"

"You haven't seen Wolfgang yet." How I came out with it I don't know. I longed with all my heart to throw myself into his arms and think only of my own happiness, but for weeks I was determined that Heiner should see *both* children before he committed himself. He *must* be sure before we married. My words, however, merely brought a laugh.

"You frightened me for a moment. What a silly darling you are, you gave me an awful shock." He stepped forward to kiss me.

But I stretched out my hand and stopped him. I was almost in tears, but was convinced I was doing right.

"I mean it," I told him quietly.

Heiner frowned. He looked angry for a moment. I had to say something to explain. "I'm only thinking of you. We must make a success of this marriage. I can't bear to let you go through what I have been through with Richard. You don't know what an unhappy marriage is. It's hell on earth for two people to be tied together when one stops loving. You must see Wolfgang first. You may not like him—he may not like you—what would happen then? Please, please do understand how careful we must be. It's not for my sake so much really, darling."

I pleaded as much as I could. He still frowned. He just hadn't had my bitter experience, and so could not understand my fears. He became silent, and on the way home did not put his arm round my shoulders. I could see he was bitterly hurt.

His mother had laid the table for afternoon coffee on the sunny terrace from which we had a most glorious view of the river. It was an uneasy meal and she tried in vain to cheer us up. She had put a new gold silk cloth on the table and the best cups with a beautiful green and gold design.

121

She told us the china had come originally from Hamburg.

I did my best to be polite and attentive and admire both the cloth and the china, but I was taut and nervous, and to my horror my hand shook so much that I suddenly spilled an entire cup of her best coffee right over the cloth and polished table. We all jumped up and tried to put things right. I was very ashamed, and embarrassed, and kept making dozens of apologetic remarks, but the cloth was ruined, and all the polish taken off the table. Quite soon after the meal I made excuses to leave early, saying that I wanted to be back in my flat before the raids began.

Heiner walked back to the bus with me. He was polite, but very cold and curt in manner. It was not a happy "good-bye". I felt desperately miserable. I had three hours' travelling by coach, and then the elevated railway through Berlin; three hours in which to think over what I had said and what result it had had on Heiner. Naturally I thought that he now no longer loved me, or wanted me as his wife. Yet at the back of my mind I knew I had done right. What use to throw myself into his arms if I felt it wrong? Anyway I loved him more than myself—why on earth couldn't he have seen it in what I said? Why had he remained so cold, and that abrupt good-bye. . .

We had a bad raid that night, and I spent three-quarters of it in the cellars. On top came a very busy Monday morning. We were having a big conference with county representatives the next day, and so all the morning the two telephones on my desk were ringing continually. There was hardly a moment to write letters awaiting attention. At last there was a respite, and I got up to go to my typewriter. Brrrr . . . brrrr . . . the 'phone again! It was maddening. With my voice full of resignation, I picked the instrument up.

"This is Headquarters Strength through Joy, Department Art," I said, in a depressed voice.

"It doesn't sound much like it," came a well-known voice

over the 'phone. It was Heiner! My heart missed a beat. He sounded so full of joy and confidence, quite different from our last meeting.

"Darling, will you have lunch with me?"

Of course I would. I was so happy the tears had come into my eyes. I thanked heaven he couldn't see them. At lunch-time Heiner told me he had talked for hours about me with his mother. She had made him see my point of view, he told me.

"Do you know what she said?" he smiled at me. "She said that only one woman in a thousand would have hesitated as I had done. She thought it was very wonderful of you and that you obviously loved me very much, and would make a splendid wife." He pressed my hand very gently and warmly as it lay on the table near his. "Darling, I've got the most wonderful idea. Let's have a holiday together, you and I and the two boys. That would be a real test wouldn't it? We should all see each other from morning till night, and find out each other's weaknesses and habits, and then we would jolly well see if we could form a family together? What do you say? Will you come?" His blue eyes shone like an enthusiastic boy's. How could I refuse?

"It's a grand idea. Of course I'll come. I wish I could kiss you now for it. Why do you say these things in public, where I can't kiss you properly?"

He laughed with pleasure. "I will give you the opportunity another time. I shan't ask you to stop either!"

We talked at once of all the necessary plans for the holiday. Heiner suggested Timmendorf on the Baltic Sea, where he had spent many holidays in his childhood and since. There was a lovely beach of white sand stretching for miles, he told me. It was ideal for children and not too overcrowded or fashionable. He worked very quickly at the idea, and in a few days all was more or less fixed. We planned to leave Berlin on 15 June. My cousin Kaethe

123

seemed quite willing to spare Wolfgang for a fortnight, as
the dates coincided with her visit to Berlin.

I now often went to Heiner's home in Kladow, and his
mother was very kind to me. Mrs. Wendel (Heiner's sur-
name) loved Hamburg and everything connected with the
navy and the sea. I was in their home when the news came
of the sinking of the *Bismarck*, and she was almost in tears
as the radio message ended. The long fierce battle with the
British Fleet was very graphically described by the
announcers.

"It's such a great death," she said to me. "To go down in
your ship with all guns firing, and to give no thought to
your own life . . . but what an awful death, when you come
to think of it. Suppose you have to swim for hours; suppose
it happened to Hermann?"

Mrs. Wendel had a large photograph of the naval hero,
Guenter Prien, in her bedroom. Guenter Prien was the
U-boat Commander who had entered the harbour of Scapa
Flow with his submarine, and sunk the *Royal Oak*. A
national hero at the time he was one of the many, I'm afraid,
who in 1941 was told "to prove himself" by going to a dangerous part of the front. I wonder what happened to the
beautiful photograph, and whether she and many others
were disillusioned by Prien, and Hitler too, in the end?

We set off for our "test holiday", as Mrs. Wendel called
it, on 15 June. She waved us off at Stettiner Station, with
little Klaus sitting on Heiner's knee and refusing to budge
from it. Wolfgang was shy. He sat by my side, and watched
Heiner without saying a word. I squeezed his small hand
from time to time. The poor child scarcely knew me either,
as he hadn't seen me for a long time.

The weather was glorious and from the first we settled
down like a real family. Heiner went off on the first day to
find the best spot to build our sand castle, and then asked
us to construct a "wall" round it. Baby Klaus looked on with
enormous interest.

Our landlady at the boarding house was an old friend of Heiner's. She had known him since he was a boy. It was all very cheerful and comfortable. She and I were getting the children ready for the beach one morning, when Heiner burst in; he was very excited and stammered:

"We're marching; we're marching into Russia."

"No! Oh, no!" said Mrs. J. "They mustn't do it." She collapsed into a chair and put her face in her hands. "It can't be true."

"Oh, yes, it can," said Heiner. "This very morning, in the middle of June, while the sun shines on the beach and we swim, our glorious troops march in to conquer Russia." He said it all in a harsh and excited voice, but, as we remained speechless, he added: "If you two don't believe me, just go downstairs and turn on the radio." But someone else in the house had already done that for us. As we opened the door, we could hear the strident voice of an announcer booming through the house, giving Hitler's proclamation to the German nation. It was, as usual, dramatic and stirring. "Russia," said our Führer, "perfidious and evil, has under the cloak of friendship and Treaty, been placing a huge army on our very borders in East Germany. My heart bleeds," he shouted at us, "but I must protect you, so I have struck first. Today our glorious armies march once more for the Fatherland. Germany cannot be overrun. Germany shall not fall under the heel of the invader!" Russia, we were told, had planned all along to attack us, the Treaty had merely been a breathing space for her to get ready. But our Führer had struck first. Suddenly Mrs. J. began to sob bitterly. Heiner tried to soothe her.

"Don't cry," he said gently. "We haven't lost anything . . . it will be all right. It always has been all right, hasn't it?"

"We have lost. We have lost everything," she said to him. "You don't understand. I know. My husband marched into Russia in the First World War, and now my son is marching in, in this one. My only son." She wept bitterly again.

125

We did our best to calm her, but it was useless. Each time she tried to stand up, she would sway, and look for support and went on crying. We didn't know what to do. We had no knowledge of Russia at all, Heiner and I, nor did the laughter and voices from the holiday-makers on the beach and the brilliant June sunshine help much. We just stood there, trying to think of the right thing to say to calm her down so that we could escape to our sand-castle and enjoy our few days of happiness together.

At last she managed to control her tears and got up. "We shall never conquer Russia," she said, in a tired, resigned voice. "I heard enough from my husband; indeed I saw enough from my husband's behaviour when he returned." Slowly she walked to the door and went to her room. We were both very depressed now, but we went down to the beach, and let the boys paddle and begin another big sand-castle. Heiner and I leaned back in our *Strandkorb* (movable wicker chair).

"I don't feel like a swim," I told him. "In fact, I feel horribly tired. Do you know anything about the husband, darling?"

"I know she has had a terribly hard life," Heiner said, "and the husband was shocking to her after he returned from Russia. Perhaps you'd better hear it, and then you'll be able to help her a bit."

Heiner then told me very briefly about our hostess. Her husband had been taken prisoner by the Russians in the First World War. She had failed to trace him. Just one notice that he had been taken prisoner, and then a blank silence. She went on persevering, but the Russian authorities refused to answer, and the Germans could do nothing. The years went by and she met someone else and fell deeply in love. She had a son, though officially she was still married to her husband. Five more years passed, and one terrible day there was a knock at her door. A pale, thin, worn out man in ragged clothes was standing outside. It was her husband. The child ran to her calling her "Mummy". You can imagine what the man felt and Mrs. J. It was a shocking tragedy for both of them. The man had been keeping himself alive during ten years of hell and privation, simply on the dream of returning one day to his wife and home. Now, he finds her happily living with another man and possessing a lovely son by him. She took her husband in; she sent the man she loved away, and she nursed her husband and cared for him until he was strong. More than that, she worked to bring him into the boarding house and the nursery garden she was running. But it was useless. The husband's shock and anger at finding himself supplanted, and the sight of the boy, made him more and more cruel and vindictive. He never forgave her and would humiliate her continuously, even in front of others. Indeed he vented on his wife, all he had suffered as a prisoner.

"So you can understand what this new war with Russia means to her. She sees the same thing happening all over again with her son, perhaps. I wouldn't like to hear what effect it would have if her son were ever reported 'missing'. I think it would kill her."

Heiner's words spoken that day on the hot, white sands of the Baltic, came true. Mrs. J's son *was* taken prisoner, and her husband too was posted back to Russia, due to his knowledge of the language. Her husband was killed in 1944, and the son still reported "missing". When the Russians advanced into East Germany and right up to Mrs. J's home, they found a dead woman. She had taken her own life. And as far as I know nothing was heard of the son. But that is looking too far ahead. We spent a quiet morning, and went back quickly to hear what we could of the new war in the east. Heiner insisted upon being optimistic.

"Come on, now," he said. "Have you no faith in the Führer at all? This is just one woman's bad luck story. Why should it happen again? Do you think the Führer would be such a fool as to start a two-front war carelessly? Either

England is on the point of surrender, or the 'secret weapon' is ready. You and I can't judge things, darling. We aren't diplomats or generals, are we? And suppose Russia had suddenly attacked us?. We *had* to act first, didn't we?"

I didn't answer, I kept hearing Mrs. J crying, and her hopelessly sad words.

"Don't spoil our holiday," said Heiner. "Whether you like it or not, the thing is done now, all we can do is to make the best of it."

"Things look pretty grim," said my next door "neighbour" on the beach as we passed.

I agreed, but only very guardedly. It wasn't wise to talk to strangers about politics. Who knew whether they would carry one's criticisms to some Gestapo ear? There was no enthusiasm about the Russian front. We said little about it, but merely proclaimed a complete trust in our Führer. He had done the cleverest things up till now, why shouldn't he continue to be clever?

Our holiday ended. A lovely holiday, in which the children grew sunburned and strong, and I laughed and played like a girl again. And Heiner put on a little weight, and was more relaxed and happy than I had ever seen him.

Back at the office I found people with many different views. There were the grumblers who kept talking of Napoleon, and what happened in *his* march into Russia, and Mr. Wolter, who was determined to be cheerful. He greeted me with: "Now don't mention the name Napoleon to me. It's banned anyway in my room. I can't bear to hear the wretched man's name again. As if Hitler hadn't looked at the map of Russia himself, or had never heard of a Siberian winter. Everyone seems to have been reading their history books suddenly, so don't you start as well. If that's all the politics Hitler knows, then we are in a mess. We won't talk politics or history."

"It's all right," I laughed at him. "I haven't come to talk

Right: The house at Berlin-Kladow which was Else's home with Heiner. Her brother Rudolf is preparing his canoe for a trip on the river.

The island in the River Havel which the Kladow home overlooked.

These photographs were taken inside the author's home at Berlin-Kladow. On the left is the dining-room with the table on which the Russians later stubbed out their cigarettes; that table Mrs. Wendel still has. Below is the lounge; the Russian doctor who took over the house laid wounded Russians on the couch for examination.

either. I've come to talk about myself. I would like to give in my notice, because I'm going to marry again."

Mr. Wolter stepped back against his light blue wall.

"No," he gasped. "You aren't going to leave me? *I* have reported to Headquarters, and am joining the army next week! If you leave as well, it will be too much for Mr. Eschenbach."

"I am not marrying until October," I told him. "That will give time to look for somebody to take my place, won't it?"

By now Mr. Wolter had recovered a little from his surprise. He seized my hand and congratulated me, and apologized for not doing so at once.

"Forgive me," he said very nicely. "I was so upset at the idea of losing you that I forgot how happy you must be."

"I feel rather nervous now that I have taken the step," he told me. "But it seemed the only possible thing to do. Older men can run this department quite as well. My wife is going to Silesia, with the boys, of course. She is taking all our silver as well. We have good friends in Silesia, they will keep an eye on her and on our small treasures. They will be safe enough in that part of Germany."

So they were, until one bitter January night in 1945, when their friends, in company with thousands of others, fled from Silesia leaving everything behind—certainly Mr. Wolter's silver!

"Tell me about your fiancé," Mr. Wolter said presently. "I would like to meet him, but I can't, as I am actually leaving the office tomorrow. What kind of a man is he? Has he a sense of humour? Does he make you laugh?" This was a typical reaction on Mr. Wolter's part. He always had to have some kind of a joke. Indeed, he summed us all up, sheep from goats; the sheep having endless numbers of jokes, the goats as hopeless people who had none. "A man's character is summed up by the kind of jokes he tells," Mr. Wolter would say; "If he has *no* jokes, then he has no character."

I went to Heiner's defence at once. I told several of his latest jokes, particularly the one about little Fritz and his grandmother. Little Fritz is showing his ancient grandmother a large school globe. She had never seen such a thing in her life. The child solemnly points out the countries of the world to her. He shows her the United States of America, and then all the red spots on the globe indicating British possessions. Then the huge size of Russia. Finally he shows her a small green spot marked "Germany". "Quick, Fritz! Quick! put on your hat and coat and run," says the old lady in a state of great excitement. "Run to the Führer and tell him what you have just told me. I'm quite sure he doesn't know how small Germany is. Quick, before it is too late!"

Mr. Wolter exploded with laughter over this. And the joke about the Nazi salute, which Heiner declared had come originally from Hitler's house decorating days, when he used to raise his arm solemnly, deciding how far up the paintwork on the walls should come. "Up to this height," he would proclaim, as he raised his right arm, with the hand spread out.

"That's a clever one," laughed Mr. Wolter. "I often wondered how he got hold of that salute, now I know."

8

Quiet Wedding and After

EVERYTHING now revolved around my preparations for my marriage. The days rushed by. I gave up my flat in Baumschulenweg, and began moving my furniture to Kladow to Heiner's villa. In the week-ends we painted and decorated a room as a nursery for my sons. They were the happiest days I had ever known.

Karl and Kaethe, however, were not happy. It came as an awful shock to them that Wolfgang would soon be leaving. Kaethe burst into tears. She knew at last just a little of the agony I had been suffering these last two years. I was sorry for Mrs. Kroll. It meant all the world to her to have little Klaus as her own child. She begged and begged me to let him stay. "The money doesn't matter in the least—it is Klaus I want," she explained pathetically. All I could do was to promise that he should come and stay with her as often as possible.

The air-raids just didn't bother me any more. I should soon be with my sons, and whatever happened in the future we should face it together and not apart.

In the late summer I went along to visit the Treitels again. They hadn't changed much, except to grow thinner.

"We shouldn't survive at all, if it were not for the goodness of an old servant of ours," Mrs. Treitel told me. She comes to see us whenever she can from the country, and always brings margarine, or eggs, or sugar for us in her handbag."

"Do they interfere with you at all?" I enquired.

"No," she said. "So far the Gestapo have left us in peace.

Many of our former friends, of course, cut us dead, but there are some faithful ones who still come at night and try to help."

I asked if the people in the house were all right to them. Yes, they were quite kind and polite. Indeed the woman had actually given her some tomatoes and a cabbage from the garden. Mrs. Treitel added quietly: "You know you can get china and clothes in return for food, don't you?"

I suppose the cabbage and the tomatoes had had to go for something warm. I did not ask that question.

"Really we are fairly quiet and happy here," she told me. "We know that Gerda is safe. I am allowed to sit in the sun in the vegetable garden behind the house out of sight, so it is not too bad in the summer days for me. But it's different for my husband. He gets so very tired. They make him work ten hours a day now. He dare not take a holiday. It is too much for Martin, he is nearly sixty now." I looked at Mr. Treitel. He certainly did not look well.

"It isn't only the work and lack of holidays," said Mr. Treitel, in his dejected voice. "It is being torn in two emotionally. I love Germany. I am a German. But now they have made me an outcast. Why? I keep turning it over and over in my mind. For generations my family have lived for Germany and worked for Germany. Now I am kicked like a dog and told I am only good enough to wash dirty bottles for sixty hours a week. It is mad! Why are they so blind and mad?" His voice had risen and was very penetrating.

"Psst!" said his wife. "Don't talk so loudly, someone may hear."

"Do you believe we shall lose the war?", I asked.

"Of course. Now that we have invaded Russia there isn't a shadow of doubt on that score."

"But surely it was better to attack than wait for Russia to attack us?", I protested.

"Germany will bleed to death on two fronts, and it is only a matter of time before America comes in against us."

"What makes you so sure about America?", I asked in surprise.

"Think hard," said Mr. Treitel. "Read between the lines. After the conquest of Poland America reacted with the 'Cash and Carry' agreements with England and France. After the conquest of France they reacted with general conscription. Wasn't that enough for Hitler to see the red light? But of course he refuses to see."

"Sh!" interrupted Mrs. Treitel again.

"Then America lends fifty destroyers to England against concessions on England's side. After the German invasion of Russia the Americans even extend 'Cash and Carry' to them. So this so-called neutral America is now delivering planes, tanks, raw material, food, etc. to England and to Russia in vast quantities. Do you imagine that in the end they won't come in and fight as well? Of course they will. How can Germany cope with that?"

It was clear to me by this time that both of them listened in to foreign stations on their radio, they sounded so like Feechen in their prophecies.

At the end of September Mr. Wolter paid a surprise visit to us at the headquarters of Strength through Joy. I was sitting with "Bachus" in Mr. Wolter's charming blue room. We were busy doing what bored us most, and what was so essential, statistics. How many exhibitions in the past six months? How many workers attended them? What results could be drawn from the attendances? What courses had been given? Suddenly the door swung open, and in came Mr. Wolter. He was in civilian clothes, and how different he looked! We both stared at him without speaking.

"Do I look like a ghost or something?" he asked.

"You look very tired," said "Bachus" quickly.

"I come from a war," was the sharp reply. He certainly looked very strange. He looked tired and haggard; he looked drained of vitality and spirit. He dropped into a chair and stared at our formidable array of papers and statistics and suddenly began to talk. Once started the words poured out of him.

"To come in and find everything just the same. It seems crazy," he said angrily. "And the war? It's just murder—plain, cold-blooded murder. There's no sense in it at all. And God?" he turned to stare hard at me; "There *is* no God. The whole thing is meaningless." He rushed into a wild description of grey bodies running like animals from one bomb crater to the next; of grenades and shells and dying men. How he had once rushed towards a small crater, only to jump on top of another soldier that moment split open with a grenade splinter. "If I had arrived one second earlier, it would have been *my* head split in half and not his," he said.

"I shot one Russian officer, and they searched his pockets afterwards for identification papers. They found a photo of his wife, a pretty woman, and two young boys about the same age as mine. He probably loved them just as much as I do mine." He put his elbows on his desk and let his head rest on his hands. And this had been the gay, optimistic man who had built up the art department of the Strength through Joy movement? Now he saw war as it was perhaps better than other men, for Mr. Wolter had an artist's imagination and powers of observation. He had rushed to volunteer for Germany and glory. He had seen the glory, but he came back a disillusioned man.

One morning I received a thick envelope from Africa. Inside were all the letters I had written to Walter, my brother's great friend. "Undeliverable" was written on each of them. What did it mean? Was he dead or wounded? I went to see my mother. It was in her house that I had last seen Walter. He too had been a volunteer like Mr. Wolter.

"Promise not to tell my mother yet that I have volunteered for Africa," he had told us. "She must not know I have volunteered for the *Himmelfahrtskommando* (Ascension Command)—that's what we call it; a ninety per cent certainty of reaching heaven at once!"

Walter was a colonial. He had a farm in Africa, and need not have volunteered at all, but he was seized with the passionate idealism of Hitler. "It is easy to die for such a man," he had said, after the Führer's broadcast.

He had told me in some of his earlier letters about the journey from Munich over the Brenner Pass. "It's so well organized, I might as well be on a Strength through Joy trip," he had written. Rome had filled him with joy. Indeed he had wished the war at an end so that he could stay there. He went on to describe Naples, the mountains, the sights, the bay, the beauty—the endless and perfect beauty. He was in Naples for a week, and was shocked at the luxuries in the shops. Then he moved on to Sicily for the final days. "Thank heaven I am ready to go now. It has softened me, this beauty and luxury and sunshine. I am busy sorting out my things. I shall take only my copy of *Zarathustra* (Nietzsche), my collection of German folk songs and a few, very private letters." He wrote very seriously in his last letter. "No man dies before his time, not even a child only one day old. There is a special purpose and pattern for each man on earth."

From Africa he had written to me that all was very different now. "We look most of the time like chocolate soldiers as the sand lies caked on our faces all day." This last bit reminded me of a strip cartoon I had seen in a Berlin illustrated paper entitled: "Daily life at 140°". In the cartoon someone is telling a line of soldiers a joke, but the faces remain carved and set, not a trace of laughter. Only in the final picture, when a brush is cleaning away the caked sand from their faces, is any man able to laugh at all, and that is many minutes after the joke has been told!

I did not hear after that. Eventually I learned that Walter was at the battle of Sollum where he was taken prisoner after fierce fighting. He was alive, his mother told me, but just as disillusioned and unhappy as Mr. Wolter.

* * *

Heiner ,and I were married in October 1941 in very modest style. It wasn't as gay or big an event as Evelyn's engagement party. I didn't try to collect clothing coupons from either relatives or friends, for everything was too difficult now that we had war on two fronts. No one could spare any kind of coupon any longer. Even my dream of a pair of new shoes had to be forgotten; shoes were the most difficult of all things to obtain now.

However, I managed to look quite bridal in the end. I made myself a long black silk skirt from two evening dresses, and with coupons bought some white lace material and made a very beautiful long-sleeved blouse. It looked quite charming. Wolfgang and Klaus both wore white suits, and they certainly made perfect pages for me. It was a very full and happy day. In the morning Heiner and I went to my parents' home in Charlottenburg, and from there to the registry office in the town hall, with just Heiner's mother and my parents and some close friends.

In the town hall Hitler's face surrounded by Swastika flags looked down on us while we solemnly promised to be faithful to each other as man and wife and obey the laws imposed on us by the State in that respect. Not a very enlivening ceremony. As we came out, we stepped, alas, into pouring rain. The whole of the Berliner Street from the Knie-square to the Charlottenburg Castle with its beautiful park was wrapped in monotonous rain and mist.

We stopped for a moment on the wide steps for protection. "Well, well," said Heiner. "It's like a Hamburg washhouse! I didn't know you had it like this in Berlin. And on our wedding day. What a shame!" He glanced down at my pretty clothes. "Never mind, darling," he said quickly. "We will manage somehow, and I can't even offer you a taxi, let alone my car." (His car was garaged owing to petrol rationing—taxis were off the street for the same reason.)

He ran off and waited for a tram to come in sight, leaving

me on the steps—then he quickly waved us on and we rushed for shelter.

It was very much a war wedding. The weather grew worse and worse, but Heiner was wonderful. He joked with the boys, making small bets with them that it would *not* be raining when we came out of the church. Then he turned to me and promised that in two years' time the war would be over, and he would give me another wedding day just as beautiful as I could wish for. He would probably have a new car by then, a much bigger one because of the boys, and then we would all go on a trip to Italy, or would I prefer somewhere else?

The boys were quite happy. They hung on his words and wanted to sit as close to him as possible. He had certainly won their hearts completely. They did not notice the tedious tram journey or the rain for Heiner was so gay.

After the church ceremony we came out again into the rain, and then into the underground, and later by bus to Kladow where we had a three-course luncheon given by my father. Finally we arrived, soaking wet, at Heiner's house. Everything was ready for us, thanks to his mother. The afternoon of my wedding day went beautifully. I took Wolfgang and Klaus into the nursery we had got ready for them. I showed them their beds and their toys. I told them that this was their new home, and that they would never have to go away from me again.

I am afraid we all got rather too happy, at least Heiner did. Looking at him suddenly I saw that the wine had gone to his head! Perhaps I looked a bit disapproving, for he grinned and told me he was stone-cold sober, and that to prove it he would walk down the blue line in the carpet without looking. He walked right off the blue line, but he was so happy about it that I couldn't tell him! We had just one peaceful family week-end without interruptions in Kladow. A war wedding, a rainy wedding, but such a happy one.

Rudolf, my brother, was not at our wedding. He had volunteered for the army again and was in Russia. He had said: "Now that we have this damned two-front war, I feel I must be a soldier again, though I loathe the idea. I'll never finish my studies now!" We had all tried to convince him that he should finish his studies first, but he insisted that his conscience wouldn't let him. "Every man is needed. You don't realize how many men will be needed on the Russian front." I argued that he would help Germany more by getting his degrees first, but he only became restless. "The more you talk, the more I realize I *must* go," he said.

So he went. His letters became less and less frequent as the awful battle across hundreds of miles went on. In December 1941 we were approximately thirty miles from Moscow. Hour after hour we sat with our radios switched on awaiting the final victory. Perhaps the end of the war now? So we all imagined in our hearts. Two years of fighting, and Europe, or all the part of it we needed, now under German domination! What an achievement.

One morning, I was in my kitchen in Kladow, preparing the potatoes for lunch when, without warning, the door swung open, and Rudolf stood here. I dropped the knife I was holding and stared blankly at him. He was smartly dressed in his military uniform, but he looked white and terribly tired. He leaned up against the doorpost after merely saying: "Hallo, Else!"

I rushed to kiss him. "Oh, Rudolf, how lovely to see you. I've been so worried."

"I'm all right now," he said very shortly but without a smile.

I called the children, and they ran in to greet him and then searched his baggage for souvenirs and presents. He cheered up a little at their exuberance, and did at last smile as he handed me a tin of corned beef and some pork fat to add to our rations.

That evening I made quite a big meal for Heiner, Rudolf

and Heiner's brother-in-law, Hermann, who, by a coincidence was also on leave. We sat there in the lounge, a typical war-time setting, with the black-out down and buckets of sand and water near the doors in case of incendiaries. After the meal, Hermann, not to be outdone in generosity, produced a bottle of liqueur. It was all quite luxurious. There was a knock at the door, and in came Dr. Schmitt and his wife, our close neighbours. Mrs. Schmitt had also brought a present to welcome Rudolf; some home-baked cakes.

"You do take risks," said Dr Schmitt sternly, as he insisted upon locking the outside door. "Don't you realize anyone could creep through your garden and listen at the door, and where would you be then I should like to know?"

Heiner and I laughed at him. "There aren't any informers in this road," we told him. "Stop being so pessimistic, and come and cheer Rudolf up. Tell him the latest Berlin jokes."

Dr. Schmitt began to smile at that. "I know a beauty," he declared. It was about Hitler's chosen successor, Rudolf Hess, who had just escaped to England and been taken prisoner there. Our Press now labelled him not only a traitor, but insane.

Hess had just landed from his plane, when Winston Churchill walked up to him and asked: 'Are you the madman from Germany?' 'No,' Hess replied, 'I am only his representative'."

Rudolf laughed the loudest. He made a note of the joke in his diary. "My commanding officer will enjoy that one," he told us.

Dr. Schmitt was warming up. "Do you know you can't get Hitler's *Mein Kampf* on the free market any longer?. It's rationed now. You have to give textile coupons for it. It comes under 'spinning material'!"

I was about to change the conversation when Rudolf shrugged his shoulders, and said wearily: "I wish I knew what we are going to do in the years to come, but I don't."

Dr. Schmitt swung round. "At last!" he exclaimed. "A young man with some sense in his head. A young man who is actually beginning to think and to doubt. In Berlin they all just work like ants from dawn to dusk and no one questions where it is all leading. They all just obey the Führer, like sheep."

"Have a drink," interrupted Heiner. "I think we all need one."

"I'll have one, but it won't help Rudolf," said Dr. Schmitt. "Or any of us. We'll all feel better but it won't change the facts."

"What facts?" said Heiner, determined to be happy. "We are at Moscow's front door, aren't we, we've only got to step inside."

"Whether we step inside or not, we've lost the war in Russia," said Rudolf suddenly.

Heiner hesitated in the middle of the room with a glass in his hand. He turned to stare at my brother.

"Lost the war in Russia," he repeated. "You really mean that, don't you?"

Suddenly I realized that Heiner had doubts too, that all the optimism and cheerfulness might be bluff, or perhaps sheer kindness on his part to help to put courage into the rest of us.

"What makes you so certain?" he asked quietly.

Dr. Schmitt could not control his impatience any longer. "For heaven's sake, isn't it obvious that we shall bleed to death fighting on two fronts at the same time?"

"Why are you so sure, Rudolf, we shall lose the war?"

"We haven't enough troops for one thing," said Rudolf. "Nor enough supplies; then look at the map. We move on over hundreds of miles in a few days, but all those places behind us have to be held with occupation troops, and all the time supplies have to be brought up to the front."

"Our victories in Russia are too quick and too many," said Dr. Schmitt.

140

"At first it was fine," went on Rudolf. "We swept on, adding towns and villages by the score. Do you know how we behaved to the civilians? Shall I tell you?" he asked. We didn't reply before he began his story.

"We behaved like devils out of hell," he said. "We have left those villagers to starve to death behind us, thousands and thousands of them. How can you win a war in this way? Do you think they won't revenge themselves somehow? Of course they will."

"You mean you leave nothing behind, no homes, no food, no animals?"

"Those are the orders," said Rudolf. "Just to leave enough for the occupying troops."

"It's utter madness," said Heiner. "Whoever gave such orders are out of their minds. Surely not the generals?"

"No," said Rudolf. "The Russian front is really in the hands of the SS, the generals have little say. It is Hitler's revenge for being told he couldn't win a war against Russia. He is trying to prove all the army officers wrong."

We sat in an awful silence for a moment. Then Rudolf went on to tell us more details of the partisans behind their lines.

"We shoot the prisoners on the slightest excuse," he said. "Just stick them up against a wall and shoot the lot. We order the whole village out to look while we do it, too."

"Yes," said Dr. Schmitt. "And I have heard too that Hitler ordered that every officer or political commissar made prisoner on the Eastern Front was to be shot immediately after questioning."

Rudolf jumped up. "No," he declared, "you are wrong there. The officers are not shot after questioning. I, at least, have seen that that's not true."

"Calm down," said Dr. Schmitt. "I only said 'ordered', I didn't say it was being carried out. Hitler signed a secret document to have it done, but the high army officers are refusing to carry the order out. That is one reason why

Hitler is getting so wild and allowing the SS and the Gestapo terrible powers in the villages after you have passed on."

"My God," said Rudolf. "If it is really true, then everything is lost not only the Russian war, but the whole war."

Heiner made a sign to Dr. Schmitt not to say anything more on that subject, but Rudolf would go on talking.

"You can't imagine what happens behind the lines. We had orders to try and clear partisans out of a wood. We combed that wood for two days in the most bitter weather. But no partisans. I was just about to withdraw my troops, when suddenly whistles began to blow, and the wood was full of Russians in a second. They were in such a terrible condition, however, that we beat them off. They had been lying in holes in the ground covered only with straw and brushwood and had had no food or drink, indeed they must scarcely have dared to take breath. They were so cold their limbs would not move properly when the order came to attack us."

"The courage of desperation," said Dr. Schmitt. "Men in those conditions will do anything."

"They do anything," said Rudolf. "When we passed through one village where the partisans had caught some of our troops, we found men stripped naked except for their steel helmets which were still stuck on their heads. A long line of them were tied together and water had been poured over them until they had frozen into a solid block of ice. You see, it's a vicious circle. We hate them, they hate us, and on and on it goes, everyone getting more and more inhuman."

Rudolf's last words echoed round the room. No one spoke. I put out a hand and touched Dr. Schmitt lightly, he was sitting quite close to me. He looked up and saw that I wanted him to try to help Rudolf.

"Yes," he said slowly, as if coming out of a coma. "It *is* a vicious circle."

"Another of our mistakes was in the Ukraine," said Rudolf, now a little calmer. "I was one of those who marched in to be received not as a conqueror, but as a friend. The civilians were all ready to look on us as saviours. They had had years of oppression from the Soviet. They thought we had come to free them. Does it sound absurd? Perhaps it does. What did we do? Turn them into slaves under Hitler. Worse, we deported their women for labour in Germany, and did not bother if they were married or single, had children or not. To add insult to injury we forced every woman and girl to undergo medical inspection. Ninety-nine per cent of the unmarried girls were virgins, but we took no notice of that, just ordered one and all to line up for medical inspection as though they were prostitutes. After inspection a clean medical report was made in their labour books, then they were loaded into waggons and transported to work for the Fatherland."

In the deep silence that followed I was very near to tears. To try and overcome them I hastily refilled the glasses and offered one to Rudolf to cheer him up.

"Come on, Rudolf, try and cheer up, we are together for only a short time. Come on," I pleaded.

Dr. Schmitt and his wife also took glasses, and Hermann and Heiner. We lifted them, and perhaps stupidly, but anyway with the best of intentions, we began to hum an old German drinking song. "Drink, dear brother, drink, and let worry look after itself." (*Trink, Brüderlein, trink, lasse die Sorgen zu Haus!*)

Rudolf took the glass and stared at me and said: "You can take my word for it, Else, if the Russians should ever knock at this door and only pay back one half of what we have done to them, you wouldn't ever smile or sing again!"

He threw back his head, and drank the wine in a gulp, and banged the glass down on the table. I was so shocked and upset that I began to cry and, to cover it up, I got up quickly and went to the kitchen on the pretext of finding some biscuits. When I returned Hermann was talking. His tales were always very amusing and Heiner was doing his utmost to encourage him to tell more. Rudolf was silent, but he did not look quite so grim now.

"As far as I am concerned," said Hermann, "one side of the war can go on as long as it likes, particularly the Italian side!"

He proceeded to read out some poems he had written in praise of Italian girls. Heiner laughed.

"You seem to be having a lot of success with the girls. I didn't realize you had so much sex appeal," he said.

"You don't need sex appeal," Hermann replied. "All you need for success with the girls and women generally is a loaf of bread or some cigarettes."

"What an awful thing to say about women," I protested in a shocked voice.

"It's true," said Hermann, still laughing. "And some of them are very beautiful and attractive as well."

Hermann would not allow the conversation to become too serious. He went on talking of his flirtations.

"They are the most marvellous dancers," he told us. "And they sing very well, too. Perhaps it's the blue skies and the warm sun." Yes, I thought, what a wonderful time he has had while we in Germany have only had rations and air-raids, no wonder he is so light-hearted. I looked at Heiner. I could see he was utterly fascinated by his brother's stories.

That night, as I lay in bed, I began to work myself up into resentment.

"What are you thinking of?" asked Heiner suddenly. I was silent. "Come on, now, out with it," he urged. "What's wrong?"

"If you were posted to France or Italy, would you be faithful to me?" I said suddenly.

There was a dead silence. Heiner did not move a muscle. It seemed like hours to me before he said, very quietly: "Darling, I just don't know".

144

He said it very sweetly and seriously, and I was so touched with his honesty that I turned over and kissed him.

"I'm sorry," I told him. "It was just jealousy and those tales of Hermann's. It was a mad question to ask; how could you know?"

I lay there for a long time after Heiner had fallen asleep, thinking of Rudolf downstairs, alone and so tragically disillusioned. My own brother, who had been so full of ideals and dreams for the future.

The next day I had to go to the city. At the Adolf-Hitler Platz I took a tram. There was no vacant seat, so I moved up the gangway towards the front of the tram and held on to a strap. Suddenly an old lady with white hair got up and offered me her seat. I was surprised, to say the least of it. I was much younger and quite strong, nor had I any big parcels, or a young child with me. The old woman looked frail. I refused quite politely, and tried to push her gently back into her seat, but she jumped up again and humbly offered it, again I refused. I used all the words I could think of to persuade her that I did not wish her to stand. Finally, as she grew so very persistent, I remarked that if she would *not* sit down, then neither would I, we would both stand and let someone else have the seat!

She stared at me, and then slowly turned and walked to the platform of the tram. It was only then that I saw a big yellow star on her dark coat, the David star of the Jews. The tram stopped and the old lady got off. I sank back on the empty seat very shocked. The passengers on the tram glared at me, and the woman next to me whispered: "If you hadn't been so obstinate that poor old woman could have stayed on. She was scared stiff. Didn't you see it?"

"I didn't know," I stammered.

"Didn't know!" said the woman contemptuously. "Where are you living? On the moon?" She then got up hastily herself, as though afraid of having said too much.

Terribly upset and confused, I gazed out of the window

145

at the people outside. Yes, there was another star, on a man's back this time; then another, on a young girl's. People moved away from them as far as possible. I began to remember the stories I had heard. The Jews were not to use the public seats in the parks. They were forbidden to visit the theatres, the museums, even the public lavatories. God alone knew where they went when the air-raids came.

In the *Kurfuerstendamm* I saw a group of Jews sweeping the roads. By now I had become completely yellow-star conscious, and was looking everywhere for Jews. I walked along to look more closely at the road-sweepers, but their faces were all turned towards the ground. Perhaps some of them were doctors, lawyers, professional men—maybe an artist or a musician was among them. They all wore dark and dirty clothes and they looked dejected and humiliated. The only bright and gay thing about them was the large yellow star of David on their backs!

At the Zoo I saw something even more poignant. The buses and trams there were full. A little boy about seven years old was waiting patiently in the queue. He held a heavy school satchel, and was probably going home from school. On his small, thin back was stitched the yellow star. When the tram arrived, he managed to scramble on to the platform. Suddenly a man rushed and tried to push his way on. Immediately the boy jumped off the platform to give the man his place. Finally, as the tram started, the child just managed to balance himself on the lowest step, with one hand gripping a pole and the other the satchel. In this dangerous position the tram moved off at full swing. Nobody put out a hand to protect him or said a word. He was a Jew; it didn't matter if he fell off or not. I thought of Wolfgang, just about two years younger. How would I feel if Wolfgang were treated like this and what kind of a man would Wolfgang grow up to be afterwards?

On my way home that day I thought, of course, of the Treitels. They were my closest Jewish friends. I must go and visit them again. I must make some tiny reparation for the rest of us. This time I visited them by daylight.

"How brave of you to come during the day," Mrs. Treitel said. "Hardly anyone comes during the day; it is too risky."

I changed colour. Her praise was more embarrassing than reproach would have been. "I only wanted to know how you were getting on," I muttered.

"Not too badly," she said. "We still have a few friends who help us with food. It looks as if things get worse every day, doesn't it? Jewish rations get less and less."

We were sitting in her lounge now. Mr. Treitel was at work, washing his bottles.

"Martin is terribly thin," Mrs. Treitel said. "He's just like a skeleton, no flesh on his bones at all. I give him the best we have but it makes no difference."

It took all my courage, but I had to ask. "Does he get badly treated in the streets, with his David star?"

"We don't wear the David star?" she said triumphantly. "No one has bothered us here. The new owners are very decent. They said as far as they were concerned they would turn a blind eye as long as we have one coat hanging in our wardrobes with the star stitched on, just in case the Gestapo come to look! Perhaps no one will betray us."

I smiled with relief. "Perhaps you will be lucky," I suggested.

"My husband would never survive that humiliation, to be publicly insulted in the streets. As for betrayal, we have made up our minds. We would rather die, if that happens." She said it quite casually, as though talking about bad weather. It seemed to matter as little to her.

That night I talked it over with Heiner. I told him about the old lady in the tram, the little boy, and then the Treitels. I poured out the whole thing.

"But, darling," he protested, "you knew all this was going on, it's not new, is it?"

147

"I hadn't looked at the stars before," I kept saying. "There aren't so many Jews here in Kladow, and it had never happened publicly to me before in a tram."

"I know," said Heiner gravely. "But what can we do? If we protest openly, we are fellow-travellers with the Jews, and we only land ourselves in trouble as well. How can we help them? Is it any use being martyred for them, and what about the boys? How would it help the boys?"

The mere mention of the boys made me shiver, and my heart missed a beat. Heiner was right, I could do nothing, except perhaps go and visit the Treitels regularly. But even that I had better do only at night, otherwise I might land myself in a concentration camp, and what would happen to the boys then?

9

Doubts and Fears

ONE of the letters I had written to Walter during the summer of 1941 eventually came into my hands again. In it I described our first fears and anxieties about the Russian front. At first we had just rumours and whispers. We were only thirty miles from Moscow, why couldn't we take it at once? What had happened? Up till now we had conquered cities hundreds of miles apart in a few days. What were our troops waiting for?

The weeks went by. Early autumn came, and still the Russians held us back. Everyone talked about it, in the streets and cafés. Radios were on all day for news. When at last news did come it was the worst the German nation had ever received. Our army was caught in the most bitter winter known in Russia for a hundred and forty years. The temperature had dropped in mid-October to as low as 58° of frost. Our troops—expecting to take Moscow that summer—were still fighting in light uniforms. We were asked to send every mortal thing we could to help them. A long list of necessities was read out daily—woollens, furs, heavy shoes, ski-ing boots, ear-protectors, gloves—everything. The Press, in commenting on the extraordinary earliness of the Russian winter, blandly informed us that Napoleon had only to contend with 25° of frost in his campaign. It was an interesting point, but hardly a helpful one.

The appeal for help was nation-wide, and I doubt if there was one person who did not respond. Half a million fur coats were sent, a fantastic number when you consider that it was wartime, and all of them quite irreplaceable. Heiner rushed at once to his wardrobe and pulled out his best and thickest pullover.

"You are a fool," said Dr. Schmitt. "It's too late to help now. By the time your pullover arrives they will be frozen to death. If you must give something, give something less valuable."

But Heiner was firm. "Fool or no, I shall give my best. Here I am sitting in a warm and cosy room with my wife, while they are fighting in this shocking cold, how can I send them old clothes?"

He took his best heavy pullover, and put it on a pile I was getting ready for the Party man to pick up.

"He's right," said my sister Hilde, who was staying with us. "They must have everything we have got. Dr. Schmitt should have been at the station and heard that man screaming last week, then he wouldn't talk about being sensible."

Hilde had actually been on a platform when a troop train came in. One man started screaming for help when he felt the train stop. A woman nearby saw the stretcher bearers throw a blanket over his head to drown his screams. Hasty orders were given to send the train out of the station again, but not before the woman had seen the lined, frozen face of the soldier, who was a mere boy. And Hilde had heard him shout: "They are going to cut my legs off . . . stop them! Help me!"

"I know," said Dr. Schmitt. "It sounded cruel, but honestly it's too late now to help. Heiner may need that pullover desperately himself. I know what is going on in the military hospitals. It is nothing but amputations of frozen limbs—legs, arms, hands, ears. They have to work day and night to save the poor devils. Often, of course, it is too late. So do you honestly think your things will reach Moscow in time?"

That terrible autumn and winter. We knew that each night trainloads of troops were arriving in the stations for hospitals. We knew the men arrived with blackened, frostbitten faces, and rotting limbs. And there was nothing we could do. Someone had made a gigantic blunder, but what use blaming anyone? It did not stop the agony, nor bring the dead back to life. Rumours, too, went around that the huge stocks of collected material never went to the front, but just lay piled up in storehouses. So perhaps Dr. Schmitt was not so foolish or cruel in his advice, after all.

Christmas came to break the horror a little. As always it brought beauty and warmth into our lives for a day at any rate. This was my first Christmas with Heiner and my sons. We had a beautiful tree and a few candles, and gave each other modest little presents. Dr. Schmitt was disguised as Father Christmas, and on Christmas Eve he knocked hard at the door and stepped in with a big sack over his shoulder. He also carried a little rod in his hand, in keeping with our German custom. Wolfgang and Klaus looked at him very seriously. They stood under the tree and sang their carols until he was satisfied, and then with anxious faces answered his questions about their little sins and failings during the year. Had they told any lies? Had they been greedy, or naughty, or disobedient? They both tried to think hard, though the twinkle behind Father Christmas's eyes was quite obvious. Soon the questions were over, and they had promised to be good in future. The rod was put away, the sack opened, and the two boys plunged into it. The sweets and gifts that poured out were a wonderful surprise to us all. Our neighbours and friends had certainly put their hearts into this Christmas for our children. We played with them for hours, wishing the lovely day would never end.

I am so glad those days are still clear to me. Heiner was so utterly good to me. He stood in the centre of the family, taking all the troubles of the war on his shoulders. He made a splendid father to the boys.

As a husband he was a surprise in many ways after Richard. One day he said: "I wish to heaven you would argue or grumble at me sometimes. You always say 'yes' meekly to everything I suggest, even when you don't approve. Why don't you say 'no' sometimes?" I looked at him in astonishment. I just didn't understand him. All my life I had been trained to accept men as they were. Men seemed to me to have a basic superiority complex, and the war had certainly increased it. One didn't dare criticize or contradict one's menfolk. I had seen it in my father from childhood upwards. I had experienced it with Richard many a time. Indeed Manfred, my sister's fiancé, was the first man I had actually noticed admiring and respecting a woman openly. Some of this I tried to explain to Heiner. It was his turn to stare at me in surprise.

"And you actually thought I was like that? That I thought women were less than servants? Darling, what a terrible marriage you must have had. Now, get this into your head. I want a real wife, someone equal—no, better—than myself. I don't want a doll or a slave. I want a woman with a heart of her own and thoughts of her own, even if they are quite the opposite to mine. Do you get it now?". He paused for a moment to look at me quietly.

"No, I'm afraid I don't," I told him.

"Well, I'll have to laugh you into it then," he said, and threw his head back. "But first promise to try and be yourself and say exactly what you think, every single day. Will you?"

I began, now, however, to try, and one day I asserted myself for the first time. It was rather funny. I was working in the kitchen, when Heiner came in and began talking about plans for the Sunday.

"In the afternoon we will have a nice long walk. I suggest we go to the Sacrower Lake this time."

Oh, I thought, these awful walks! How sick I am of them!

"No, *not* another walk! I am so tired; all I want is to sit down on Sunday afternoons. I have to stand in queues all the week and walk miles looking for extra food."

"Good lord," said Heiner, and burst out laughing. "Why on earth didn't you say so before?" He had his arm round me now, and was kissing me. "Look, we won't go for a walk on Sunday. We'll sit in the lounge or garden and read or listen to the radio, is that better?"

"Much better," I said in relief.

"I know," he said. "Let's take it in turns. In spring and summer we'll sit in the garden one Sunday to please you, and go for trips the next Sunday to please me. How's that? Could you bear that?"

I told him that I could bear it very well. It wasn't that I didn't like the trips, it was because I was very tired.

The New Year brought news of our new ally's successes— the Japanese successes. Pearl Harbour, the conquest of Singapore and Rangoon, then the conquest of Mandalay. Looking again at our maps we now wondered at the minute size of Japan and the huge conquests she was making against America.

The Press couldn't praise the Japanese enough. They seemed the most remarkable fighters in the world. We heard astonishing tales of selfless heroism; of tiny planes with one pilot who flew *himself* with his bombs straight at the target; of "human torpedoes" in which the Japs guided their weapons to the enemy ships and died with them. It was fanatical courage and made me shudder. To love your country so much that you wanted to die like that. Somehow this seemed horrible.

The Japs, however, were not only fanatically heroic, they were also clever. On the very eve of the German-Russian war they had signed a treaty with our enemy—Russia—to guarantee neutrality. It was a brilliant stroke. Japan at any rate was not going to have a two-front war. Not that it helped them in the end.

In the spring of 1942 my mother-in-law wrote from Hamburg that she was coming to visit us, and would be bringing a friend of hers, a Mrs. Mahler.

Heiner was slightly amused. "That's typical of Mummy," he said. "She can't stay in one place for a moment. The longest I have ever known her to stay still has been for three months, then she is up and off on her travels again. I should have thought her beautiful flat in Hamburg would have kept her quiet in wartime. I suppose she will be out and about showing her friend all over Berlin."

He was wrong in that last idea. They did not want to see Berlin when they arrived. They wanted to see Himmler! Mrs. Mahler was desperately unhappy. She had begged my mother-in-law to come to Berlin with her to try and talk to Himmler. It seemed that her youngest son Werner had been arrested by the Gestapo. He was a musician and had played with a band in a seaside place on the North Sea. Most unfortunately, he had suggested they played an English dance song. It was not sung, merely played by him on his violin, and it was tremendously popular with the audience. Perhaps no one knew it was English, they simply liked the melody. The next morning the Gestapo stood at his bedside, and Werner disappeared.

Mrs. Hahler was a tall, fine-looking woman, with perfect Aryan colouring and blue eyes. Each morning since her son's disappearance she had set off to try and trace him. She had stormed every official citadel, but wherever she went she got the same reply. "We cannot interfere with the Gestapo."

Finally she had decided to come to Berlin to see Himmler himself.

"I shall go down on my knees to him," she said to us. "If he has a heart at all he must listen and set Werner free. Werner is only nineteen, he didn't see how serious it was."

Heiner and I did not know what to do to comfort her. What could we say? We knew she never stopped thinking and worrying about her son. At last Heiner got up and went and fetched one of his hidden "treasures", a bottle of liqueur he had got hold of by the "exchange" system. It had been put aside for my birthday, but he didn't ask my permission to use it now, he knew I would be only too pleased. Mrs. Mahler drank a glass, and began to talk more quietly.

"I curse myself all the time," she said, "that I never forced him to join the Hitler Youth. But you see he just wasn't the type. He has no feeling for military things at all. He is a musician but he is not a traitor. He had no idea that to play an English dance tune would label him a traitor to his country." Mrs. Mahler broke down and began to cry again. I remember her hands. She had long and beautifully shaped hands. As she sat there she kept trying to adjust her hair, taking out a pin and putting it back again.

"Where is he? Where can they have taken him? What are they doing to him?"

We couldn't answer, nor could we persuade Mrs. Mahler even to take sleeping pills at night.

Needless to say, Mrs. Mahler did not manage to see Himmler. At night we would hear her marching up and down her room, talking to herself, planning the things she would say to Himmler when they met. Things that would melt his heart, words that might save her son. Sometimes I feared she would go mad with grief, but at last my mother-in-law convinced her that it was useless to stay in Berlin any longer. She told Mrs. Mahler of a rumour she had heard that her son might be travelling through Hamburg to the Eastern front. This was enough to get immediate results. Mrs. Mahler was packed in a few hours and they set off back to Hamburg.

Later on I heard the dramatic end of the story. After weeks and weeks of waiting daily at Hamburg station, Mrs. Mahler was brusquely informed that her son would be on the second platform of the Central station in about half an hour's time. The message came early in the morning, when she was at home. Without waiting a moment, she seized hat and coat and rushed into the street. There were no taxis, and so she scrambled on to a crowded tram. Breathlessly she arrived at the Central station, and rushed to platform No. 2. It was empty. She waited. At last a train pulled in and a group of young men, heavily guarded, were marched on to the platform. She ran towards them. Her heart told her that Werner was among them. She stumbled over a suitcase and fell heavily to the ground in her excitement. But she got up quickly and ran on.

"Werner!" she cried out.

Her son was there. He turned round. What she saw in his face made her stop dead. He looked utterly different, just like a stranger. He did not move one step towards her. He was unshaven, dirty, and utterly exhausted. His eyes were cold and hollow, and had the expression of a very old man who has seen everything, and cares for nothing more. There was not a trace of a smile to greet her. She saw bloodstains on his clothes. They have beaten and tortured him she thought. Oh, God, please don't let me cry, it might be bad for him. At last Werner spoke. He didn't say "Mother", or "Hallo", or give any kind of greeting. All he said was: "Did you bring me some bread?"

The words hit her like a blow. How could she have forgotten about food?. Of course he was hungry.

"No," she muttered. "I haven't any with me. The news came so suddenly."

"You forgot," he said sharply.

"But I'll go and get some now. Wait here. I won't be a moment."

She turned quickly and rushed to the shops. She had of course no ration cards with her, and there was no time to return home. She had to try and get bread without a card. At the first bakery they merely laughed at her. They were suspicious, too. Didn't she know that she could not get bread without a card? She offered her handbag, anything, if they would only give her half a loaf. Then they became angry and told here there was a policeman near who might report them all. Would she please leave the shop at once?

Mrs. Mahler raced to the next bakery, but this time it was in a quiet, side street. She just threw her handbag on the counter, took her coat off and left it lying there, seized a loaf of bread and ran. They must have thought she was mad. She did not care. She returned to the platform with the loaf in her hand. The men had gone, and the train. She never saw her son again, nor did she ever get news of him. She was told eventually that he was put into a special company on the East front. A "probation" company it was called which was regarded as a death sentence. The so-called "probation" companies were always thrown into battles or given tasks in which there was no chance of survival.

In 1943 Mrs. Mahler lost her Hamburg home in the big air-raids. She is living now with her husband in a tiny flat there. Both of them have heart trouble. No one today even mentions the name of her son, nor is there a photograph of him to be seen. Mrs. Mahler hoped against hope that her son might be among the prisoners of war returning from Russia in 1955. But it was not to be and she became very ill indeed. I suppose she still hopes against all hope that even today she may hear of Werner again.

There were terrific Japanese successes in the Far East in the spring of 1942. Things went very well on our own African front and much better in certain parts of Russia. We didn't pay much attention, therefore, to a tiny notice in the papers that summer saying that the Americans had landed on the Solomon Islands. I looked at the map and couldn't even find the spot they had landed on.

"How honest the military headquarters are," I said to Heiner. "Fancy mentioning the name of a spot so tiny we can't find it."

Heiner agreed with me, but as ever Dr. Schmitt was very suspicious. "Perhaps they mention it because of the people who listen into foreign broadcasts. It's not wise to tell us all the good news only or try to underestimate the results of the raids. Did you know that fifteen thousand people were killed in Cologne in the last raid, and more than two hundred and fifty thousand are homeless as a result of one raid? They are starting daylight attacks now. Perhaps it's as well to try and focus some of our attention on the Pacific, even if it is only a very tiny victory for America."

None of us at the time knew of course that the "tiny victory" on the Solomon Islands was going to become an important base for the Americans, from which they were to carry out their future operations in the Pacific Ocean. The conquest of little Guadalcanal was indeed one of the turning points of the war in the Far East. At the time, we, in Germany, merely admired the honesty of our military reports in telling us about it.

General Rommel was our great hero of the summer of 1942. In July he achieved the final victory in Africa, or so we thought. He broke through to El Alamein not far from Alexandria. This meant that Egypt and the Suez Canal were now opened up to us.

Once more we swung into a mood of hope and jubilation. Even the sceptical Dr. Schmitt admitted that the prospects of breaking through to Egypt, Palestine, Syria and Iraq were imminent, and that perhaps we should then soon link up with Japan and so "close the ring".

"Provided, of course," he added, "we have the necessary troops and equipment."

In Russia we now pushed forward to the Caucasus between the Black and the Caspian Seas. It was a proud event when the German flag was hoisted on the Elbrus in August 1942. As a result of these successes, our rations were increased. Bread went up from two to two and a quarter kilos (about five pounds), and meat from three hundred to three hundred and fifty grammes per week (about twelve ounces). We all began to be full of optimism.

"Wouldn't it be marvellous if peace came this summer?" I asked Heiner, as I returned from a shopping expedition in which I had been cheerfully discussing the extra rations with other housewives.

"Do you know what I would do first?" I continued.

"What would you do?"

"I would make a bonfire of all your socks and the boys' and all your old underclothes. Then I would go off and get lots and lots of new things, ending with. . ."

Heiner interrupted me. "I know, ending with a new fur coat," said Heiner laughing. "On second thoughts perhaps peace wouldn't be such a good idea. I can't say it looks as though it would be very cheap for me! I am to get a couple of pairs of new socks and some new underwear while my wife gets a fur coat. What a prospect!"

Then he, too, did a bit of day-dreaming.

"I tell you what I'll do. I'll get a new car, the very latest design, and much bigger than the one in the garage now." He grinned at me. "What would you say if I spent all the money on a nice new car and you had nothing?"

"It would mean a battle," I said firmly.

Heiner burst into laughter. "A third world war between us, would it?"

"Yes," I said. "You told me to say what I thought."

"I did, indeed," he said, kissing me. "I can see you are going to be an expensive wife." He seemed very pleased about it.

And so was I. "I've had to be a pretty cheap one up till now, haven't I? You can't buy me a thing, however much you may want to!"

"One day I'm going to enjoy making up for it all."

But all this was not yet to be. I went on darning and patching. Our hopes on the Eastern Front again began to fade as all news was now concentrated on Stalingrad. Was this to be Germany's Waterloo? It looked like it. By the end of October 1942, the largest part of Stalingrad belonged to us, but the Russians went on offering street to street resistance. It was all hand-fighting now.

In November the Russians started their counter attacks on a big scale. I learnt after the war that General Halder was dismissed at this time by Hitler for his warning that, by the end of 1942 Russia would have vast new quantities of materials and freshly equipped troops to throw into the war. Hitler would not listen and went on with the Stalingrad battle.

Halder was right. The fresh Russian troops cut off the German Sixth Army, parts of the Fourth Tank Army, and some Rumanian troops from our communication lines. There was still a possibility of retreat, and General Paulus, in charge of three hundred thousand men, asked Hitler for their withdrawal. Hitler refused. So all the three hundred thousand were lost either in the battle or later on in prison camps. Terrible stories came to us later on of our wounded men lying in the snow without food, without medical attention, and without hope of either, just lying there in the ruins of Stalingrad. Only those who have known the torture of a Siberian winter will know what they must have suffered.

We all had friends on the Russian Front and we tried not to talk too much about them to each other. But one day an old friend of mine—Edith Wieland—wrote, begging me to visit her, as she had just lost her husband in the battle. I found as she opened the door, a thin, old woman in black, not the proud, confident Edith I had known She began to cry as she asked me inside.

In the lounge she showed me her husband's last letter from Stalingrad. He asked her to forgive him for anything he might ever have done to hurt her. He had never at any time wanted to hurt her. It was for her alone that he was now living and he loved her more than his life. This was no empty phrase he wrote because they were now facing death, and it would only be a matter of days or weeks. But as long as he felt his death served a purpose he would be willing to give his life for the Fatherland. He implored her never to give up, no matter what might come, and to bring

160

up their children—the youngest only two months old—in the spirit they had agreed upon.

I was utterly shaken. I could see him standing before me in his officer's uniform, so proud and with the Iron Cross on his chest and the stars of a Hauptmann. He had been a strong and virile man, honest as the day.

"Was he wounded when he wrote this letter?" I asked Edith.

"No," she said quickly. "I have been told he was not wounded. He met his death with open eyes. He was perfectly well and strong."

I looked down at the carpet. What kind of death then had he met? As if Edith could guess my thoughts, she said: "They have written that death came instantaneously. He got a bullet through the head as he came round the corner of a house."

While I was searching desperately for the right words, Edith spoke again. "There is one thing that haunts me. I have heard a rumour that they could have escaped, but that Hitler forbade it!"

I was frightened. I had not heard that rumour myself at the time. "No! Impossible!" I said. "It would be plain murder. Hitler would never do such a thing. You know that, surely?"

Very slowly Edith lifted her head. "I am not so sure," she said in a low voice. "I keep re-reading that sentence in Albert's letter ('as long as I feel my death serves a purpose') that doesn't sound a bit like Albert. It sounds as though his confidence was waning, and he was beginning to doubt."

It took all my energy and powers of persuasion to convince her that Albert had been too honest and straightforward to tell her to bring her children up adoring Hitler if he no longer believed in him. They had both been heart and soul in the Führer's dream of a great Germany. Albert *must* have had faith till the end, I kept telling her.

I did not see her again. I heard that she lost her home in

F

161

air-raids and that her little son, Albert, was killed by a grenade splinter from the Russians. There must have been thousands like her, dying for the Führer's mad dreams.

They fought to the last in Stalingrad, as Hitler ordered. On the 31 January 1943, General Paulus signed the capitulation. Ironically enough Hitler had only appointed him a Field-Marshal just two days before he surrendered. Ninety thousand men went with the Field-Marshal into captivity; the remaining two hundred and ten thousand in the attack, it was said, were all dead. A hush fell over the country, in the Press and on the radio.

"How romantic they were centuries ago," said Dr. Schmitt. "In those days they made up poems: 'Into the valley of death rode the six hundred.' No one seems likely to write a poem today about the two hundred thousand men who died for the Führer in the town of death."

"Perhaps two hundred thousand is too many for a poem," said Heiner.

The evening the news of the capitulation came through none of us talked much. We were too depressed and anxious. Suddenly I asked Heiner if he wouldn't start improving our garage so that we could live in it?

"What on earth do you want to live in the garage for?"

"When the Russians come perhaps they will allow us to live in it," I said slowly. "Do you think they would?"

Heiner burst into laughter. "You certainly haven't got the heart of a lion," he chided me. "You give up at once. Just because we are defeated at Stalingrad doesn't mean that the Russians have got to Berlin!"

"Not yet, but I have an awful feeling that they will. One day they will be here," I said.

"Don't be absurd," Heiner retorted. "Stop being pessimistic. Do you know more than Hitler then?"

He refused to talk about the garage. I can still hear his laughter as he called me his "silly, sweet, little coward," and tried to change my mood.

Edith Wieland was not the only friend who sent us mourning cards. I heard from an old college friend Gerda that she had lost her two brothers in Stalingrad. Gerda's father was a priest of the Evangelical Church in Berlin. He had four children, three sons and one daughter.

When I went to their house I ran into the eldest brother. He was one of the last wounded to be flown out of Stalingrad. I was appalled when I saw him. His hip had been totally smashed, and he was now disfigured and could not walk without crutches, but his spirit was not broken. Indeed, he said fiercer things to me than had ever come my way before. Things that made me think very hard afterwards. At first the atmosphere in the house was tense and uneasy. The father sat there silent and morose. The mother kept trying to bring him out of his lethargy to talk to me. Then Gerda pulled me on one side and explained.

"Father thinks he is the cause of my brothers' deaths," she said. "You see he wrote to the military headquarters pointing out that he had three sons serving in Russia and asking for one of them to be posted to a quieter front. The reply to his letter was a flat refusal. He now blames himself for being so outspoken. He feels he has murdered his own sons."

But as the time went on and nothing could draw the old man out of his gloom, Gerda's brother turned to me and burst out violently: "I may as well say it, it's no use you trying to cheer us up. Germany *must* lose the war."

I nodded sadly. This was the theme song of many young wounded men today. He looked at me keenly.

"You've got me all wrong," he said loudly. "I don't mean from the military angle at all. I mean from the Christian angle. For the sake of Christianity, for the sake of the world, it is better that we lose the war!"

I sat up and said. "What on earth are you talking about?"

"You understand me perfectly," he said grimly. "It's no use playing hide and seek with our consciences, now or at any time. I have faced my Stalingrad already. I have met death face to face. There was nothing noble about it in Stalingrad. We just pushed the dead aside and piled them up. There was no time to say goodbye to a friend or mutter a prayer." He spoke quickly and with violent effort. The sweat began to break out on his forehead.

"Come and lie down," said his wife very gently, moving across to him. "It's not good for you to get so excited."

"Oh, for heaven's sake, let it come out for once," he said. "I have escaped. I am crippled for life, but I have now plenty of time to think. Perhaps that's the only time any of us do think. I find that I would rather die in a concentration camp than lift another hand to help Germany win this war."

I had never heard such things before, a German who wanted to be vanquished. I stared at him in silence. He was talking directly to me.

"I tell you, Else, I have been through my Stalingrad and seen the truth, now you have got to face yours. Each one of us must face it in the end."

We still sat in silence not daring to interrupt him.

"Do none of you realize what life would be like if Hitler did win the war?"

I had to admit that I had never thought of that.

"I thought not," said Gerda's brother. "We are all built like that, we Germans. We have no vision, no imagination at all. We don't see until we are knocked down, that's why we are guilty. We never see where our acts will lead us.

"One thing is certain to happen if Hitler wins. Christianity will disappear from Europe, if not from the world. Hitler's race theory will stamp it out. You can't have lots of German gods and one God as well. Do you imagine for a moment Hitler would allow the Christian churches to continue? I have seen too much in Poland and Russia. Hitler crushes everything that gets in his way."

I wanted to argue. This seemed the most terrible accusation I had ever heard. But before I could get any arguments ready, the voice went on.

"Have you forgotten Pastor Niemöller? He is still in a concentration camp remember. You protested in 1937 over his arrest, didn't you? You ran quickly enough to put your name on the lists of people asking for his sermons. Do you remember that last sermon?"

I did. It had been printed, and many of us had copies still. Pastor Niemöller had taken his text from the Acts of the Apostles, where Gamaliel, pleads to save the Apostles from death. "Leave these men alone, for if their counsel be of men it will come to nought. But if it be of God, ye cannot overthrow it. Or if you fight it, then, you fight against God." Niemöller, in his sermon, had gone further than Gamaliel.

"Neutrality like Gamaliel's is not enough. Neutrality only becomes enmity in the end. The words of Jesus Christ are valid now. 'He who is not for me is against me'."

In that sermon Niemöller told his congregation that even at the Communion Service there were three young Gestapo officers whose job it was to spy on the congregation. He tells of six women and one man who were arrested merely for distributing leaflets about the "Confessing Church", as this movement of the Evangelical Church was called.

He finally warned his people not to be blinded by a wise and clever detachment, nor to listen to reassuring phrases, but to face life the hard way. "Man shall not live by bread alone, but by every word that proceedeth out of the mouth of God."

Those words came back to me vividly. Some of them Gerda's brother now re-quoted. I was ashamed.

"So you had forgotten Niemöller. For you, too, his sacrifice is in vain."

"No," I cried, "that's not true."

"Isn't it?" asked Gerhard. "Then why aren't you by Niemöller's side?"

"I can't," I said.

"But you can sit and admire Hitler and wait for more victories?"

"I have two children," I reminded him.

"Pastor Niemöller has five. Be honest. You are like those who pass by on the other side of the road. Don't deceive yourself you are really the Good Samaritan; you can watch the wound bleeding and go on without doing anything."

With trembling hands Gerhard reached for his crutches, and with his wife's help got up. His pale cheeks were a hectic red now. He raised his voice.

"We are all the same. We are all like Parsifal—we can all stand and look on while Germany bleeds to death in a wicked cause. Just as Parsifal became an outcast from the Knights so too will Germany become an outcast from the world. All because none of us stood up and halted the wickedness."

Tears came into my eyes. It was a terrible condemnation. I turned my face quickly as he limped across the room. I could not bear to see that broken body.

"You don't understand," I murmured to him. "You don't know what it is like to have two children."

"But I understand," said a soft voice quite near me.

I looked up. Gerda's mother stood beside me.

"I am a mother as well," she said, and began to cry.

Suddenly Gerda's father got up from his chair and came slowly and heavily across to his wife. He put his arm round her and led her away. Then he turned to me and spoke at last.

"It's all right," he told me. "We do understand. We are all of us guilty, and we do at last confess it."

Perhaps it was at that moment that the idea of writing this book first came to me. Gerda's parents did not survive the war. They died in April 1945. Gerda's father had to put on uniform and become a *Volkssturmann*. This was the corps of Hitler's last defence, composed of men of no matter what age, no matter how ill. The people called it the army of the

166

grandfathers. Gerda's mother was burnt to death when their bombed house collapsed on them. But the crippled Gerhard survived and today has two happy, healthy children. Gerda too is still alive in East Berlin. She is a nurse in a hospital. She has never married, and she is separated from all her friends. A very lonely life.

I was haunted by Gerhard's words all the way home. I had surely done my best in the past? Didn't one's children always have to come first? Yet he had said to me: "*You* are one of the middle-of-the-road people, just like all the rest. You want to eat your cake and have it, be a member of the Confessing Church and yet be silent when you see what Germany is doing. You are just a middle-class woman, ready to do anything for a quiet life."

It was the most horrible thing he could have said to me, for middle-class was used by Hitler of those people who always did the best and cleverest things for their own skins. When had I heard it used about us before? Suddenly I remembered. It was a very long time ago, in the winter of 1918 just after we had lost the First World War. I was a little girl of about nine years old, and I was hearing rifle shots for the first time in my life. I was playing with my brother and sisters in the nursery in Berlin-Charlottenburg, when I heard screams. Like a flash all of us ran to the door to see what was happening. What we saw was rather comical. My father was rushing from room to room closing the windows and letting down the blinds with a noise like thunder. My mother raced behind him to help, but always arrived a second too late. Close behind them came our servant Anna. She seemed to have lost her wits completely. All the time she was wringing her hands and crying, "*Ach Gott, ach Gott!*"

We children ran after them, staring and asking questions, which no one would answer. At the same time we could hear banging and screams from the street outside.

"Keep away from the windows, go back into your nursery,

don't dare go to the front of the house, there may be splinters," my father shouted at us; "do as I tell you at once, Else," he said.

But Anna was too curious to be treated as a child. She went to one of the rooms and peered through the blinds.

"Control yourself," said my father. "Don't behave like that in my house."

After a time the noise stopped, and the street was as silent as the grave. My father went and looked out but hastily dropped the blind back into place.

"Get on with your work," he told us. "It was nothing much. Just a small police matter, I suppose; nothing for children to worry about."

My mother was crying but she did not say anything to us but merely fo'lowed father out of the nursery obediently. Later on that day I managed to get the true story out of Anna. She said there had been a mob of people dragging a group of officers along the street, insulting them. They had torn off their shoulder flashes, hit them, spat on them, and finally put one of them up against the wall just opposite our house and shot him. The mob had been crazy with hatred, like a pack of wild animals, she said.

"I did not know people could behave like that," she kept crying to me. "He was a very young officer. He was tall, and handsome. He smiled at me," said Anna. "He saw me peeping through the window. He smiled. It was a horrible smile. I think he hated me, but I wasn't doing anything, was I?"

No, I thought, on that painful journey home, she wasn't doing anything, and Gerhard had said I was not doing anything either.

Those officers of the 1914-18 war had fought for Germany and come back as defeated heroes, then the mob had turned on them in a moment of blind reaction.

My conscience about my own part in my Church was so stirred that I had to talk to Dr. Schmitt that evening.

"There's no doubt," said Dr. Schmitt, "indifference and silence are perhaps worse crimes than any others but what can we do now?. It's too late. We are in the same position as General Paulus at Stalingrad. We have to go on. If a brave man gets up and speaks the truth he is only 'liquidated'." He turned to his wife. "I wonder if the Lion of Münster has been arrested yet?"

"Who on earth is the Lion of Münster?", I asked.

"You *are* out of things," said Dr. Schmitt. "Your crippled friend is right; you and your children and your husband, that is all you know about."

Mrs. Schmitt interrupted quickly. "The Lion of Münster is Count Galen, the Catholic Bishop of Münster. He is speaking openly against the Party. It's a miracle he hasn't been put into a concentration camp."

"It's no miracle," said Dr. Schmitt. "They would love to treat him the same way as Pastor Niemöller, but they daren't. Things are a bit different now. Münster is deep in the heart of the Catholic country. It's been terribly bombed too and more and more people are losing their homes. It wouldn't be wise to take their bishop from them. People who have lost everything are dangerous. They are ready to risk their skins, start a revolt, anything, if their last hope is threatened."

"Yes," added his wife. "Catholics can be fanatical. They aren't tolerant or indifferent like Protestants. If the Party touches their beloved bishop, it might be the last straw. Would you like to hear some of his sermons?" She went out of the room.

"Of course we would like to hear the Lion of Münster roaring," said Heiner.

"The sermons are sent everywhere," said Dr. Schmitt. "They are even going to the soldiers at the front. Radio London has spoken of them, and there are photos of the Bishop in the *New York Herald Tribune*."

"And he is still at large?" asked Heiner in astonishment.

Mrs. Schmitt returned with some of the sermons, and began to read aloud. After a few moments Heiner and I were both silent.

"None of us is sure," said the bishop, "however faithful or conscientious a citizen he is, that he will not one day be fetched from his home and locked in the cellars and concentration camps of the Gestapo. I am quite certain that this will happen to me today or tomorrow. And so because I may not then be able to speak to you I am warning you now. If the public continue on the road they have taken then God's judgment will fall on them. This road leads to total misery and the ruin of our people and country."

In one of the sermons the bishop accuses the Party of confiscating one convent after another. "We must face the fact that the Gestapo will continue to confiscate our convents," he said ... "Our brothers and sisters; children of our families; faithful Germans; will be thrown into the streets and chased like vermin from our country."

He gave the full facts and figures in all the sermons. The names of the confiscated convents and the number of the members of each Community who had been expelled. But all through the bishop was wise and careful. He never put himself up against the law of the country.

"We will obey the Party as far as legal government is concerned, but there will be no community of spirit.

Finally, in one of his latest sermons the bishop tells his congregation to hold on, to become hard and firm.

"At this moment we are not the hammer but the anvil; others are hammering on us. By force they will bend our people, ourselves and our youth away from the straight and true path to God. You ask the smith and he will tell you that what is forged on the anvil gets its shape from it. The anvil does not have to strike back. All that it needs to do is to hold firm and remain hard. . . . The anvil lasts longer than the hammer."

Mrs. Schmitt told us that all Catholics awaited the

bishop's arrest hourly. The bishop himself reckoned it was only a matter of hours or days before he was taken. But, astonishingly enough, nothing happened. However, he seemed determined to become an inmate of a concentration camp. He continued with his public attacks. His churches were so full that the congregations overflowed into the streets at each Mass. In August 1941 he had taken up another subject. He spoke of euthanasia, of the liquidation of "unproductive life", and of the murder of inmates of mental homes then being encouraged. Although the Party had tried to keep these actions secret, Bishop Galen had brought them before the public. He spot-lighted them in his sermons, giving an exact report of what was happening, and quoting from the Penal Code of Germany to show the legal position of those unfortunate people. He actually sent registered letters to the County Court of Münster, and the Chief of Police. "These actions are not only contrary to the laws of God, but also to the laws of Germany." He maintains that this was plain murder and asks the President of the Police to "protect the threatened members of the German people, and to inform me of the measures you are taking."

When the bishop got no reply, he went further, and his sermons and his letters began to cause great anxiety to the highest Party members, including Goebbels, Himmler and even Hitler himself, but they simply did not know what to do to silence him.

Speaking of euthanasia in the hospitals, the bishop said: "Are these people a machine that does not run any longer?; or an old horse which has become incurably paralyzed? (referring to the neurotic, old, and insane); or a cow that can't give milk any more and must be disposed of. If we all acknowledge . . . the principle that an 'unproductive' human being should be wiped out, then woe to us all when we are old or decrepit. Woe to the invalids who have put their strength into their work and production. Woe to our soldiers who come back crippled or disabled. What of those who get

171

illnesses as they grow older? Soon all will be liquidated?"

Heiner and I sat there listening. We had never heard such things discussed publicly before. Perhaps we should have been even more astounded if we had known that the Lion of Münster had actually sent a telegram to Hitler at the Chancellery in which he demanded that Hitler protect the freedom and the property of the German people *against* the Gestapo! That telegram was couched in correct and legal language demanding that the head of the state do justice to the people he ruled! We stayed some time with the Schmitts, listening to those sermons then went back to our home. To think that such a man was still at large, still preaching, and still telling the truth.

"It's fantastic," I said to Heiner. "His courage! I wonder how much longer he can go on?"

Courage is catching to a certain extent. Anyway I decided to go and see the Treitels again, and to take them some food and eggs. Heiner and I were now keeping a few hens to help out with our rations. I decided again to go by daylight, not so much from sheer bravado, but simply to avoid being in Berlin during a possible night air-raid. I looked round carefully as I pressed the bell on the garden door of the Treitel's home. It seemed an eternity before it opened. A lady opened it. It was the new owner of the house.

"You wish to see Mr. and Mrs. Treitel?" she asked in surprise.

"Yes, aren't they in?"

"No," she replied slowly. "They are not in. Would you mind coming in for a moment?"

I followed her into the lounge.

"They are both dead," she said.

"Both of them?" I echoed mechanically. "Why? How did it happen?"

It was a short story. One evening, quite out of the blue, the Gestapo had arrived and arrested both of them.

"I watched the Treitels coming down the stairs," said

172

the lady. "They were very pale but quite composed. My husband told me to go away, but I refused. He said we would all get into trouble if the Gestapo saw us but I just couldn't stand behind a closed door and let them go like that, without a friend."

"It was very dangerous," I said.

"I know but surely someone has got to show a heart some time? Perhaps Mr. and Mrs. Treitel saw the fear in my eyes. They passed me without a word."

"They didn't even say good-bye?" I asked.

"Mr. Treitel turned his eyes away but Mrs. Treitel looked me full in the face and smiled. Perhaps it was to thank me for being there, or perhaps she wanted to show that she wasn't afraid.

"I stood behind the curtains and watched as closely as I could in the dusk. They climbed into the Gestapo car and were driven away. You can imagine how terrified I was when shortly afterwards the bell rang again, and the officer was back. My husband whispered : 'They have given us away.'

"I went and opened the gate for them. 'Sorry to bother you again,' said the officer, 'but those swine are dead!'

" 'Dead?' I asked.

" 'Yes, dead! They have committed suicide in our car, the filthy devils.' It seemed that while sitting in the car the two of them had taken poison. Their bodies were still in the car outside. It was too much to bother to get rid of the bodies, they said, it would mean doing the same trip twice, as they had to confiscate all the property immediately on their death. 'So may we come in, please?' they asked me! The bodies lay huddled in the car outside while the Gestapo took an inventory of the property and sealed up the room; then with a 'Heil Hitler' they drove away."

Unable to say a word, I just sat there with the basket of eggs at my feet. Then I remembered. Mrs. Treitel had warned me at my last visit. 'We are prepared for everything, even for the worst,' she had said. I suppose Mr. Treitel couldn't face his wife going through the torture and humiliation that he had known at Gestapo hands; they would be separated and that would have been a torture for her. I admired her so much. I never heard her complain. She kept her dignity and her cheerfulness until the last. Perhaps it was better for her to go like that, with her husband by her side, one does not know what might have been in store for her.

10

The Horror of Hamburg

THERE were some very frightening words on people's lips in 1943—"unconditional surrender". We did not know of course that Churchill and Roosevelt had come to this decision in January 1943 during the conference at Casablanca, but somehow the fear of total defeat was already creeping across Germany.

It increased with the great disaster in North Africa, the defeat of Rommel's forces at El Alamein by the English 8th Army, led by Montgomery, and by the American and other Allied Forces led by Eisenhower. General von Arnim surrendered with his two hundred and fifty thousand men. Our first reactions were it can't be true; it just isn't possible. Dr. Schmitt said: "What I want to know is how long can we allow two hundred and fifty thousand men to be lost? Why did the military chiefs permit it for a moment?"

"No use asking that. None of us know," said Heiner.

"Oh, yes, we do. We know why they were lost, but what we need to know is why we *allow* it to go on. We lost the men because Hitler again refused permission to withdraw while there was time. Again he shouted 'no surrender'."

"What, the same mistake as in Stalingrad?" asked Heiner.

"Yes, the same mistake," said Dr. Schmitt. "Some corporals never learn, either from their own defeat or from the enemy. At Dunkirk Churchill ordered his troops to withdraw. He did not say; 'Stand and fight to a finish'. He got his men out, and they lived to come back and fight us in North Africa."

Hitler's orders became more and more difficult to under-

175

stand. From now on it was not a long list of victories, but a long list of defeats. In July 1943 the Allied Forces landed in Sicily, and later defeated the Germans in Italy and put the country out of the war.

In the Pacific the Americans had one victory after another and pushed the Japs farther and farther back. German forces in Russia were defeated everywhere.

One day I asked what had happened to our great German fleet.

Heiner said, "Gone with the wind."

"Gone to the bottom of the sea," Dr. Schmitt corrected him. "Our fleet can't cope with this new radar invention. By the time we have put our counter-apparatus into mass production the war will be over!"

There was little doubt that the Allies now had superiority in every kind of weapon and equipment.

It was in August 1943 and on a very hot day, that real family disaster came upon us. I had just taken the children up to bed, and was sitting in the lounge doing some mending, when we heard footsteps outside. We looked out. Heiner's mother was wandering about, utterly exhausted. She scarcely seemed to know where she was.

"Mother," called Heiner, and ran to her.

She came in and sank down slowly on our couch. She was shaking all over. I ran quickly to the kitchen to bring food and coffee and Heiner went to the cellar to get brandy. Mama did not speak for a long time. At last she stirred and looked at us. Then she held up her handbag. "That's all I have saved," she said.

"But have you no suitcase or anything else?"

"Nothing else in the world. You haven't been in Hamburg. It's a miracle to be alive at all."

We gave her food and drink, and we washed her hands and face. She was too exhausted for us to allow her to get off the couch. And then, as the hot August evening died away, Mama told us her story.

176

It started with the description of a very simple but peaceful dinner she and her friends had had on a beautiful July evening at a restaurant by the River Alster. They had sat there on a terrace listening to the people in the small boats below, singing and playing their accordions. The stars were out, the moon had not yet risen and there was no hint of war at all. They toasted the weather. "To rain on Monday, but not before," they joked. There had been a long spell of hot, dry weather, and they wanted just one more day to enjoy it.

"No wonder they call Hamburg 'Little Venice'," one of Mama's friends said. "I wouldn't change Hamburg for anywhere in the world."

He didn't have to. He died a few hours later that night in the fires of Hamburg.

Just before midnight the first alarms went off. Mama did not bother to get up. They had not had an air-raid for weeks. The Allied planes were too busy in West Germany and Norway, and Belguim and perhaps Sicily. No doubt this alarm was for just one plane and she was not getting up for one plane. Somebody banged loudly on her door. She sighed. Why couldn't they leave her alone? But she got up, she would be in trouble if she didn't.

"I thought you were in," said the air-raid warden. "Hurry up now. They have announced a big formation of bombers on the way."

Mama dressed, took her suitcase full of valuables, opened all her windows as a precaution against explosions, and went to the cellars. All people in Hamburg got up and opened their windows obediently. A few hours later this ventilation helped the fires to sweep through the town even more successfully. The noise of anti-aircraft artillery became stronger. Once more Mama went to the windows to look for planes. What she saw made her shake with fright. There were white and red target bombs all over the sky. She rushed down to the cellar.

177

"There are Christmas trees everywhere all round us," she called out. We had nicknamed the target bombs "Christmas trees" because of their brilliant lights and shape.

The warden was annoyed. Mama was causing a panic. But she insisted upon telling the others. "There's a Christmas tree right above us," she declared.

"That's a lie," shouted the air-warden. "Calm down now."

His further words were drowned in a deafening crash. The cellar floor shook and the lights went out. Women screamed as they heard the heavy rumbling of falling masonry. "We are being buried alive; we are hit; it's right on top of us," came the terrified whispers in the dark. The warden did not lose his head. Calmly he asked for silence so that he could hear what was really going on. They heard more explosions, a new wave of planes roaring over them. It got very hot down there, but no one moved. Then another wave of planes swept over, and finally a fourth one. The cellar grew hotter and hotter. One woman fainted. The warden carefully opened a door. The raid had now lasted one and a half hours.

Then he and a few other men went slowly up the stairs and into the street. A few moments later they came running back to say that a land-mine had fallen in the next street and everything was on fire, and that the houses on either side of them were also burning but theirs was still intact.

In infinite relief Mama got up and carrying her suitcase went out into the street. Outside it was far brighter than day. The sky was vivid yellow with flames, the house in front was burning as though seeped in petrol, and those to left and right of her were the same. Desperate people were throwing out belongings through the windows; cases, carpets, chairs, tables; anything they could save Someone, an old man, began to push a piano out of a side door. He was a composer trying to save his greatest treasure.

Mama spoke to a man standing near her. "Where's the fire brigade? Why on earth don't they come?"

"Are you mad?" asked the man. "The fire brigade? Do you think there are enough brigades for each house in Hamburg? The whole city is burning. As for fire brigades, they are racing from miles away to help us. Didn't you hear the announcement over the radio? They are coming from Bremen and Lübeck and Kiel to help us. All through the raid they have been coming."

Mama had not heard. The electricity in her house had gone long ago.

"There are fire brigades in the next street," the man pointed out. "Incendiaries have fallen in front of a house and phosphorous bombs as well. The phosphorus is dripping on everything. All the people in the cellar must be trapped."

"Can't we help them," said Mama, and put her suitcase down.

"Impossible," said the man. "It's like a furnace. You can't get near the house at all. Besides you would faint if you heard the screams coming from the cellar. I can't listen to children screaming like that."

Just at that moment a man came along shouting out: "Come on and help! We are trying to dig through to the cellar. Everyone come and help."

The man next to Mama forgot his fears and began to run. Mama too, leaving her suitcase in the cellar again, came up and rushed to the next street. Everyone was in a frenzy to help. Women were carrying buckets full of stones and cement as the men dug away at the cellar walls with any implement they could lay their hands on. The air was full of dust and the heat was so intense that men were stripped to the waist and were covered with sweat. A woman came up. "It's hopeless," she said, wiping her face with the back of a grimy, dusty hand. "They don't answer any more. We have been tapping for half an hour now."

The firemen came. "It's no use. Stand back all of you. They don't answer any more. The next houses are burning, we must try to save those."

179

Mama went over to one of the firemen. "No use at all?" she asked in a whisper.

"None," said the fireman briefly. "They must have boiled to death in their own blood," he added in savage horror.

"Didn't I tell you?" said the man, who had been standing with her before. "It's hot enough to roast anyone alive."

There seemed nothing she could do so she decided to go back to her home and lie down. Not to sleep (she couldn't sleep while Hamburg burned), but just to lie down a bit to stop her legs trembling. She went round the corner towards her home. Huge clouds of hot smoke whirled in her face. She stumbled over something. "Look out there," a shout came from above. She looked up. A fireman covered all over with fine white ash looked down at her.

"You're working here?" she asked. "This is my house."

"Well, it's burning, your house or not," said the fireman.

"Oh, no!" screamed Mama, and was wide awake in a moment.

She ran towards her home pushing the fireman's hands away from her as he tried to stop her. The smoke was the worst part at first, she could not see through it at all. She got at last to the third floor. The staircase was like an ants' heap, with people running up and down in long streams carrying their belongings. Suddenly she was stopped by a voice screaming: "Help . . . help me! Phosphorus!"

Wasn't that her neighbour's voice? It was. The woman came rushing down the stairs, her clothes burning brightly. In horror, Mama pressed herself against the wall. One fatal drop of phosphorus on her own dress, and she too would be burning like a torch. The woman rushed on, still screaming. Terrified, Mama gave up. If there was phosphorus about, then she could not go into her flat. But her suitcase and her coat? Where were they? She remembered, they were still in the cellar. Down she went and grabbed them and out into the streets again.

There was now no fresh air in the streets, just smoke and

180

flames and dust. All the people had blackened faces. They all really looked like chimney-sweeps. A wave of hysteria rose in her. She dropped the suitcase and sat down on it and began to laugh. She couldn't stop. Then she began to cry at the same time. The neighbour she had seen burning on the stairs was brought past her on a stretcher under a blanket, her face was now red and streaked with black. Mamma laughed, on and on, nothing could stop her.

"That's the second one who has gone mad tonight," she heard a voice say. She looked up and stared into the blackest face of all. A man was bending towards her. It was a doctor. She screamed with fright, and then fainted.

When she came to she was still on the pavement, but not alone. Neighbours from her house were grouped all round. Some sat on carpets and suitcases, others on coats or bundles. They were quite silent, just sitting there staring at the burning city. The hysteria gone, she began to cry quietly. Everything was gone. All the things she and her husband had worked for and collected.

The woman next to her had two children pressed tightly against her. "Here, drink a cup of this, it's real coffee. It will do you good. We all thought you had gone mad."

She took the flask and drank. It refreshed her, she felt better. The giddiness went.

"I suppose it was too much for you," the woman said kindly.

A fireman came up. "You'll have to move on. The roof will be down in a moment."

They all got up then and began to walk off carrying as much as they could. The children started to cry. A man who had dragged out a green velvet chair tried to pull it along with him, then stopped. "Have to come back for it later," he said. "Must find somewhere to sleep first."

Where to spend the night was the first question in everyone's mind. The desolate troop of homeless people wandered on through the early morning. As they turned a corner, another group of bombed-out families met them.

The woman with the two children stopped first. "It's hopeless," she said. "The houses in that street have stopped burning. The children have got to rest. I shall stop here, and they can sleep on the pavement in front."

Mama walked on. She wondered if her friends in Elmsbüttel were still alive, the friends she had so merrily arranged to meet that evening in the Alster restaurant. She walked on very slowly, hoping and praying that they were all right, and she could stay with them.

It was midday when she reached Elmsbüttel. She looked down the long street, and for a moment it was like one of those nightmares when you are running about lost and find the streets and houses and numbers changed as you reach them. For as she moved up the street she found only ruins. Where was her friend's house? Surely it used to be there? She moved on hastily. Perhaps she had made a mistake. There was nobody in the street. Then she saw a notice chalked up on a wall; "50 to 60 Dead People", and a long arrow pointing into an entrance. Numb with fear, Mama put her suitcase down on the pavement and followed the direction of the arrow. She opened a cellar door. Sixty tiny burnt human beings lay around on the ground. They looked about half their normal human size.

In a panic she slammed the door and stood leaning against the post. Her first reaction was one of intense relief. She turned and ran up into the street, leaving the horror behind. She wanted to shout out: "I am alive! I am alive!" A second later her mood changed. Her friends were dead, burnt to death in the most horrible way. She had no friends. She sat down on her suitcase and began to cry for them. She kept trying to forget what they must have suffered and remember only that they were now out of their agony. The hours crept by and still she sat there now worn out with loneliness and sorrow. But she could not make herself move. There was nowhere to move to.

Presently a woman came by and stopped and asked her if she had had anything to eat that day? No, Mama had not, nor did she really care. But the woman insisted, and took her to a large place where hundreds of bombed-out people were lying on the ground being served with food.

Lying there with the other people Mama began to pick up bits of information about the raid. The Catherine Church was burnt out completely, also the Nicholai Church. The Hagenbeck Zoo was destroyed, and hundreds of animals killed. Two tigers had escaped and been shot while loose in the park. A buffalo had rushed madly down the Kaiser Friedrich Street and been shot. The worst problem in Hamburg was the water supply, the people told her. Only a very few districts still had any regular water and gas supply. The afternoon came and still she lay on the grass. She didn't know what to do or where to go. She saw one truck after another loaded up with people and driven off. Where were they being taken? No one seemed to know. Suddenly the sirens sounded again. Everybody jumped up. What did the enemy want now? Hadn't they done enough?

This time the harbour was attacked, the dockyards and factories in Wilhelmsburg. This raid lasted well over an hour. When it was over Mama decided to go in search of other friends on the far side of the city, friends she had not seen for some time. Anything was better than lying here homeless on the grass. She walked and walked, carrying her suitcase and the coat. It was still very hot, and the fires behind her were still burning. But this time she found her friends safe and their home intact. She was given food, allowed to wash in a minute basin of water, and then put to bed. That night there was no air-raid, nor on the Monday.

On the Tuesday night, 27 July, the bombers came back. In that raid over forty-five thousand people in Hamburg died. Mama and her friends went down into their cellar. The air warden stored sand and water and piled up tools ready for any digging that might be necessary.

It was the worst raid Mama had ever known. For hours they huddled there, with bombs crashing nearer, and the ceaseless rumblings of falling masonry. Then there was the loudest crash of all. The air warden ran out. He came back, his face grey. "Leave the cellar at once!" he called. "A phosphorous bomb has fallen at the entrance door. Quick, all of you..."

An indescribable panic started. Mothers grabbed children and rushed madly away. People fell over each other and Mama was separated from her friends. She didn't see them again. Out in the street people just rushed blindly away from the bomb, thinking of nothing else. An old man came near Mama, who was now standing dazed and alone. "Come with me," he said. She picked up her suitcase and followed him. It was unbearably hot in the street.

"I can't go through this. There's a cellar there not burning, I shall go down there," she told him.

"Don't be a fool," he said. "All the houses here will catch fire soon, it's only a matter of time."

A woman with two children joined them. "Come on," said the old man. "This looks the clearest way."

There were walls of flame round them now. Suddenly into the square came a fire engine drawn by two startled horses. They swerved aside, and one of the terrified children rushed down a side street. The mother followed, leaving her boy behind. As the first child reached a burning house, some blazing wood fell near her, setting her clothes alight. The mother threw herself on top of the child to try and smother the flames, but as she did so the whole top floor of the house opposite crashed down on the two of them.

The old man grabbed the boy's hand firmly. "You come with us," he ordered.

"I'll wait for my Mummy," said the boy.

"No," said the old man, trying to make his voice sound harsh. "It's getting too hot here. We will wait for your Mummy farther away from the fire."

Mama intervened quickly. "We will find the best way out, and then come back and fetch your Mummy."

"All right," said the little boy.

They went the same way as the horses, thinking the animals' instinct might have led them to safety. The boy fell down but got up, then fell down again.

"We can't go on like this," said the man, pulling them towards a cellar. "There's water here, pour it over your coats, and we'll put them over our heads and try that way."

Up in the square again, the man took a hasty glance round and then grabbed the boy's hand. "Now—come this way," he told them. Mama grabbed her suitcase. "Put it down," shouted the old man. "Save yourself, you can't bring that as well."

But Mama would not let go. She took the boy's hand in her left hand and the case in her right. Out in the square it was like a furnace. Sweat poured down her body as they began to run. The smoke seeped through the wet coats and began to choke them. Only for a few yards could she carry the suitcase, then she dropped it and left it without another thought. The little boy ran between them, taking steps twice as fast as their own. He fell again and again, but was hauled to his feet. Were they still on the track of the horses? They didn't know, for every moment or two they had to turn to avoid burning wood and pylons which hurtled down from the houses around. Bodies were still burning in the road. Sometimes they stumbled against them. But on they went, with the little boy's feet running tap, tap, tap between them. A dog was howling madly somewhere. It sounded more pathetic and lost than they themselves. At last they came to a small green place, and ran to the centre of it and fell on their faces, the little boy between them. They fell asleep like exhausted animals, but only for a few minutes. The old man woke first.

"Wake up," he said, shaking them both. "The fire is catching up with us."

Mama opened her eyes. They were lying in a small field, and the houses on one side were now alight; worse than alight; some kind of explosive material was there as well, it seemed. A great flame was shooting straight out towards them. A flame as high as the houses and nearly as wide as the whole street. As she stared in fascination the giant flame jerked back and then shot forward towards them again.

"My God, what is it?" she said.

"It's a fire-storm," the old man answered.

"The beginning of one. Quick, come along, there's no time to lose. In a minute there will be dozens of flames like that and they'll reach us; quick, come on, we must run. I think there's a small stream on the other side of this field."

Mama got up and bent over the boy. "Poor little thing, what a shame to wake him." She shook him gently. "Get up! We must run again."

The child did not stir. The man bent down and pulled him to his feet. "Come on, boy," he said. The child swayed and fell again. The man sank to his knees beside the child and took his hands.

"Oh, no!" he said in a shocked voice. "No, it can't be. My God, he's dead!" The tears began to pour down his blackened face. He bent down lower over the little figure and began to whisper to it.

"You were a good little boy, a very brave little boy," he said, stroking the child's face with a woman's tenderness. "As long as Hamburg has boys as brave as you she won't die." He kissed the child's face very gently. "Sleep well, little boy," he whispered. "Sleep well; you got a kinder death than your Mummy and sister. They were burnt alive like rats."

Mama became nervous; another tongue of flame shot out from the side street. The roaring of the flames became stronger. The old man seemed quite oblivious now of their danger.

186

"Come on," she called out. "The boy is dead. We can't help him any more. Come on, we must go on."

The old man did not look up. "No," he said. "You go on by yourself. I shall die with this little boy."

Mama yelled through the roaring wind. "You're crazy! Come on!" The old man did not answer. He kissed the child's forehead again.

In despair Mama grabbed the man in her arms and tried to pull him away. Sparks were now beginning to reach their coats. Suddenly a hot gust of wind blew their coats off their backs, sending them blazing through the air. This brought the man to life again. He jumped up and started to run. As they raced across the field, the flames crept behind them. Once they fell and then got up and ran on. The field seemed wider and wider as they raced towards the stream, but at last they reached it. Unable to say another word, they both fell on the banks and slept, or perhaps they fainted first and slept afterwards.

When they regained consciousness it was daylight, and they stumbled down into the stream and washed their faces and hands. The water stung their scorched skin, but they did not mind. The old man told her he had lost two grandsons and his daughter-in-law in the fires last night. "My son is in Russia. I don't know how I shall tell him when he returns," he said.

After a rest they decided to walk back into Hamburg. It seemed suicidal, but they both felt they must go and see what remained of the city. It was a terrible walk. They passed through one big square where corpses were piled up, corpses burned beyond recognition. Soldiers and police were sorting them out and loading them on to trucks.

"All of them were standing in the middle of the square when a fire-storm caught them. No one escaped," a woman said.

"Didn't I tell you?" said the old man to Mama. "A fire-storm finishes everything and everybody."

187

The woman standing near them shivered. "I heard scream after scream. I shall never forget those screams. If there were a God, He would have shown some mercy to them. He would have helped us."

"Leave God out of this," said the old man sharply. "Men make war, not God."

Two soldiers came up. They were breathing heavily and carrying charred bodies. They dropped their load on to a lorry, took out some cigarettes and offered them all round. Mama had never smoked before in her life, but this time she did.

"How many dead here?" asked the woman in an ordinary voice. She might have been asking a baker how many rolls he had baked that morning. The soldier replied in just the same businesslike manner. "Up to now, I reckon, five hundred."

"How many more do you think are still lying around here?"

The soldier gave a look round. "About eight hundred altogether in this square. I should think."

"I'd rather be on the Russian front," said the other soldier.

"How did you escape?" asked the old man, turning to the woman.

"Just luck, I suppose," she said. "I went to one of the public lavatories when our cellar was burned out. It was crammed in there, and at first we tried to keep the taps running to damp our clothes and handkerchiefs to put over our mouths because of the smoke and hot air. Then the men tried to cut through the pipes of the toilets to reach the water. Then a phosphorous bomb dropped right in the entrance. Children yelled like animals and we all panicked. One woman next to me took a knife and cut her child's wrists. Then she cut her own, and slipped down on her, calling out : 'Darling, my darling, we shall soon see Daddy now.' I shall never get the sight or the words out of my mind.

"She wasn't the only one who killed herself down there. I saw a man climbing on top of the partitions between the toilets—there was a bit of air and space up there. I tried to do the same. I kept slipping, until an old woman told me to climb up on her neck, she said it didn't matter, she had had a long life and I was younger! That's how I survived really. I lay there until the fire outside burnt down, and then I got out. Only a few of us survived. We left about sixty dead down there."

After a time Mama and the old man walked on to look for something to eat and drink. They found an open square where the army had arrived with food and water. There were no plates, no spoons, no cups, just lorries full of large tanks. They got water when they had found someone to lend them a mug, but they were forbidden to wash. When dusk came on the second day Mama's spirit was broken. She shook hands with the old man and walked off alone into the night. The old man wanted to stay in Hamburg, he had told her. He couldn't drag himself away. Mama felt she must go on, get away from Hamburg and from everything connected with it. So they shook hands and parted.

It took a week to get a train to Berlin. During that time she slept in barns and fields and begged for food and drink from door to door. When she boarded the train she found a compartment full of women describing their awful experiences. Mama listened, and then told her own story. They sat there, dirty, bedraggled, and with only a handbag or an odd coat each. Nothing more. All except one woman in the corner of the carriage who sat absolutely silently, and with a small suitcase across her knees. She told nothing of her experiences, just sat there staring out of the window while they talked. At last one of the others turned to her and said:

"Well, at any rate *you* managed to save something out it all. You've been luckier than some of us, haven't you?"

"Yes," said the woman suddenly. "I have been lucky. I've

saved the dearest thing in the world to me. Do you want to see it?"

"Of course," they all said.

Quickly she opened the suitcase. They got up to look. Inside lay a small brown body. The skin was taut over the shrunken face and body, just like a tiny Egyptian mummy.

The young woman broke into uncontrollable laughs. "That's my daughter. Isn't she sweet? She has such beautiful fair curls and blue eyes, hasn't she? Her eyes are bluer than the skies. She's grown a lot this last year. She's just twelve years old, you know. But now she's shrivelled. I can carry her in my suitcase now."

She burst into mad laughter which made their blood run cold.

"Sleep well, my darling," she said, and patted the little body in the suitcase. Then she closed it and became silent.

Mama ended her story at last, and we put her to bed and went to our room. Altogether, it has been said, fifty-five thousand people died during the air-raids on Hamburg, but on the night of 27/28 July forty-five thousand people lost their lives.

The newspapers at the time had, of course, another story for us. "Strong bomber formations of the enemy continued their attacks on Hamburg last night. Further demolitions were caused, and extensive fires in some districts. The population suffered losses. Night fighters and anti-air artillery shot down forty-seven of the attacking bombers."

Mama's story made me worry terribly about my own parents. They still had the big flat in Charlottenburg, and my mother was there. My father was as usual travelling around. At the moment he was in Austria. My mother was very brave, and casual over the raids, and this increased my anxiety. So I got hold of my sister Hilde the day after Mama's arrival, and we set out to persuade my mother to leave Berlin. We had to talk hard and convincingly.

"I would rather stay here among my own things," Mother

kept saying. "It doesn't matter if I die now, you are all grown up. Just leave me here. I'm all right. If it comes, it comes."

But we just couldn't bear to think of her one day going through what Heiner's mother had experienced. We promised to keep an eye on the flat if she would go and stay at her sister's villa on the Baltic Sea. At last we won the day. My mother was wrenched from her home and put on the train. We waved and kissed her good-bye. Hilde now came to live with us permanently in Kladow.

11

Beginning of the End

EVEN more terrible air-raids came in 1943. One great city after another was heavily bombed. Irreplaceable historical monuments were destroyed; churches, cathedrals, castles, in such places as Frankfurt, Cologne, Nüremburg, Münster, Dresden, Münich, and of course Berlin.

Something must be wrong with our Luftwaffe, we thought. Dr. Schmitt insisted that the "accidents" to Air Force Chief Jeschonnek and General Udet were in actual fact suicides on account of their failure to hold back the raiders. Heiner only smiled at this and said Dr. Schmitt was a born pessimist. "You're only happy when everything goes wrong," he told him.

We celebrated Christmas together but with much more austerity and with air-raids all the time. When 1944 came we scarcely bothered to have any hopes or make any resolutions.

"It's just a case of holding on, now," Heiner told me, as cheerfully as he could. "It can't be so very long, you know."

As I kissed Heiner good-bye each morning now I always had the thought at the back of my mind that it might be a permanent parting. I would put the thought out of my mind quickly, and turn back to the house and children. It was no use to think on those lines. Better to work hard in the house and try and plan a good meal for the evening. Sometimes I begged him to telephone me after a very bad raid, but he refused.

"If you saw what I see day after day at the hospital, during and after the air-raids, you wouldn't ask. The 'phones

192

are ringing all day about accident cases. We can't have them used for private calls. One delayed 'phone call and a life might be lost."

"But can't you tell me exactly where you will be going each day? If I knew which hospital you would be in, that would help a little," I begged him.

"I'm afraid I can't," said Heiner. "I just don't know half the time. What would happen if we all rang our wives after each raid?"

He was right of course. I must try to be brave, I thought. I became more and more taut and nervous at night time, and would stand during a bad raid by the boys' beds in the cellar with a pillow in my hands, ready to throw it across their heads should the roof be hit. This exasperated Heiner, and he tried to stop me doing this.

"You must pull yourself together. We are all frightened, but we have got to make the best of it. For goodness' sake, sit down," he shouted at me one night.

But I wouldn't leave the boys' sides during a raid, however much Heiner objected. I would sit there listening to the planes roaring overhead, the pillow lying on my lap. For a time Heiner gave up and left me to my own devices, but when my brother came on leave he had reinforcements. They sat there one night, Heiner, Rudolf and my mother-in-law, all mocking and laughing at my nervousness. I hated it. They kept playing games and talking loudly just to make it worse. I wanted them to be quiet, so that I could hear how close the planes were getting. I wanted to be able to hear that light, high whistling noise, but the others were determined I shouldn't.

The only person who was really sympathetic was Hilde. She would sit quietly doing some darning, and just look up at me now and then with a gentle smile. I know I ought to have done some mending as well, but I couldn't make myself. Besides, my hands used to tremble so much, and that would have made Heiner angrier than ever. I would

G   193

hide my hands under the pillow so that no one saw them shaking. Heiner wanted to know where my faith in God was, that I was so afraid. I couldn't answer. How could I know whether God was going to let us all die that night or not?

"I don't mean that at all," Heiner said. "I mean whatever God has decided about your life and the boys' lives will happen whether you shake with fright or not. Why not put your life in God's hands and show more dignity? Isn't that your creed?"

Heiner was, of course, a fatalist. He was just like his mother. He laughed and walked upright until the bitter end; he always hoped. I was bitterly ashamed of myself. I could see that I was a terribly bad example to everyone around me but I couldn't stop trembling. As soon as the sirens started a feeling of numbness would creep all over me, and I would begin to shake. I am still the same today. Years later I heard a siren in the streets of London over a small fire alarm, and to my horror I burst into tears in the open street.

As the raids grew in intensity many of the transport facilities broke down, and Heiner had to walk part of the way home. Gradually all the big railway stations were wrecked: the Stettiner, the Potsdamer, the Lehrter and the Charlottenburg and the Friedrichstrasse. The Foreign Office was bombed out—Dr. Schmitt said he did not mind that!; the Ministry of Propaganda, Dr. Schmitt said he did not mind that either. Then the new Chancellery in the Wilhelmstrasse and the Air Ministry. "We are better off without them," said Dr. Schmitt grimly. The only official buildings he was sorry to lose were the University Library and the Opera Houses, one in Unter den Linden and the other in Berlin Charlottenburg.

As the air-raids grew in intensity and frequency, my mother-in-law became more and more restless. She had heard news that rebuilding was going on in Hamburg. "I haven't come to Berlin to be plunged into a worse hell than Hamburg," she said one day. "Mrs. Mahler writes that I can join her in a big flat they have found if I like."

In a way I was glad that she decided to go. She was always complaining that I was too fussy a housewife. She did not like me to polish the floors each day, and always said so. To my mind they *had* to be polished each day. I realize now that I was very silly and very stubborn, and I only hope that Heiner made secret allowances for me at the time. We were all tired, nervous and strained. I clung to one way of keeping my spirits going—my idiotic polishing. Mama clung to another—her love of Hamburg. Heiner had his own optimistic thoughts.

So I went on polishing, and Heiner went off to his dangerous daily work at the hospitals. The food situation was now deteriorating rapidly. The rations were by no means sufficient for anyone's health. Outside the rations there was nothing to come by except in the "exchange way" on the black market. I wrote to my aunt in Silesia asking if she would help with some parcels. Feechen replied that she *could* help with food if I could come and fetch it in person. She dare not send anything through the post.

I was frightened at the idea of leaving the boys behind, and I certainly did not want to leave Heiner, but we needed food. So off I went, and Mama was left to organize things. She would return to Hamburg when I came back.

I was absolutely astonished as I stepped out of the train in Haynau. Nothing had changed at all. Not one house bombed, not one stone out of place, not one window broken. Everything was just as neat and tidy and perfect as it had looked years ago. The people were normal in appearance, no tired eyes and worn faces.

To be honest, the sight of so much prosperity and peace angered me. I could have kicked myself for the feeling, but there it was. My aunt, knowing nothing of these thoughts, gave a party to welcome me. Families from some of the big estates all arrived in beautiful clothes, looking in good health and in cheerful mood. They stared at me as though I were a rare exhibit in a museum. They asked questions about the raids.

"I really don't know how you stand them for a moment," said one lady, as she nibbled a delicious nut-tart with a layer of rich cream. "Do please tell us some more details of the air-raids." She complimented my aunt on the tartlet, and turned again to me. "Your stories are as exciting as the cinema."

I was relieved when the party was over. How I kept my temper I don't know. That night I made up my mind. I could not stay a day longer.

There was a particularly heavy raid the next day on Berlin. I made this an excuse to leave at once. Feechen wished me to stay and build up my strength, but she quickly understood when she saw my awful anxiety. She gave me a very large parcel of food. All the families around had contributed something towards it. I was very touched, and very grateful, and I felt all the better for having made my peace with Silesia in the night.

I took a train via Breslau in order to see my friend Paula Gluch, who lived there with her two children. She was standing on the platform to greet me, looking as radiant and beautiful as ever. We spent two hours together in the beautiful city.

At Breslau in Silesia I again broke my journey to see my cousin, who was a leader of a big camp of Land Youth. It was all very pleasant and well organized. I joined for a time in the singing and the sports. Everything was gay and charming, and I found the Hitler land girls some of the nicest I had met. When I got back to Berlin there was a letter from my sister Evelyn inviting me to her wedding. I talked it over with Heiner, but we decided I had better not go. Mama was leaving for Hamburg, and I could not leave them all alone.

During the early summer of 1944 Dr. Schmitt and Heiner were always talking about Hitler's secret weapons. Heiner believed in them. Dr. Schmitt seemed to think they would come too late. But on 14 June 1944, the V-bombs started over England, and Heiner was jubilant.

"There you are," he said. "It doesn't cost us a single man, and England will be knocked out of the war."

"Wait and see," said Dr. Schmitt.

How they used to argue, those two. First the hope of the secret weapons, and then the results of the landing of the Allied Troops on D-Day. The news was broken to us very briefly, and quietly. The Press said the Atlantic wall would prove too well organized, and that the attack was merely a "nuisance raid" on a big scale. Heiner, with his usual optimism, backed the newspapers.

"We've had years to build up the Atlantic wall—it will hold," he boasted.

"Your husband will be the foreman of the angels in heaven," said Dr. Schmitt. "I have never known such innocence, or such faith."

Whatever might come of the Atlantic wall, Heiner and I decided we had better snatch a little peace that summer for ourselves and the two boys. So we set off to the Baltic to stay with my mother. It was still as lovely on the sands but the food was in short supply and poor in quality and no good coffee. But there was sunshine, the sea and sleep, oh, that blissful and night-long sleep. Suddenly, however, even this fishing village was disturbed. Orders came through from Party Headquarters that every man there between the ages of sixteen and sixty had to report to the Party office. There they were sorted out and put on transport for the eastern front. It came as suddenly and dramatically as that. Every man was to take a spade with him to dig the East Wall.

This shook even Heiner. "I can't believe it," he said. "There must be some mistake." He went off to question one of the old fishermen himself.

197

"It's true, all right," he told me. "That old man has got to go as well. He's sixty-five. They have now put the age limit up."

There was nothing for me to say. I took Heiner's arm, and we walked along in silence. "At least we have these two weeks here, darling," I said, as we came up to the children. The fortnight went so very quickly, before we knew it the holiday was over, and we were on our way back to Berlin. My mother stood at the corner of the tiny station and waved goodbye to us. A breeze from the sea played with her pretty, silvery hair. She kissed me very fondly. "We don't know when we shall see each other again."

"No," I replied from the open window of the railway compartment. "We never know."

That was my real goodbye to my mother. I never saw her again. She stayed on in the east, refusing to move, even as the Russians approached. When the Russians left her house after occupation, she quietly committed suicide. There was no coffin for her, so they wrapped her in some paper and put her body in a hole which my aunt herself dug in the garden. There was no priest at her funeral, nor is there a cross where she is buried. There was snow on the ground at the time. My mother's grave has never seen a single flower.

Soon after my mother's death, my aunt was taken away and put in various camps from which she escaped after five years. As far as I know the villa now belongs to a Polish family. Perhaps Polish children play on the grave? My mother had five children. She made so many sacrifices for us, but I doubt if any one of us will ever succeed in putting a flower or a cross on her grave. They would not allow it now. Sleep well, darling mother!

We had only been back a few days in ruined Berlin when we were interrupted by a sudden radio announcement—a highly important political announcement. I jumped up. Infinite relief swept over me—it must be the announcement of an armistice. It must have been a bitter decision for us, but thank God it had come at last.

It was *not* an announcement of an armistice. Instead it told us quite simply that an attempt had been made to assassinate the Führer by means of a bomb on 20 July 1944 in East Prussia. But the plot had failed. Hitler had escaped with slight injuries. Providence had saved our Führer, but woe to his murderers! The Party would know how to deal with them. Colonel von Stauffenberg and a few others had already been shot.

I was completely flabbergasted. So too was Heiner. Even Dr. Schmitt had little to say. Not that we were the only astonished people in Germany that day, very few people had heard outright criticisms of Hitler. They did not know that high ranking Army officers and others in key positions were openly condemning him.

Neither Heiner nor I had heard one whisper of the secret resistance movement that had been going on for years. Members of this movement included many of the old nobility of Germany. There were others from all walks of life; ministers of religion, officers, undergraduates, and simple working men.

We learned many details of the failure of the plot from Dr. Schmitt. It seemed that the bomb lay in a brief-case which Colonel von Stauffenberg calmly put under the conference table as close as possible to Hitler's feet. Then came a slip. One of the officers present got up to examine the map, and kicked against the brief-case, sending it a foot or so away, thus Hitler did not get the full blast when it exploded a few moments later.

"And Stauffenberg?" we asked.

"Well, the Count watched the explosion from a distance, and being sure the Führer was dead, jumped into a car and raced for Berlin to give the news. There he was arrested and shot."

Hitler reacted with his normal brutality. Two hundred

men were tortured and hanged immediately after this attempt on his life, and in the purge that followed more than five thousand lost their lives by April 1945. Even today I find it hard to believe that Hitler ordered his victims to be hung from butchers' hooks and had a film taken of their death agonies, and that he and other Germans enjoyed looking at these films afterwards.

When later on we learned of the power and size of the resistance movement we were completely astounded. I had not the slightest idea of this resistance movement against Hitler.

After the failure of the assassination, the Gestapo rounded up "Circle of Kreisau" and similar groups. One of the Circle—Pater Delp—wrote from the jail in Berlin. "God has tested me thoroughly to see if I still stand by my faith . . . that only with Him can man be master of his fate and have life abundantly . . . Sometimes it was difficult for me . . . I have tried again and again to believe and preach that there are only two things a man—if he be man at all— has worth living for and to live with . . . worship and love. Everything else is valueless."

Pater Delp was hanged on the same day as State Commissar Goerdeler, 2 February 1945.

The Protestant clergyman, Dietrich Bonhoeffer, died in a concentration camp as late as 9 April 1945. Quite frankly he said: "If a madman is driving the passengers in his car to death, one must not only prepare to bandage the wounded or bury the dead, one must snatch away the driving wheel from him."

Our life in Berlin now sunk to a mere animal fight for existence. It was too hectic and exhausting. Each day the questions for me were, will there be a raid? Will we be bombed? Will there be enough food for us? And Heiner would he return alive that evening?

I could hardly find time to write Evelyn to wish her happiness on her marriage. It was going to take place in

Aue, and they were to have one week's honeymoon before Manfred went into the army as a doctor. My present to them was a dozen silver forks and knives which I had received for my own wedding but never used. It was a very valuable set, and I knew they would be delighted.

Instead of the happy letter or card I expected in acknowledgment, there came a long letter from my mother. What she wrote contained the most terrible news. Manfred was dead. There had been an air-raid on Goettingen, and he had been blown to pieces. Evelyn's despair was indescribable, my mother wrote that she had never seen such grief. She dared not leave her alone. So ill did Evelyn become that when she recovered she had but one thought in her head, to be married in name to Manfred, even though he was dead! In those days it was permitted. Special arrangements had been made so that a bride and groom could be married after one of them had been killed. This happened in Evelyn's case. She was dressed totally in black when she went to the registrar's office and leaned heavily on my mother's arm. Manfred's parents—dressed in black too— accompanied her. Evelyn was sobbing all the time, and could hardly answer "yes" when the Registrar asked her whether she were willing to marry Manfred.

My mother wrote that it was the most eerie day of her life. But it was real. When Evelyn buried Manfred she buried her own life as well, her dreams and her hopes of human life. Since that day she has never cared what happened to her, she refused to take shelter in air-raids, and she did not wish to live. She remained in East Germany when the Russians entered, and never having been a Party member was allowed to build up a surgery of her own. It gave her no joy at all, though, in fact, it was the fulfilment of a life's ambition. "It is all quite empty and meaningless now that Manfred is dead," she wrote to me.

She is still plodding on in East Germany—eleven years later—and working extremely hard. She is strictly rationed for food, as are all people in East Germany, and have been for eighteen years. She longs to see me, she says, as she lives completely alone, but that is impossible. I cannot go to East Germany, she cannot leave to visit England. Perhaps we shall never see each other again.

One night my sister Hilde did not return as usual to sleep with us. The next afternoon there was a knock at the door. Hilde stood there, grey and worn out.

"Don't come near me," she said quietly, "until I've had a bath. I'm completely filthy. I don't want to spoil your beautiful carpets. I'll leave my shoes here."

After a bath and a rest she told me the news. Our flat in Charlottenburg was burned to the ground. All night Hilde had done her best to search for children and pull household goods out of the flames. She had had to listen to the terrible screams of the people burning in the streets.

My mother took the loss of her beautiful things very calmly. "Don't worry, my dear," she wrote. "What do beautiful things matter in the end? All that matters is happiness. May you and Hilde never know the terrible agony that has come to Evelyn—that is all I worry about. May the rest of you be spared that."

In one of those winter nights at the end of 1944 Heiner suddenly turned to me and said: "I've thought it over, I *can* do it."

"Do what?" I asked in bewilderment.

"I could build the garage so that we can live in it when the Russians come."

So even Heiner at last accepted final defeat, even he saw that the war was lost. I felt infinitely sad to see such faith destroyed. I wanted to comfort him, but would that help? I couldn't give him back his faith.

As the winter went on our gas and electricity was so often cut off that cooking of any kind became impossible.

"I'll try to build a stove in the entrance hall against the chimney there," Heiner told me.

It didn't look very smart, but it worked. We cooked what food we had on a fire of wood and refuse from bombed plots. Indeed it worked so efficiently that the Russians found it a splendid stove, and used it continually after they arrived!

Heiner and I spent hours that winter sorting out potatoes in the cellar. They had sent us a full winter's supply, and most of them, part-frozen on arrival, had now thawed out and gone rotten in the heat of the cellar. But rotten or not we had got to eat them, as they were now our staple diet. I had heard that they tasted less unpleasant if soaked in vinegar water and then dried. We tried that, but found it better in theory than in practice. The potatoes not only smelled horrible while they cooked, they tasted even more disgusting afterwards. Wolfgang and Klaus refused theirs, and started to cry because there was nothing else to eat.

In despair I followed other women's examples, and began to sell my clothes for food. This helped us over the worst. Heiner was speechless when he discovered what I had done.

The weeks went by and still no rumour of an armistice. Every day the enemy planes came over. "Hitler won't give up until the whole of Germany is one vast rubble heap," Dr. Schmitt said grimly. No, Hitler would not give up. He went on asking us for sacrifice after sacrifice. The Press told the Berliners on no account to worry about their children evacuated to the east. "All the children are being well cared for in camps," they were assured.

But were they? There is a different story to tell now. Hitler was so mad and stubborn in his determination to hold out to the last ditch, that even the children were sacrificed. Kept in camps and homes until the Russians actually approached, a terrible stream was then let loose to fly westward at the last moment. Along icy roads the refugees poured, the old people dying on the roadside, the young mothers carrying children or pushing them along in any available cart. Many children died of exposure; mothers just left them on the sides of the roads, there being no spades to dig graves.

A farmer's wife in East Prussia told me a most terrible tale. She, Mrs. Buckow, was in the refugee line with her ten-year-old son when they were overtaken by a Russian column on a narrow bridge over a river. The fugitives pressed themselves tightly against the balustrade of the bridge to allow the troops to pass. Next to Mrs. Buckow stood a young woman with three children, the youngest a baby in a pram. Suddenly one of the Russian soldiers, hearing the cries of the three-year-old girl, came over and looked at the pram. He spoke broken German. He told the young woman he wanted the pram for himself. The mother began to cry and implored him not to take it. The Russian became angry and impatient. In despair the woman fell on her knees and begged for mercy. The Russian was furious. He swept the boxes and bags from the pram, flung the blankets on to the road and the baby after them. When the mother saw her baby lying there screaming she went mad, picked it up and rushed to the side of the river and threw it in. She then grabbed the little girl of three and flung her, too, into the river. The screaming boy (the third of her children) had run away, but she caught him and hurled him into the river. Then she jumped in after them. The Russian soldier had gone, taking the pram with him.

The grey column of human agony moved on. Nobody said a word. What shook Mrs. Buckow most of all was the fact that nobody bothered to see what happened to the mother in the river. Nor did anyone try to save the little boy, even though he screamed for help. They had all got used to people in pain and people dying. Nobody stopped, and nobody helped.

"All that could have been avoided if Hitler had allowed us to leave our homes in time," Mrs. Buckow said.

She told us of the utter confusion and lack of organization. No news, no advice, no help anywhere along the route.

"We met people, for instance, who told us Breslau was the safest spot to make for. Then later on we met people just coming from Breslau, who reported that there was utter chaos in the town, and that the population were being told to leave at once."

I wondered, as she told me this, what had happened to my beautiful friend Paula—she who had never suffered anything in her life. Had she, perhaps, gone to Dresden? Dresden was still considered safe, possibly owing to the architectural fame of the town and the great pictures which drew people from all over the world. But in the end Dresden also received its share of bombing. There were two hundred thousand refugees in Dresden when, on the night of 13 February 1945, the fire-storms fell on the town. There are no figures of the numbers who perished that night in Dresden, for the simple fact that the chaos was so complete no one knew who was in the town and who was not. Identification being impossible, and a decent burial out of the question, benzine was poured over the corpses, and all of them were set alight. Officially it was reported by the German authorities that the casualties were four hundred thousand. The British gave the numbers as two hundred and fifty thousand. No one will ever know the truth. Most of our news about Dresden came from Evelyn who was working there in a hospital.

Gerhart Hauptmann, the famous German poet, saw Dresden's end from one of the surrounding hills. He watched it burning for five whole days. He saw it in ruins. He had a stroke. After his recovery he wrote an appeal to the world in which he said. "He who has forgotten how to weep, learns again at Dresden's ruin. I know that in England and America there are enough good people to whom such glories as the Sixtinische Madonna were well known. I am at the end of my life, and I envy my dead

friends who have been saved this terrible sight. I weep, and
I am not ashamed of my tears. The great heroes of old were
not ashamed of tears, were they? I am nearly eighty-three
years old, and I am standing before God beseeching him
with my whole heart to show His love more clearly, to show
mankind how to purify ourselves, to show us how to reach
our salvation."

I did hear of my friend Paula after all. Some weeks later
her husband Kurt arrived, limping and grey, at our door.
He had been wounded and lost a leg. Paula had gone to
Dresden, and then with her two children had fled from
the town on to the open roads. Low-flying enemy planes had
caught them. Throwing herself on top of her children she
had been splayed with bullets and slowly bled to death. A
peasant woman, seeing she was dying, had taken her papers
to the Red Cross and had rescued her son as well. The little
girl had died with Paula on the road. The boy had been
terribly wounded and had screamed and clung to his
mother as the peasant tried to lift him. In hospital they had
given the child injections to try to save his life, but he too
had succumbed in the end to exposure and loss of blood.

Kurt accepted some soup I made from black flour, and
he washed himself; I could not offer him a bath. Then,
thanking me, he limped off down the road. I never saw or
heard of him again.

In February 1945 my dear brother Rudolf arrived. He
did not bother to knock, he just came and stood against
the front door, breathing very heavily. I caught sight of
him as I came up from the cellars where the children slept
each night. As I ran to welcome him the thought flashed
through my mind: "He's deserted; I must hide him." Then
I saw that he had a stick in his hand.

"A bed, Else," he said wearily. "I only want a bed. I have
been walking for days. The hospital had to be cleared as
the Russians came." Limping painfully, he followed me
down the cellar steps. I made him up a bed. "Help me off

with my boots," he asked. Both his legs were horribly swollen. The left boot took many minutes to get off, but the right one I couldn't budge at all.

"I shall have to cut it off," I said presently.

"No, you mustn't cut it. These are all I have. I can't get any others." He begged me to try again. When finally I got the boot off, Rudolf fell back on the bed, his face whiter than the sheets. He made no attempt to undress. I covered him with a blanket and went to fetch food. He was asleep when I returned, completely exhausted.

Slowly my brother recovered. He had not told us how seriously he had been wounded. We now learned he had had many operations on his leg, and that the wounds kept festering. They had moved him from one hospital to another as the Russians advanced. Each time the wound had opened again. All the other wounded men were in the same state as he was.

"We divided ourselves into two parties in the last hospital to wile away the time; the Black and the White Party. The Black Party had given up all hope of winning the war; the White Party still swore that Hitler's secret weapons were on the way to us." Rudolf was trying to joke now.

"And were you Black or White?" asked Heiner.

"Neither," said Rudolf. "The war has already been lost, but I have my vows of allegiance to keep, success or failure doesn't matter. I must go on."

One evening Rudolf said: "There came a time when even the White Party could not hope any longer. We were told to get up and dress as best we could, and come to the operating theatre. There they told us the Russians had advanced very suddenly, and that we must get out that evening. There wouldn't be enough transport for all of us, so the 'easier cases' would have to walk. I was, of course, one of the 'easier cases'."

They set off at night with just their papers, ration books and some food. It was snowing and icy cold. Rudolf said the aching of his wound was so terrible that the cold did not matter much, in fact it kept him concentrating on which hurt most, his leg or the cold. What he soon saw on the roads made him forget some of his own pain. Joining in with the wounded soldiers were columns of other people, refugees—old men, old women, children and sick people—all struggling along through the night. He saw them fall out on the sides of the roads and lie there to die, without making a sound. Once or twice he went to try and help. Then he became used to it all and just looked and limped on himself.

"They were in worse plight than I was," he said, taking off his glasses and polishing them vigorously. "Why didn't they evacuate them in time? Why didn't they clear the hospital weeks before? All of them could have been saved."

This terrible cry . . . why were so many lives lost? Why was everything done too late? From every side people were now asking this. We heard tale after tale of the suffering in our hospitals. In one hospital in East Germany they were given but two hours to clear the wounded and crippled men. A nurse told me that she was standing in the entrance of her hospital, waiting for ambulances to collect the wounded in her ward, when a soldier rushed in, saying: "the Russians are here, on the outskirts of the town; come on quick." He tried to grab her and push her into an ambulance with him. "My wounded," she had protested. Her ward contained terribly wounded men, some without any limbs left at all; shattered torsos.

"Quick," said the soldier again. "There's no time to get them away. Don't you understand? They are lost in any case, they won't live much longer."

Losing her head, the nurse allowed the ambulance soldier to force her on to a truck. Behind her she heard the screams of the crippled men.

"Don't leave us. Take us with you. Don't leave us to the Russians. Mercy, mercy."

She said she would never forget those cries; she could still hear them now. If she had stayed she would have died a terrible death with them. She knew that only too well.

It sounded pitiless to our ears at the time. It still does. But there was no pity left in Germany in those days. Everyone was for himself. No one stood up and showed an example of courage to the soldiers and civilians, or if they did, it was just one isolated case affecting but a few people. The best Army officers had been "liquidated", and the Party leaders merely blared out false hopes of secret weapons arriving in time; and between them the true spirit of Germany died.

"We left the helpless by the road while the stronger ones walked on, each for himself," said Rudolf.

"All one can hope is that God let them have a quick death when the Russians came," I answered him.

Rudolf gave me a half-smile.

Heiner and I and Rudolf and the children were soon alone. Hilde went to the Harz Mountains with her firm. My father returned from Austria, where the bombs were now falling on Vienna and after staying for a few days in Berlin, decided to move west to Thuringia. Then Dr. and Mrs. Schmitt also went away.

"The rats are leaving the sinking ship," said Heiner bitterly. It was not a pleasant feeling. Were the Russians so very close then? What about the children? On 7 March we heard that the Americans had crossed the Rhine at Remagen, where the bridge had not been destroyed.

"Darling," said Heiner, "the Americans are coming first." He seized my hands and danced wildly around the table with me. "You see, they will race along and reach Berlin first. Everyone likes to be first into a capital city. They won't let the Russians take the glory."

From then on we studied the maps feverishly each day. Heiner got special maps of Germany, and followed very carefully the progress of the armies. It seemed as clear as

209

daylight that the Americans would arrive first in Berlin. Again and again the German soldiers threw themselves against the Russians to hold them back. The Russians did not stop, but our attacks did at any rate delay them. We were now absolutely certain that the Americans would be here first.

Rudolf was more sceptical. He was much better now. His wounds were healing, but he still could not walk without a stick. He was allowed to stay in our house. He had to report to the military authorities twice a week. When the radio announced that boys aged sixteen were to be conscripted to hold the Russians back, he groaned and buried his head in his hands. "This is murder," he moaned. He got up from his chair and, saying he did not feel well, he went to his corner in the cellar and made out his will. He handed it to me in a sealed envelope that evening.

Heiner no longer danced round the dining-room table with me, nor did we look at his maps. The awful and incredible thing was happening. The Americans were *not* coming first, nor the British. Both enemy armies had halted at the Elbe.

When first this news came to us we thought the troops perhaps needed a rest. We waited anxiously, one day, two days, three days. The Americans did not move. Heiner was pacing up and down the room on that third night. "They are deliberately handing us over to the Russians," he said. His thin face was strained and grey. A few days later he came home smiling a little, and kissing me said: "I managed it after all. It wasn't easy, it cost me quite a lot."

"What did you manage? What are you talking about, darling?"

"This," he said triumphantly, and pulled some papers from his pockets and waved them at me. "You know what they are? Tickets? Real railway tickets that will let you out of Berlin, and a telegram as well!" He was as happy as a

210

little boy. I just couldn't make head or tail of it. "A telegram?" I repeated stupidly. "Tickets?"

"Yes, a telegram from our friends in Wesermünde. They
will put you and the boys up in their house."

Gradually I got the story properly. Heiner had organized
our "escape" from Berlin through his office. He had not been
able to bear the thought of our falling into Russian hands,
so he had pulled every string he knew, and spent every mark
he could lay hands on.

"And you? You will come with us, of course?"

"Oh, no. That's impossible."

"But you will try, won't you?"

"No. I can't come. I can't desert the hospitals now."

"Then *we* shan't go either," I said calmly.

Heiner's face began to grow red with anger. "You will
do as I say, all of you," he ordered.

"I shall not," I said just as firmly. I saw Heiner open and
close his fists in an attempt at self-control. "Will you please
tell me *why* you won't go?" His voice was sharper than I
had ever heard it before.

"I won't go because I won't leave you alone. I won't go
away now that things are bad whatever happens to me."

"Whatever happens to me," repeated Heiner. "Stop being
heroic, do you hear me. 'Whatever happens to me.' You
know quite well what will happen if the Russians come.
Rape, murder, starvation for you and the children, that's
what will happen to you. And I won't have it. You will leave
Berlin at once!"

"No," I said again. "I will not leave you. We must stay
together. That's where I belong, with you."

"And the boys? What will happen to the boys? Are you
ready to sacrifice them as well?" He had me there of course.
Torture for the boys, slow starvation for the boys, could
I face that? For a moment I wavered, then I looked at
Heiner again.

"We will stay together. If we have got to die, it's

better to die together than apart. It's no use, Heiner, please don't go on fighting me."

But he was too angry. He turned and rushed out of the lounge, slamming the door violently. I heard him running about the house banging doors and cupboards.

I remained staring out of the window at the peaceful River Havel. What had I done?. Decided whether my sons were to live or die; had I done right? What would happen if we stayed here?. There was still time to call Heiner back. His last words as he left me had been: "It will be on your conscience!" They were terrible words.

But there was something above conscience, surely, there was love. How could I leave Heiner when he needed me most. And what would life with the boys be like if I did run away just to save our skins? No, my place was here with Heiner, and the boys were best with their mother whatever happened to her.

In the night I made my peace with Heiner. He had not spoken a single word to me during the whole day, not even during the air-raids in the cellar in the evening. But that night I began to plead with him once more to see my point of view and at last he answered.

"But I only want to do what is best for you and the boys," he said. "Don't you see what I feel? How could I do my work during the day if you and the boys were being tortured. What use would that be to any of us?"

At last I broke into tears. "I can't leave you. I can't be apart from you. Please don't be angry with me. I can't go away and leave you in Berlin alone. Darling, please understand."

Suddenly Heiner put his arms round me violently, and held me so close that I couldn't breathe. "Else, Else, my darling. I didn't know you loved me like that," he said. "Why didn't you make me understand at first? All right, darling, we'll stay here together, then."

Rudolf came home one evening and told us that this

would be his last night in Kladow. All the less seriously wounded in hospital had been told they must fight at the gates of Berlin. They had decided he was one of them.

"But you can't even walk without a stick," gasped Heiner. "How can you command troops like that?"

Rudolf laughed grimly. "You would be surprised if you saw the men they have sorted out. Only one arm? That doesn't matter, you can still carry ammunition, can't you? Wound in the back? That's all right as long as you don't show your back to the enemy! We'll see your bandages are changed regularly!"

We both stared at him incredulously. It was murder— nothing more nor less. Slowly, and I suppose just to break the unbearable silence, Heiner asked: "I take it you are going to meet General Wenk's army?". Every day we heard on the radio that General Wenk was coming with his army to relieve Berlin.

Again Rudolf gave that short, bitter laugh. "That's what they told us in the hospital. General Wenk is marching to the aid of Berlin with his army. The SS General Steiner will unite all troops in and around Berlin to meet him." Rudolf's voice went on in a monotonous tone as though he had learned it all by heart. "Once these armies have united we shall beat the Russians, they will run like mad with our secret weapon pursuing them. We shall chase them over the Oder, out of Silesia, out of East Prussia, Poland, Lithuania, and on right into Kurland. In Kurland another German army will receive them and destroy them completely! The army in Kurland is not like mine—it is not an army of old men and invalids. It is a healthy well-equipped army, and so on and so forth." Rudolf ended this declaration with a "Heil Hitler".

"But," Heiner interrupted, "if we have a whole army standing in Kurland and in good condition, why isn't it here to defend Berlin?"

"There is only one thing wrong with the army in

Kurland," said Rudolf. "A small thing, but quite important, that army is cut off. Don't you see that?"

"No," said Heiner. "I don't see. There is still the sea open to them. They could all be brought by ships to Berlin."

Rudolf turned a bitter look on Heiner. "You will never make a soldier. You ask questions. Soldiers only listen and obey. I have told you that under Generals Wenk and Steiner we are to chase the Russians back from Berlin and into the arms of the army of Kurland. There is no query about it at all. That is Hitler's plan and that must be followed. If you query this plan, or attempt to shirk your part in it, you may end on a lamp-post. I passed one poor devil in his soldier's coat hanging on a lamp-post quite near the hospital. There was a neat notice under his feet saying that anyone who cut him down would be severely punished. Round his neck was a small card saying : 'This is how we deal with traitors.' God knows how long they will leave him there rotting in the wind."

"Do you understand now what is going on?"

"So Hitler is quite determined to fight to the last," Heiner said. "He has declared he will stay in Berlin and not surrender. Not even if the whole city is blown to pieces around him? Is that it?"

"Round him?" Rudolf repeated. "You mean *above* him, don't you? You don't imagine Hitler is sitting in any ordinary air-raid cellar, do you? He is sitting in a concrete dug-out eighteen yards below the surface and with walls eight yards thick, and in every luxury and comfort. He has no need to fear bombs or fires."

"You have changed a lot, Rudolf," Heiner remarked.

"I know," said Rudolf. "I tried to be loyal for years. I even tried to obey orders against the Russians. But now that I see what is happening I can't be loyal any longer. Hitler is killing Germany to feed his own vanity. If you had seen those hollow-eyed men in hospital today you would feel as I do. We were all mustered out like sheep to

214

stand in front of an SS officer telling us about the Führer's plans. How we would beat the Russians with the secret weapon. How the Russians would turn and run; and do you know, some of those poor sick devils *still* fell for it! They still believed in the Führer; they had to. They would have gone mad if they had faced the truth. The truth is that Hitler is mad himself, so mad he is going to hurl all of us to destruction, himself as well. By the way, the SS officer finished his speech with the words: 'Never before have we been so near to victory! Sieg Heil!'."

Heiner and I laughed at this. Rudolf did not.

The next morning he shook hands with Heiner, who left quite early, and he said "If I report to you at the Pearly Gates, will you, as 'foreman of the angels', let me in?"

"You are too rough and grim for the angels, I'm afraid," said Heiner, giving a smile in return. "But I promise that I'll try to make an exception in your case. I have very good connexions up there, and I'll try and find you a peaceful corner somewhere. Is that all right?"

They both laughed. These were their last words to each other. I got ready a good meal for Rudolf before he left. I sacrificed another tin of meat and tried to be as light-hearted as I could. But he remained silent and gloomy with me. When he went, I remained standing at the door as he limped down the steps into the garden. At the bottom step he turned once more and said: "When the war is finished I shall not give myself into Russian hands. I have seen too much of what they can do."

Quickly he turned round and limped off to his last battle, his stick making a sharp tapping noise as he went. I did not run after him. I did not even cry at the time. I knew I should never see him again, and there was nothing I could do to prevent him going, and nothing adequate I could say. He was going to die, and all I could do was to lean there against the wall of the house and watch him hobbling away into the distance. It was a sunny day. Spring was in the air and the birds singing. But I was turned to stone in my pain. Rudolf, my brother, whom I loved so deeply, was leaving and was going to die. He died in one of the desperate battles round Berlin.

Years later I heard that he died in the last battle near Berlin and that he was buried there in East Germany. So I cannot look for Rudolf's grave either, or put a flower on it. I shall never get a passport to visit that grave either. In the evening I told Heiner of Rudolf's last words from the garden. He was as shaken as I was. In the night, and during an air-raid, he said to me: "Darling, promise me something?" I said I would, whatever it was.

"If ever I am taken by the Russians, never give up hope of my coming back, will you? Will you promise to wait for me?"

"Of course I'll promise, but please, please, don't talk like that, not today just after Rudolf has gone," I begged him.

As I cooked on my primitive stove in the entrance hall— and not very efficient cooking, as it was difficult to keep it burning evenly—the guns of the approaching Russian armies grew closer.

"The houses not bombed out in the raids will soon be finished off by the Russian shells," Heiner said to me.

The newspapers of course still kept printing stories about a "final victory" with the "most gigantic defeat of the Russians at the gates of Berlin." They also threatened that to shelter soldiers overnight without official leave was assisting at desertion. "This will bring a death sentence!" they told us.

Terrible stories were published about the cruelties of the approaching army. The midday paper (12 *Uhr Blatt*) in March 1945 wrote a violent leader telling us to crush the Soviet beasts at sight. "If you don't wish your wives and daughters raped and then shot by these criminals, fight with every ounce of your courage."

To spur us on there were photos of men going out to fight

the Russian tanks on bicycles! It told, too, of boys in the Hitler Youth throwing back a mature Soviet regiment and killing a hundred and seventy Russians. The surviving boys got the Iron Cross (second class). The bravery and discipline of the Hitler Youth girls helping the wounded and supplying ammunition to the troops was also praised.

Goebbels continued to pour out his ravings. "Never, never, will we sign our own death sentence. We shall go on suffering. I know millions of Germans are behind me in this. Life would not be worth living if we gave in . . . it would be worse than hell."

"Easy for some to talk," I said to Heiner. "Goebbels is perhaps sitting in Hitler's concrete 'castle' as he says this. They would not talk like this if they lived in the underground shelters of Berlin day and night."

Indeed the lives of the people of Berlin were one continual nightmare. The incessant raids, and the almost complete lack of food and domestic necessities made any kind of normal living impossible. Sometimes the Berliners still cracked their jokes, however. One night Heiner came home and told me about a doctor next to him in an air-raid shelter. He started praising Hitler and Goebbels, waxing very enthusiastic, and ended his speech with: "Where would we be if our Führer were not with us?"

Heiner said he felt rather bored and so just nodded politely. He found the doctor's remarks in rather bad taste, and was in fact looking for a seat somewhere else, when he was given a dig in the ribs.

"Wake up, I want an answer. Tell me, where would we be without our Führer?"

Heiner was both annoyed and embarrassed. He shrugged his shoulders and said, "I don't know."

"I know," the doctor said abruptly. "At home in bed."

Most of the schools were now closed. Whenever possible teachers arranged "home lessons" in private houses to groups of children collected hastily between the air-raids.

I did not allow Klaus and Wolfgang ever to move far away
from the house and never to go into an open field because
low flying aircraft fired at anyone in the open. As for queue-
ing for food, that was the worst strain of all if you had
children at home. I might be standing an hour in a queue
and working my way slowly to the front when the sirens
would go. Immediately all the mothers broke from the
queue to rush home, I with them. This was always a
dangerous thing to do. So there were no rations or "extras"
that day. One night there was no air-raid at all. It was in
April. We slept right through the night in peace and woke
in astonishment to find it was almost time to get up.

"What bliss," I said to Heiner. "I had forgotten what it
was like to sleep through a night."

"Yes," he said, "but I don't like the noise of the guns."

The guns were certainly closer than ever that morning.
I turned over and said: "If the planes don't come during
the day either, you should be able to come home a bit
earlier, and we could have another night's sleep." For a
moment Rudolf came into my mind. Perhaps he was fighting against the Russians while we were sleeping in our
beds.

When Heiner came home that evening the news was not
good. "The Russians are shelling the town, that's why
there are no more air-raids, the bombs might hit the
Russians."

Berlin was now burning continuously. As one fire died
down, another broke out. No kind of fire service could cope
any longer. I implored Heiner not to return the next morning.

"The Russians must be almost round the whole city," I
said. "The shells seem to be exploding everywhere."

"I must go back," he told me. "The hospital is in a most
terrible state. I cannot let them down. Even if I have to
walk I must go."

A great many items of news came that day over the radio.

We heard of Roosevelt's death. Then the minor fact that Hanna Reitsch had joined Hitler in his "castle" cellar. Then that Goering had gone, and Greim had taken over as Air Marshal. One reason given for Goering's departure was his "heart attacks". Nothing impressed me any more. All I felt was fear of what was to come; of a terrible, inevitable end.

While we all sat there listening to the awful noises of Russian shells, a fantastic last minute fight for power was going on around Hitler. Hitler himself was now completely mad. From his cellars he issued (we learned later on) the craziest orders, to burn and destroy the whole of Germany at once. He called it his "burnt earth" order. "Everything in Germany was to be burnt or destroyed—all bridges, electricity supplies, gas supplies, water supplies, still existing food stores, fields, factories, transport. The enemy would find only 'burnt earth' in Germany."

This was apparently his last order and message to his country before his suicide. The final shriek of a man gone mad with vanity and a lust for power.

Heiner came home eventually that night to say that the Russians were in the southern suburbs of Berlin. The people there had taken to their cellars with as much food as they could collect, and they planned to stay there as long as possible. He then promised that tomorrow, 27 April, would be his last day for going to the hospital. It was useless arguing or begging. He said he had given his word to come back the next day to help, and he would not break it.

The evening came and the explosions of shells became louder and louder and Heiner did not return. In terrible anxiety I went to friends in another street for any kind of news. The man of the household had returned himself hours ago.

"Are you going back tomorrow?" I asked.

"Not on your life," came his quick reply. "The bridges over the Havel have been blown up. Besides, it's impossible

219

to work in the city. A shell exploded right in my office."

Very frightened, I put my question. "What are the chances of my husband getting back to Kladow tonight?"

"Very slender," he told me. "I don't see how he can get across the river, unless he swims," he added with dry humour. "It would be a pretty cold swim."

How could Heiner go on working like this, when shells were exploding all round him? Didn't he realize his life was important to his family? It was rather the reaction of a mother who is angry with a child who has been lost or run into danger, you want to smack it because of the shocking anxiety it has caused you.

My anger against Heiner's devotion to duty soon died down. I walked back to our home in growing despair. Mr. M. tried to comfort me as I left by saying: "All of us have had to go through the gunfire. Perhaps your husband is really safer in hospital than out of it. The Russians are very suspicious of civilians, they may be kinder to hospital staffs."

The boys were sleeping peacefully in the cellar as I went in. I sank down and buried my face in the cushions of the couch, and sobbed and sobbed. I was quite sure Heiner had gone for ever. It was now hours after his normal time to return. If only I could 'phone to him, but they had taken away all the telephones from civilians.

My head was still buried in the cushion when a hand touched my shoulder and I heard a voice say: "Darling!" It was Heiner! He was bending over me. He looked very dirty and dishevelled, but he was alive and unhurt. I laughed and cried at the same time, and pulled him against me. He was shaking as much as I was.

"I only just made it," he said after a moment or so. "The idiots had already blown up the bridge when I arrived. There were a number of us standing there and were absolutely cut off."

He then told me how he started to walk along the banks

to try and find a boat. They couldn't find one for the army had commandeered all boats a few days before.

"I wasn't the only husband, you see, who worked till the last minute," he said with a smile. "Finally we found an old fisherman we thought looked likely. At first he refused to talk at all. Then one of the men opened his case and produced half a pound of butter. Another one took off his wrist watch, and said; 'This might save your life when the Russians come!' That did the trick. The fisherman changed his tune. Yes, now he came to think of it there *was* a boat not very far from the very spot we were standing on! He had hidden it from the army. We went and dug the boat out and rowed across the river. There weren't any buses on this side so I walked home. It took about an hour and a half."

We were sitting now, leaning against each other on a corner of the couch. "I'll get you food," I said, and went to warm something up on the hall stove.

"First, I've got a nice present for you," he said.

I came back, thinking it was food of some kind. To my intense disappointment he took a small wireless crystal set out of his case and triumphantly put it on my lap.

"What a silly you are," he teased me, when he saw my face drop with disappointment. "Can't you see what a comfort this will be? We are going to be besieged, so this is the only way we shall know what is happening in the outside world."

12

My Husband's Tragic Death

VERY late on the night of Heiner's last trip to Berlin there was a loud knock on our door. We sat quite still for a moment. It couldn't be friends, for no friends called so casually or so late. What had we done wrong we wondered? The knock came again and we went upstairs together.

Outside stood a civilian and an SS man. I went cold with fright, but they smiled and hastily explained that all they wanted was the key to Dr. Schmitt's house. Heiner asked for a few details.

"I can't hand it over just like that," he told them. "I am responsible to the owner."

The civilian then explained that he was a civil servant in Kladow, and was in charge of requisitioning houses for bombed-out persons. He showed papers to confirm this. So would we please hand over Dr. Schmitt's key to this SS man and his wife?

Heiner gave the key over. He had no choice in the matter at all.

"Strange," he said, when they went away. "There are hundreds of bombed-out families with several children, and yet they put just one man and his wife in that big house. They certainly look after the SS all right."

We slept well that night. Heiner was safe; there were no air-raids, and he was not going to work in the morning. It was enough to bring peaceful sleep to us both but other noises of battle reminded us of what was to come.

The next morning somebody again knocked at our door; the SS man, now in civilian clothes, and his wife. They wished to speak to us. Heiner led them into the lounge. I looked at them both with curiosity. The spring sunshine showed their faces very clearly. She had a coarse, hard face, and wore clothes far too elegant for either a besieged city or a country that had been rationed for five years. Her voice was coarse and her language vulgar and harsh. The man, on the other hand, wore a shabby, soiled suit, and looked poor. Watching his face I decided that he had a horrible personality, and I did not like the hard, watchful look in his eyes—the eyes of a man who cheated and who expected to be cheated in return.

At first he spoke about the weather, as if we were all politely seated in an English drawing-room. "Yes, it was a surprisingly nice April, with spring well on the way." He said that he did not think the political situation looked quite so rosy, but that could change overnight. People were getting a bit difficult to handle, he had noticed. The Party had no patience with that kind of thing. He burst into a dreadful story of punishments he had himself inflicted on a group of men recently. It was a short story and ended with details of fiendish cruelty. Involuntarily I shuddered. The wife looked at me and smiled. The SS man got up.

" So long," he said cheerfully, and left us.

Normally we did not lock our house door during the day but that time we did. Slowly we went back into the lounge. For a moment we did not speak to each other, we were thinking over the terrible crimes that might have been committed so close to us. Heiner stared out of the window at the Havel which was reflecting the blue sky. "Such dreadful things should be reported," he said grimly. "If that story were known they would be expelled from the SS."

What idiots we both were! It still did not occur to us that these two who had just left were no exception, but were part and parcel of the whole policy of the SS. That their cruelties were not only known, but actually approved of at Party headquarters, and that all over the country these cruelties were now increasing hourly as our defeat and bitterness closed in on us. There was no time, however, for further thoughts on the subject. All of a sudden Kladow was full to overflowing with German soldiers. They were worn out and dejected. Some of them were very young, not more than seventeen perhaps. Some looked very ill. Daily I wondered if Rudolf were among them, perhaps quite close to us. The shops in Kladow closed and so too did the post-office. One morning I was in the entrance hall cooking a very thin potato soup when Heiner rushed in.

"Quick," he said. "Give me a bucket."

"What is it?" I asked.

"Butter," he shouted gleefully. "I'm 'organising' some butter for us."

When he returned he was not quite so happy. All the same the bucket was a quarter full of real butter. It was like a gift straight from heaven.

But Heiner was furious. "Those gangsters," he stormed. "Nothing but grab, grab, grab, nobody else matters at all."

It took me some time to calm him down. "But you've got a lot" I said.

"We could have had the whole bucket full if they had been fair," he kept saying. "It would have lasted us weeks and weeks."

The story came out in bits and pieces. He had gone into a big garden in our neighbourhood where high-ranking officers of the Air Force used to live. Heiner had wondered if by any chance they had left anything behind in their hasty retreat. In the garage he had discovered a huge quantity of butter. Delighted, he had rushed home to me, but not before knocking on Mr. M's door to spread the good news. Together they had been dividing up the spoil, when in rushed the SS man's wife. She immediately demanded her share. Heiner, of course, gave it to her. Exactly the same as his and Mr. M's. But she exploded with fury. Didn't Heiner realize who she was, the wife of a

Party official? She should have more than they so Heiner gave her more. That was not good enough. Had it not been her husband who had blown up the bridge over the Havel to hold back the Russians? She must have more than the two of them put together.

Heiner protested that she had no children, whereas they had. That made no difference at all. She threatened to fetch the military police and have him court-martialled for stealing military property. Anxiously Mr. M. had trodden on Heiner's foot at this juncture. She got the biggest part of the half ton of butter, and the two men walked off with a quarter of a bucket each. I still went on trying to calm Heiner, and saying what wonderful use we could make of what we had got.

"That's not the point," he persisted. "It's the selfishness and corruption and threats that make me boil. If I give her enough she will shut up. If I don't, then she reports us. At least she could have agreed to a third, but no, she must have double the amount of both of us, and only for herself and that filthy husband of hers."

Mr. M. came in a few moments later. "It was just about time you gave in," he told Heiner. "In another moment we should both have been strung up on the nearest lamp-post. It just shows her intelligence that she could be proud of the fact that *her* husband blew up the last bridge over the river. As if that would halt the Russians, all it will do is cut off all our food supplies from now on."

That night we did not sleep so well. I woke first. The gun-fire had come considerably closer. I roused Heiner. He sat up with a jerk, listening intently.

"Quick," he shouted. "Get your clothes and dress downstairs, the shells will be on top of us in a moment."

He was right. It was the most terrible sound in the world. We could not even sit on chairs in the cellar as the whole house shook when the shells exploded, so we lay face down on the ground and did not even notice the icy cold of the cement. We lay, Heiner and I, by the side of the low bed on which the boys were sleeping, and it was to me an absolute miracle that they still went on sleeping—yet they did.

How long we lay on the floor I don't know. It seemed like eternity. Heiner, who had known some of the fighting at the end of the First World War, said he had never heard anything so frightful as this. In the morning the firing stopped, and the SS man came over. This time he seemed in quite a hurry. He handed back the key, and asked us to keep an eye on his belongings, as he and his wife had to leave at short notice. Soon afterwards the German officers went through the town and requisitioned many houses for the coming battle.

It was hard to imagine a battle of any kind at the moment, hard, because at that moment outside in my garden, it was such a gentle spring day. Birds sang, the first flowers were fresh and fragrant, the trees held their light green veil of opening buds, the waters of the Havel glistened peacefully. Was it really possible that in a few hours Russian troops would be trampling through this garden and destroying it.

Heiner had the same strange and divided feelings. The Russians were already in Potsdam, which was about ten miles away. We did not stay long in the garden. The gunfire started again and we fled to the cellar. This time the boys were awake, and Heiner and I had to use all our self-control to hide our fear from them. The firing was not quite so heavy as during the night, and Heiner held their attention by telling them about the different types of guns. Suddenly there was a very loud crash. The walls shook and we heard the sound of splintering glass. Our windows I thought. Heiner stopped his talk and said: "And that was a grenade, and pretty near to us."

We ran upstairs and looked outside. A grenade had exploded between our house and Dr. Schmitt's, but ours had received the lesser damage. Now it was quiet again, then sounds in the distance.

"Listen," Heiner said to the boys. "That is firing; rifles and machine-guns. They are fighting in the woods now."

I felt paralyzed with fear. If the Russians were in the woods they would soon be here.

We looked at each other. Then I had a thought. . . .

"Quick," I said to Heiner. "Come in here a moment, I want to talk to you."

"Heiner," I began very cautiously. "*Please* do as I ask, go into hiding until the Russians pass on."

"What? Are you mad? Leave you here in this mess? Alone with the Russians?"

He was wildly excited, and would scarcely listen to my reasons. At last I got him to listen quietly to my plan.

"There's that narrow gap in the roof above the stairs, you could just squeeze into it and sit up once you were inside."

While he turned this over in his mind I kept reminding him what happened to German civilians when Russians caught them.

"But what about you?", he stammered at last. "What would they do to you?"

I implored him to be reasonable. What could any of us do if the Russians entered the house? We had no guns. If they wanted to rape me how could he stop them? He would merely be shot defending me.

"Be sensible, darling," I kept imploring him. "You can't help me, and you only risk your own life. If you promise to love me whatever they do to me, I will try to be calm and not make things worse for us all than they are."

Heiner did not answer. He just stared at me.

"I will go to a doctor as soon as I can afterwards," I added.

Heiner broke down at that. He fell on his knees and put his head in my lap. I bent over him and quietly stroked his hair.

"Darling, it may not happen. They may be all right, but there's much more chance if I keep calm and you are out of the way. We mustn't make them angry."

At last he got up. "Perhaps you are right. I'll try and stay up there but I may not be able to." He took a blanket with him, and I took a jug of water and a few slices of bread, and some of the "organized butter". He found he could just fit himself into the hole in the roof.

There was now nothing to do but wait for the final battle in Kladow to begin. We brought the boys up from the cellar to let them play in the air and light, as they were so white and heavy-eyed from living underground. We opened the shutters across the windows, and played games. Except for the distant noises of machine-gun fire there was peace round our house on a lovely spring day. But not for long. Suddenly there was the tramp of heavy boots round the house. We peeped through the curtains; German soldiers! We opened the windows to speak to them. To my horror they wanted to come into the house to use it to fight from. Hearing my conversation the boys ran into the garden.

"Oh, you have children?" said the eldest of the group. "All right, then we'll leave you in peace. But have you got a boat?"

"Yes, but not here. Farther down the river at the bottom of the hill," Heiner told them.

"They've all gone from down there," said the soldier. "We searched the whole bank."

"Where do you want to go?" we asked.

The soldier shrugged his shoulders. "Haven't a clue."

"But aren't you joining up with General Wenk?" I said. "They said so on the wireless days ago."

To my astonishment, one of the soldiers burst into tears. We all stared at him. He pushed his steel helmet well over his face, but we could see the tears pouring down over his thin cheeks. He looked not a day more than seventeen. None of the other men said a word to him. Indeed they all looked exhausted and fed-up enough to cry.

The older soldier pushed his helmet high and wiped the sweat off his forehead. "They've been telling us that tale about General Wenk for weeks. What do they take us for? General Wenk won't come. God alone knows where he is. The Russians are everywhere. They're just playing cat and mouse with us. And so we go on . . . fighting to the last man." His voice rose in mockery of Hitler's speeches. "Fighting to the last little boy, they ought to say." He turned and looked at the weeping soldier. The awful bitterness in the soldier's voice, still urging his little group on to some kind of action, brought tears to my eyes.

And General Wenk? He had taken the law into his own hands and decided *not* to sacrifice his army by leading it into Berlin. Hitler raged and screamed in his cellar, but General Wenk stayed away and saved a few hundred thousand lives. The SS General Steiner did not turn up either. So Berlin was now defended only by grandfathers, boys, and invalids from the Russian front.

We watched the soldiers walk back through the garden. They hadn't an earthly chance, and they knew it. Then the firing flared up again from the woods. We closed the shutters and fled to the cellar with the children. There we stayed, crouched on the floor all the rest of that day and through the following night. When the second morning came we heard loud, hoarse shouting from the Russian troops and there was the sound of rifles and machine guns.

Heiner and I stood in the lounge and looked out. The Russians were swarming into our street, running, shooting and shouting. I nearly screamed aloud in terror, then I remembered Heiner.

"Quick," I said to him, "upstairs."

He turned round, his face ghastly pale. He flung his arms round me, and held me close for a second, then he rushed up the stairs towards his hole in the roof, and I snatched up a book from the bookcase and went down to the cellars. I was too agitated to look at the boys, but merely opened the book and began to read aloud to them. It was a fairy story book. I had grabbed it at random from the children's bookshelves in my panic.

The fairy story was about a princess who was born blind. Wolfgang and Klaus became fascinated. It wasn't often I had time to read to them nowadays. There I sat in the cellar just saying the words and trying to keep my voice steady, with one ear listening for the Russians and the other trying to hear whether all was well with Heiner.

The poor shepherd in the story had just seen the beautiful blind princess and decided to give his life so that she might see, when we were interrupted by a sharp banging on the door which I had locked and bolted.

"That must be the Russians," I said in the calmest voice I could manage. I went upstairs, telling the boys to stay absolutely silent in the cellar. Two Russian soldiers stood at the door with their rifles and guns loaded and pointing at me. I stood and stared and so did they for a second. Never shall I forget that moment.

Then, in broken German, one of them said: "Arms up!" I held my arms up. The Russian stepped forward and searched me thoroughly for weapons. He took nothing from me, not even my wrist watch.

When they were satisfied that I was unarmed, one of them spoke again. "Where is the man?" he asked.

"There isn't a man," I replied.

"Yes there is."

"No."

"We'll find him. Show your house!"

They indicated that I was to go through the house with them. I had to go ahead, and they followed with the rifle and gun behind me. While we went through the rooms I kept wondering if someone had betrayed Heiner. Why had they said : "Yes, there *is* a man." Suddenly I noticed Heiner's hat hanging from a peg by the front entrance door. Had they noticed it? I was seized with cold fear.

Now they wished to see the cellar. The staircase was dark as the electricity was cut off. I could sense the Russian behind me becoming nervous. Then I felt the gun pressed against my neck. It was a clear warning that if I was leading them into a trap, I should fall first!

I opened the door into the cellar. A candle was burning there, and the two small boys were standing with their mouths wide open and staring at me and the soldiers. They looked so thin and pale and frightened they might have been carved out of stone. Immediately the Russian saw them, he took the gun off my neck and broke into loud laughter. "Oh, children!" he shouted. The other Russian smiled and let his rifle drop to his side. Then he turned to me and indicated that the search was off, and I was to return upstairs with them. Actually I was more nervous on the way upstairs than on the way down. In reaction my legs shook so much I nearly fell twice on the steps. They took me outside the house and stood me up against the door post, aimed and shot . . . not *at* me, but to each side of me. Then they turned and left me standing there, turned to stone now, in relief and astonishment.

The moment they had gone I rushed back indoors and to Heiner. He was in a far worse state than I was. He thought the shots he had heard were the end of us all. When he recovered a bit, we went down to the boys and hugged them. We kept telling them there would be no more raids, no more shooting, and that they could sleep upstairs in their beds again.

Wolfgang and Klaus were not much impressed.

"But what happened to the blind princess?" they urged. "Did she get her eyes back again?"

The next morning Kladow seemed strangely silent. We peeped out again through our shutters. Brilliant sunshine outside, but not a sign of either Russian or German soldiers.

"We don't know a thing," said Heiner. "Who won the battle last night? Where are they all?"

Then we saw something lying in the road some way off but Heiner would not leave the house to investigate. "Don't be mad," he said to me. "Leave well alone and wait and see what happens next," as I made as though to go out myself. An hour passed and still nothing happened. Heiner started busying himself in the cellar. Very quietly I unlocked the front door and slipped out and into the road. It was, I found, thickly strewn with pieces of German uniforms. What we had seen from the window was a heap of discarded coats. Now I knew for certain who had lost the battle. I bent down and picked up one of the coats. It was in good condition. The thought crossed my mind that I could make something warm for the boys out of it, perhaps a pair of trousers each. Hastily I grabbed three military overcoats and ran back to the house.

Heiner was angry. "It's a mad thing to do. If the Russians find them they'll think we are hiding German soldiers here, or have given them civilian clothes in exchange. They'll shoot us."

"I'll cut them up quickly and burn the rest of the material," I promised. "I'll hide the part I cut out too. The boys *must* have some new things; they are in rags."

"All right," said Heiner in the end.

All that long morning we four sat indoors behind closed shutters and locked doors. So too apparently did the rest of the street. No one dared to come out. No one dared to contact a neighbour. We just sat indoors and waited to see what happened next.

In the afternoon, there was a hard knocking on the door. Heiner ran up to his roof-hole to hide and I opened to them. This time there was a Russian guard and a German civilian whom I had never seen before in Kladow. He informed me curtly that the house was requisitioned for a Russian doctor and his staff, and that they would arrive in half an hour's time. We were to leave at once.

I began to plead. I had two children I told him. We had nowhere to go. He shrugged his shoulders. "What can I do about it?" he asked coldly. He was just turning to go when I had an idea.

"Can we please stay in the cellar? We could keep completely out of the way."

The German spoke to the Russian guard. Then he turned back and said that the doctor himself was coming to inspect the house, and could speak some German; I had better try pleading my cause with him. Off they went. I went upstairs to Heiner and we tried to plan. But what could we do? It all rested with the Russian doctor. And even if I were allowed to stay in the cellar, how could I get food and water up to Heiner? Again I went down to the cellar for another bout of waiting. This time I didn't read to the boys. I just moved about nervously, tidying things, and rehearsing my arguments and pleas.

The Russian doctor came quite quickly. He was a well-educated and reserved type of man and seemed to like the house very much. At last, and when he had seen everything upstairs, I began to plead.

"Please, I have two small children; please can we stay in the cellar? We have a side entrance; we could go out through that. The cellar door could be barricaded up, and we need never bother you at all." That's how I began. Other arguments I, of course, used about cleaning and cooking and gardening for them if necessary.

The doctor began to hesitate. I could see he didn't really like the idea at all. But at last I could think of nothing else except to bring the children up to plead for themselves. They came up and stood there together, and said, "Good evening", very quietly and timidly. He looked at them, seeing no doubt the fear in their eyes, and the signs of semi-starvation and tiredness on their faces.

"Oh, all right, then. You can stay, but for goodness' sake keep out of our way. I don't want to catch sight of any of you, do you understand?"

I began to thank him profusely and his face at last relaxed into a smile. At this I dared to ask one more favour.

"And what is that?" he said, taken for a moment off his guard.

"My husband," I began.

"Your husband?" he said, his voice changing rapidly. "And what about your husband?"

I told him that Heiner was crouching upstairs under the roof, and had been for days. The doctor's face grew red with anger. I rushed on to tell of Heiner's work in the hospitals, of how he had stopped till the last minute because of the wounded.

"The hospitals? What does your husband do then?"

I told of Heiner's work—no doubt I rated his qualifications pretty high, but that didn't matter much, anything to maintain the sudden interest I had aroused.

"Send for him," said the Russian suddenly. "I would like to speak to him."

In an astonishingly short time Heiner and the doctor had become, if not friends, at any rate friendly colleagues. They began discussing technical treatments and hospital equipment, and I was almost forgotten. Suddenly the doctor stopped talking and turned to me.

"You can stay in the cellar. Your husband must not go outside the house, but you can take what you need downstairs in the way of cooking things, but don't take any furniture."

Suddenly the boys shouted: "They're coming." I glanced up. They were indeed coming. Not just one or two soldiers with the doctor, but what looked like a whole regiment driving over our garden and up to the front door. How on earth could all these men sleep in the house? We opened the front door to them, gave one look at their expressionless faces, and fled to the cellar. The house was theirs from now on.

In the cellar we sat and listened. A terrific noise was going on over our heads with the trampling of what sounded like a hundred feet. Doors banged, heavy things were pulled about and coarse, strange voices shouted. I thought of my polished floors. What a waste of energy they had proved. Would there be any floors at all left I wondered.

I had put lace curtains across the cellar window and we watched the Russians or rather we watched their legs and feet. We saw horses trampling down our rose beds, and a truck go straight over our fence. Within a few days the beauty of our garden had been wiped out as though it had never existed.

That night we could not sleep, and I did not even undress. The noise was awful, and there was loud music as well. Were they dancing? Certainly they were drinking as I could hear the shouting become wilder and wilder. I became more and more nervous. The Russian doctor had promised that no one should molest me, but I knew the reputation of the Russian soldiers when drunk. How long would I be left in peace even with Heiner's protection?

The next morning was little Klaus' birthday. My heart was very heavy and sad. There was nothing for him at all. No gifts and no food worth eating. All we had for that day was some very watery flour soup. Indeed I wondered how on earth I should cook even that, as our only stove was in the entrance hall upstairs. Last night Klaus had been jumping up and down on his bed shouting: "Tomorrow is my birthday," and I would give him nothing.

Heiner looked at us all and dressed slowly and thoughtfully. Then he opened the cellar door and went upstairs to the Russians. After a time he came back. He was smiling from ear to ear. He had some bread, some hot water for our substitute coffee, and even some jam. Klaus began to sing with delight. "It's my birthday," he kept shouting at us. "I knew there would be something on my birthday." Heiner told me the Russians had told him to come back at lunch time. That sounded very hopeful, perhaps they were going to be kind to us after all.

Some of this optimism affected the boys, for no sooner was my back turned, than both of them slipped up the cellar stairs and went to visit the Russians. Not daring to show myself I sat on the top step and hoped to grab one of them as they passed. But I need not have worried. After a time they returned quite merrily on their own with their hands full of sweets!

"The Russians are very nice. We are going back another day," Wolfgang announced cheerfully.

At lunch time Heiner brought down a dish full of marvellous food—potatoes mixed with big lumps of meat and some carrots. We hadn't had such a meal for months and months, no meal ever tasted better than that lunch in our cellar on Klaus's sixth birthday. One thing was now quite obvious to us the Russians were not nearly so bad as our propaganda had painted them. They gave handfuls of sweets to enemy children, and handed out good food to grown-ups. This was not the treatment we had been warned to expect.

We were of course very lucky to have the Russian doctor in charge. The men were well disciplined, and the officers had complete control over them. Only one incident upset me. One day, while Heiner was upstairs, a Russian soldier slipped down to the cellar and gripped my arm and tried to become intimate with me. I screamed and shouted for help. Fortunately Heiner heard and came rushing down followed by the doctor. When the doctor saw the situation he shouted at the soldier and ordered him out of the house altogether. He had to live in the garden from then on no matter what the weather was like. I was amazed at the time. I did not know how severe the penalties were for disobeying an officer in the Russian Army.

We were very lucky having the Russian doctor with us. In the other houses the men went in and out, and raped girls and women just when they liked. They behaved worse than animals in many cases. In the next road to ours, some of them tried to rape a woman and her husband rushed into the room to save her. One of the Russians was so furious that he shot him, and then raped the woman in front of the dying husband. I met her some time later. She had a little son and was in terrible despair. All she could say was: "If only I hadn't screamed. If only I hadn't screamed." She dragged herself along, looking utterly dejected, with the little boy holding her hand. I heard she left Kladow soon afterwards.

One of the most frightening things in those days was the fact that we were not allowed to lock our doors. All the women had to sleep completely unprotected and the Russians had access to anyone they liked. If they found no woman in the place they would often wreck the furniture in their rage.

In the centre of Berlin the battle was raging and Hitler was still alive. Many of the Berliners had fled to the tunnels of the Underground to escape the shelling and firing. The coaches of the underground railway had been turned into hospital wards, and thousands of wounded were lying there. Bombed-out families lay on the stone platforms; some had a little food, some had none. But all were in despair, poor and hungry, trying to keep alive just a few days longer.

Their end came violently and suddenly. They looked up with strained eyes one morning and saw a great flood of water roaring through the tunnels towards them. The river walls had been blown up and the tunnels flooded. Thousands were drowned like rats in the tunnels underneath Berlin.

We did not hear of Hitler's actual end for some time. We did not know that he had committed suicide, or that he had married Eva Braun. What we did hear came to us in a communiqué from Military Headquarters signed by Hitler's successor Admiral Döenitz on 1 May 1945. "Leading the heroic defenders of the capital, the Führer died. He has sacrificed his life for his people, and saved Europe from Bolshevism. This example of 'Faithful unto death' must be obeyed by all soldiers. It is an order."

An order that was not obeyed for Berlin capitulated the next day 2 May 1945.

The Russians went mad with victory. The soldiers in our rooms behaved like children. Wolfgang and Klaus were thrown handfuls of sweets. Naturally they, too, went wild with delight.

Berlin had now ceased to be the capital of Germany. It was now an occupied city with the hammer and sickle, and soon the Allied flags, hanging everywhere. It is still to us a tragic city, the scene of conflicts between east and west. None of us know how many years it will be before the whole of Berlin is really German again or, when this happens, whether the young people growing up under the Soviet ideology will feel part of their own country.

The Russians started to celebrate at once. The Russian doctor invited Heiner to his party in the evening. I laughed when Heiner told me.

"Don't be absurd," I said. "You're not going, of course? You can't sit there celebrating your own defeat, surely?"

Heiner flushed. "Do you think I *like* the idea? But if I refuse? How far does that get us?"

He was right, I realized. How far would it get us to sit bunched in the cellar all night with only our pride to keep us alive. Anyway the doctor's invitation was partly an order . . . he *wished* Heiner to be present, and that was that. He left it as late as possible before going upstairs even though the Russians kept shouting for him. He had become very popular with the men as he helped with the stove, and with many odd jobs they couldn't manage. The doctor called him frequently to discuss new X-ray treatments in the hospitals. In fact they almost regarded him as a friend and not as an enemy by now.

How ironic it all was. One moment I was laughing bitterly, the next I wanted to cry. Heiner had gone upstairs into all that noise while I sat with the boys who couldn't even sleep. But I wasn't alone for long. Heiner came back. He looked rather serious.

"Well?" I asked. "What's the news this time?"

He hesitated.

"Out with it," I said.

"Darling, you are invited as well."

"Good lord!" I said, and jumped to my feet. "Are they crazy? Can't they leave one of us out of it?"

Heiner said. "Please, darling, do be sensible. They don't mean any harm. They like you, you know."

"Tell them I'm ill," I told him. "Like me?". I began to laugh hysterically. "Do you really want me to go up and be pawed about by a lot of . . ." I hesitated to find an ugly enough word.

Heiner was utterly shocked. "Else, you've got me all wrong. It isn't that at all. They think you're an artist, and they respect all artists. The doctor told me one of his colleagues is coming tonight who attended lectures at the University in Berlin, they both want to meet you."

I began to cry. Heiner went on urging me to go upstairs. "It will make all the difference to our existence down here," he said at last. "Surely you can put up as bold a front as I can? Think of the boys; they will take it as an insult if you don't come up." There was nothing for it then but to go. I tucked the boys up, kissed them good-night, and walked upstairs with Heiner.

Our lounge was crammed full of Russian soldiers. They were all smoking and drinking. As I came in every man turned to stare at me. At first I thought I was the only woman present. Then I saw the nurse Heiner had spoken of several times. She was the Russian doctor's "girl friend", and they were sleeping together quite openly in my bedroom upstairs. I realized that she was not at all pleased at my appearance. Any kind of competition for the men's attention was a nuisance. It showed very plainly on her face. I ignored the men's looks and smiles and walked straight over to her. I greeted her enthusiastically and found that she could speak some German. I explained that I was not feeling well but had come upstairs so as not to hurt anyone's feelings. Could she please help me to leave as soon as possible.

She was quite delighted and smiled at me. "Of course," she said. "You must stay while we are eating and perhaps you had better have a dance or two with the special guests invited, but keep an eye on me and I will tell you when it is all right for you to disappear." Then she added very pointedly. "If you don't go when I give the hint, it's on your own head. Once the men have had too much to drink, they'll never let you go."

I took it as a warning, and thanked her.

We sat down to a meal at once at my table. There was no cloth on it nor any table mats. I did not know whether to laugh or cry when I saw a Russian with a dish of hot food, slap it down on the polished surface. Many white rings were already burnt on it—so I supposed a few more didn't matter. I must put up with minor things like that, but winced as each new hot pan went down on that lounge table!

Another shock was the meal itself. We were given one plate each but nothing more. No spoons, knives, or forks. The Russians just dipped into the bowls with their fingers and took out what they wanted. I looked at Heiner. The look in his eyes said: "When in Rome, do as the Romans do." So I fished into the bowl and got a nice large piece of meat. There was bread lying around on the table. I took some and ate it with the meat. Then I gnawed at my bones just as the others did in true animal fashion. The only habit

I just couldn't follow was to throw my bones under the table when I had gnawed them sufficiently. I laid mine at the side of the plate instead.

All through the meal the Russians smoked vigorously. The cigarettes were put down on the polished table. In fact by the end of the meal my lounge table was just one vast ash tray with burns, and stubbed out cigarettes. If it all seems very vivid for a thing that happened so long ago, it is simply because I still *have* that table. We were given vodka to drink. It burnt my mouth terribly and Heiner could scarcely swallow it. But the Russians urged us again and again to drink, and found our gulps and grimaces highly amusing.

After the meal we danced. I danced with the doctor and with his colleague. The latter spoke fluent German, and was an excellent dancer. He told me of his life as an undergraduate in Berlin. He said he hated war, and he hated to see Berlin in ruins. But what could one do? He shrugged his shoulders in resignation. His extraordinary tolerant attitude amazed me. He did not seem to blame us for the war or to be vindictive over our past treatment of his countrymen. Nor did he make me feel that I was celebrating a national humiliation. He behaved just like a charming, friendly human being enjoying a dance and a conversation. Whether he would have remained like that I do not know, as during our dance he received a note from one of the Russian soldiers, and stopped.

"I am so sorry," he apologized. "The dance was delightful, but the war is not quite finished," he added a trifle grimly, and turned round to leave. He made a very deep impression on me. He seemed a gentleman in his attitude to life.

All this time I was, of course, keeping a wary eye on the Russian nurse, and quite soon she gave me a sign to come over to her. I asked her at once if she would escort me to the cellar to keep up the bluff that I was feeling ill. I also begged that Heiner might be allowed to leave as well. I could see Heiner had already had too much vodka, and heaven only knew what would happen to him if they started playing around.

"I can't do anything about your husband," she shrugged. "And it's better if I don't interfere. He will have to look after himself."

We parted on the cellar steps, and I thanked her profusely. Then I lay down on the couch and just listened to the noises above; stamping, singing and shouting. It made a frightful contrast to my own depressed thoughts. What was happening to Heiner? Why didn't he come? Hour after hour I lay there. It was dawn when Heiner appeared. He could hardly walk. I helped him to undress, but he could not lie down. Then he was terribly sick.

For three days the Russian troops were allowed to celebrate in Berlin. The houses had to be left open and the Russians could help themselves to anything they fancied. "Berlin is yours," the troops were told.

The children and I stayed in the cellar, all day and all night. Heiner got what food he could for us. At the end of the "celebrations" I asked he doctor if I could allow the boys out of doors, and if we could possibly have some water, as we had none.

"We have no water, no gas and no food to cook," I said to him.

"All right," said the doctor. "Go and get what you need, but your husband must not leave the house, it will not be safe. Don't be away long."

I scuttled off as quickly as I could to find food and water. The tales I heard from other women soon made me realize the danger Heiner was in. The Russians were grabbing all healthy looking German civilians, and shoving them in lorries to be carted off. Most of them were never heard of again.

I saw dead German soldiers lying on the streets as I went through. They lay on the sides of the road, no one daring to come out to bury them. Passing a window of a house I looked up and saw the face of a dead soldier staring out. He was propped up against the window frame still wearing his helmet. His face was grey-yellow and apparently no one in the house dare touch him.

I could get no bread. There had been a few loaves at the bakers but by the time I reached the head of the queue they were all gone. When I turned to walk away a woman came up and called on us all to try and find bandages for the wounded. I went home at once, got what I could, and returned to a doctor's house. The doctor, a tall, strong man of about fifty, had always been known for his toughness and humour in the district, but today he had changed. When he saw me and the things I had brought he suddenly broke down and cried bitterly.

"Thank you," he began, and then: "But what is the use? What can I do? Hundreds of wounded, hundreds of dying, and no food, no drugs, just a few clean bandages."

"Can I do anything?" I asked.

"No, it's too late. Go back to your children and try to keep them alive."

There was no food to be got in our shops, but the Russians provided regular meals at lunch time for the German population. We took dishes or bowls and got food without questioning, and it was good food too. As for the children, they followed the Russians about as though each one was a Pied Piper of Hamelin. Sweets, bits of food, all came their way. The children were quite fearless and the Russians showed nothing but kindness to them.

But the bicycles! That was another matter. No bicycle was safe from a Russian. It was to them some kind of miracle. The way they learned to ride them was the funniest thing to watch. They stood and stared as a cyclist came along, and then rushed up and grabbed the bicycle. Seated on the saddle, they would push off to try and ride down the road, only to fall off immediately. They would fall a hundred times, and still get up and try again, until at last they had mastered it.

A wrist-watch was another miracle to them. I saw Russians who had strapped a dozen watches on their arms all ticking away at slightly different times—gold watches, silver watches, platinum, aluminium, chromium. They went to any lengths to add to their collections, holding up women in the street until they produced one.

The Russian doctor only stayed in our house for three weeks. Then he left with his troops, his trucks, and quite a nice collection of loot from the neighbourhood—bicycles, mattresses, a sewing machine and toys for children. When they had gone we rushed upstairs to look at our home. Three weeks' occupation had made quite a difference to its appearance and condition. The first thing that met us was the most awful smell, a mixture of sweat, perfume and toilets.

"Open the windows," Heiner called out, and we all ran to open each window in the house.

"Now for the worst of it." Heiner walked towards the bathroom and lavatory. He stumbled back, coughing. I stood behind and looked over his shoulder. Then I too had to lean against the wall. The Russians were not what one would have called "house-trained". Indeed, they must never have seen any indoor sanitation before. Everything had been wrongly used. The toilet had apparently been used to wash in. I heard afterwards they had been delighted by the brisk shower of water that came down on their heads when they flushed it. The bath had been used as a toilet pan. Heiner shut the door abruptly. "You go down to the cellar. I will call you when the worst is over."

When the nastiest part was dealt with I began to scrub. For days and days I scrubbed on my hands and knees. Then we took down the curtains (curtains that had been used as pocket handkerchiefs by the Russians) and washed them! As for the books, they lay all over the house. They had been taken from the shelves and searched for any pictures of nude women which they apparently found highly diverting. These pictures had been torn out and some were left stuck on the walls.

It took me many weeks to put the house in order. In the meantime I got a taste of what ordinary Russian occupation meant. The soldiers were roaming about the town with little to do. Our doors had to be left unlocked and our houses left open to them. Heiner insisted, however, on going out and taking his bicycle with him again.

"Please, darling," I kept saying, "please, just walk, if you must, but don't take your bicycle."

"Nonsense," he told me. "I can't go on skulking away in the house. We have got to start building up again. There is so much to be done." Off he went to the centre of Berlin and started to work again.

A new city council was formed in Kladow. We were even allowed our own mayor, one of the former gardeners in the park! An astonishing number of Germans became communist overnight! They walked around with red armlets on and did their best to make life awkward for the rest of us. One of their first orders was that we were to bring all radio sets to the town hall. Anyone who held back a set would be severely punished. At home we had four sets. Two of our own, one that belonged to my brother, and a fourth belonging to my parents, all went to the town hall. This was a small punishment, however, compared to what was happening in Berlin. There the Russians had commandeered everything. All factories were now in Russian hands. Most of them were dismantled, and the machinery sent away at once to Russia.

"If they go on like this, we shall never build up again," said Heiner. It went on until even the rails of the railways leading to Berlin had gone. "Russia needs railways," they said, and just left us a single track to the city. Slowly it dawned on us what the Allies meant by "unconditional surrender". It meant that everything was lost. We were to be reduced to a primitive people, without any material possessions left to us, or the chance of building up possessions again.

We found that the first batch of Russians that had entered Kladow were the *elite*. The next lot of troops were of a different type. Every family was examined, not by Russians, but by the new German communists among us who had changed coats so quickly. They were of course far more cruel than any Russian. They had in their hands a list of Nazi Party members from the past. Soon every Party member in Kladow had gone. All were rounded up, loaded on to waggons, and sent to Russia. Most of them never returned. Kladow became emptier and emptier. We went about in terrible fear, even more terrible than before, as this time it was right in our midst—a next-door neighbour might be the one who would give your husband away.

Thank God neither Heiner nor I were on any black-list they had compiled. They cross-examined us carefully but in the end assured us we should be left alone. They took none of our valuables. Other acquaintances were not so lucky. Some families lost not only husbands and fathers and sons, but also furniture, valuables and clothes.

Looking back I see that this was Germany's greatest tragedy for hardly had one dictatorship passed before a worse one took its place. Now it was dictatorship by the enemy. Members of the communist party got the only pickings to be had. They got bread, fats and extras; we had nothing. If they saw anything in our home, or on our persons, they wanted, they found some way to get it. The least resistance or objection and a member of the family disappeared to Russia.

There was just one vague hope on the horizon; the hope that the rumour of British troops on the way might be true. The whole question centred on Gatow aerodrome. It was rumoured that British troops wanted it for their 'planes. If it were true then surely the neighbourhood would also come under British occupation. We heard of negotiations between the Russians and the British. Then that they had stopped. And then one day it happened. Heiner came cycling back to the house from the town hall to say that the Russians were moving out!

"Perhaps others are coming in," I said despondently. "For heaven's sake, don't get optimistic too soon."

"It's all right," Heiner told me. "There's a notice board in the town hall, the Russian troops are withdrawing, and the British will be arriving tomorrow."

I don't think any occupation troops were greeted with such joy as those British soldiers in Kladow. Women threw bunches of flowers at them; children rushed to greet them.

That evening the British soldiers walked round our suburb, talking and smoking. They did not molest anyone. They distributed cigarettes and chocolates and soon had a trail of children behind them. Now after a long time Heiner and I knew freedom and peace. I can't express how happy we were. We had hope again and felt we could plan for the future.

The British troops were indeed a change from the Russians. Screams from women in the night ceased and the looting of watches and bicycles, and funnily enough the red arm-bands from some of the new German communists, disappeared! Only one enemy remained; hunger. The water supply came back and in August we even had gas to cook with. But we had nothing to cook on it, not even potatoes or vegetables. Often I was so faint with hunger that I had to walk slowly and close to the walls of the houses when I went out in case I needed to stop and lean against them. My finger-tips were full of pus and I had to bandage them continually. This made housework and washing-up very slow and awkward.

Heiner's ears began to discharge. He had no pain in them, but they became so bad he had to use ear-covers.

When he shaved and nipped his skin the scar would not heal. At night he had to lie down on the couch before he was able to sit up and take what food there was.

The boys, too, had scars on their legs, full of pus which would not heal. I had to bandage them day by day. They were always begging for something to eat, some potatoes, a piece of bread, but I had no bread to give them. They were now so weak that they did not bother to play any childish games. When they were indoors they would just lie on the carpet saying they felt tired. We went to the doctor. He took a curious view. He gave us some tablets but added that they wouldn't work a miracle. What we needed was food. We weren't really ill, we were just starved. "Eat more butter," he added ironically, as we went out.

One day in August we were at lunch, if you could call it that. I had some potato peelings with which I had mixed other vegetable parings and minced the whole lot together. As I had no fat I had put them all in a pan and tried to roast them up with some malt-coffee powder. I had kept Heiner and the boys out of the kitchen while I cooked this mess, because it smelled so awful. But Heiner was not deceived. He ate it—indeed we all ate it, every single scrap, but it was frightful. Suddenly Heiner banged his fist on the table and jumped up. "I'm going to get something to eat. I can't stand this any longer."

I jumped up too. "No, Heiner," I said. "Don't be mad. What are you going to do?"

"I'm going to the Russian zone. There's an old woman there who has a big garden. She gave me potatoes and vegetables last year maybe she'll give us some now."

"No," I said again. "It's too dangerous. They'll kill you if they catch you. We can manage. We'll go to the British and beg."

"We shan't get anything from them; they are not going to feed us. They have only enough for themselves."

He reminded me what a good friend the Russian doctor

had been, and how well we had got on with the Russians in our house.

"They liked me all right, they won't shoot me. I'll manage. If I don't go we'll soon all be starved to death anyway."

He got his bicycle from the garage and I gave him a blouse of mine as a gift for the woman with the garden. It was a pretty blouse and of good material; it might perhaps soften her heart a little.

"I ought to get some good vegetables for that," said Heiner, smiling cheerfully.

We all stood round as he strapped his rucksack over his shoulders. The boys were very happy and he was full of wild promises of the nice things he would bring them back to eat. But I felt depressed and despondent.

"Cheer up," he told me, as he kissed my cheek and waved merrily to us. "It won't be long before I am back with the dinner!"

He waved once more as he turned the bend in the road. Then he was gone.

The afternoon went but Heiner did not return. The boys refused to go to bed as they wanted to wait for the nice surprise. They had talked of nothing else most of the day. When it got really late I prepared a water-flour soup for them, and promised that if they would go to bed I would wake them up for a feast when "Vati" returned.

Slowly the light faded. Heiner did not return. I became restless and kept going to the dark windows and wandering about the house. The night fell and still no sign of Heiner. I was certain now that something terrible had happened to him. I had felt it vaguely as he rode off, now I was quite sure.

The boys slept peacefully and the clock ticked relentlessly. Presently I fell on my knees and prayed. I got up eventually and walked out into the garden and then into the street. There was utter silence; no one seemed alive in Kladow except myself. And so the night went on.

At six o'clock the next morning there was a loud knock

on my door. I rushed to open it. Heiner? No, a policeman stood outside.

"My husband?" I said quickly.

"May I come in?" he said. "Perhaps we had better sit down."

I knew then what his news was going to be. It showed in his face.

"My husband has had an accident?" I asked, for the policeman was just nervously sitting and looking round the room.

"Yes, there has been an accident," was the evasive answer.

"Is he in hospital? Which hospital?" I asked many questions very quickly.

"It has been a severe accident," the policeman hesitated. "He has concussion."

Still I had to go on trying to drag the details out of him.

"Concussion? A street accident? Is he very bad?"

"Not a street accident. It happened in the woods. He rode his bicycle over a tree-stump and fell."

"Over a tree-stump and fell and got concussion!" What a ridiculous story. As if a man could get concussion that way. I jumped up.

"I am coming with you to see him," I said. "Just wait a moment while I dress properly."

That brought out the truth as last.

"You can't see him. He's dead."

I sat down very slowly as the words sunk in. I didn't cry out or make a gesture of any kind, just sat there, looking ahead, completely numbed.

"Shall I get you a glass of water?" asked the policeman.

"No, thank you," I said mechanically. Then I began to question him again. I wanted the truth. The complete truth. *How* had Heiner died? Had the Russians killed him? Had there been a fight? Had the woman given him away?

The policeman stuck to his original story. Heiner had ridden his bicycle over a tree-stump and fallen off. As for going to see him that was quite useless and would only upset me more. But I went on persisting in my demand. I must see my husband. He must be allowed to have a proper burial. I must see my husband. At last the man gave in. "All right, then," he said. "Go to the police at Glienicke, that's where the accident happened. They will take you to your husband's body."

I took the boys to a neighbour for some kind of breakfast and rode off on my bicycle to Glienicke. I still felt absolutely numb with pain and shock. Only one thought was in my mind, I must see Heiner again. I rode on and into the Russian zone without caring. It was quite a dangerous thing to do. A woman with a nice bicycle was a great enticement to any Russian but I didn't bother this time. I found the police in the village and met their cold looks with indifference.

"I wish to be taken to see my husband's body," I told them. They refused point-blank. It was too far away, and what was the point of it anyway? He was dead, and they could give me the death certificate there and then if I liked.

"I wish to be taken to his body," I said again. "I am his wife, and it is my right."

They became angry then. But I insisted. We argued for a long time but in the end I won. The three men got up and we walked towards the woods. None of us spoke a word. It was quiet and hot in the wood. The August sun had been shining for many days on the trees. I smelt the warm scents as we walked along.

Then we turned a corner in the path, and I saw Heiner. He lay sprawled across the pathway in a pool of blood. He had been shot in the head and his brains were scattered on the ground. Over his eye was a hole where the bullet had gone through. His rucksack lay not far from him still filled to the brim with food. Some pears had rolled out of it. The bicycle had gone.

I did not kneel down beside him because of the blood.

So I bent and kissed his cold, stiff hand. The "foreman of the angels" had been shot dead, on his way back from getting us fruit and vegetables of which we were in such desperate need.

At last I got the truth from the police. Two Russian soldiers had seen him with the bicycle and had demanded it. Heiner had refused and tried to laugh it off. He had told them the war was over now, and they couldn't have it, so they had shot him and got it that way. It was as simple as that.

13

England Has Been Good to Me

TWELVE years have passed by since that day in the woods.
I went back and carried on the struggle for my boys' lives
as best I could. With other Berliners I plunged from the
"hot" into the "cold" war that came afterwards. I struggled
on through the Berlin blockade of 1948 and was working
in Gatow aerodrome when the air-lift started, and the
Allied 'planes roared in.

It was an unforgettable night, when the 'planes brought
us food and help. We stayed on till midnight preparing
meals and finding accommodation for the crews. It was
good to have been in that all-night shift. I felt that Heiner
was working by my side urging me on in this magnificent
gesture of defiance of the Communist blockade.

*   *   *

A very few years ago I came to England and began to
build up a new life here with the boys. It has not been easy,
but it began with a very good omen, an omen of kindness
and fair play that I certainly did not expect.

I had hurried from the ship to the waiting train. I asked
someone if this was the right train, and jumped into a
compartment, and settled down. I noticed as I put my
luggage on the rack that the compartment was very nicely
upholstered. I had heard in Germany that the English no
longer had third-class compartments like ours, but this was
really luxurious. I began to talk to the lady opposite
me and discovered she was a German too. Presently the

253

ticket collector came: I handed him my ticket. He bent down.

"This is a first-class compartment. You have a third-class ticket, madam."

His words frightened me. I changed colour and looked round the compartment. What could I say, that I was a foreigner and had made a mistake? He would reply: "Foreigner or not, you can read numbers, can't you? Look at the number on the door."

I got up quickly to reach for my suitcase. "I am so sorry," I began to mumble, feeling all eyes in the compartment upon me. I fully expected a fine, my name and address taken, and some unpleasant words.

Instead, an astonishing thing happened. The ticket collector bent down, put a hand on my shoulder and said very quietly: "Stay here. I'm sure you didn't realize . . . but be more careful in future!", and off he went, whistling a tune.

It sounds a silly tale to English people perhaps but you have not had years under a terrible regime. I felt I had cheated the railway company and that therefore I should be punished, the more so because I was a German. Instead I got kindness, a smile, and a very pleasant ride in a first-class compartment to which I was not entitled!

That first little omen indicated other kindnesses to follow. For England has been good to me in many ways. I have been able to give German lessons; I have demonstrated German cookery on T.V., and much of Klaus' and Wolfgang's education has been in English schools. There is in your country great kindness and generosity towards a former enemy.

I have also heard, of course, other opinions of us. I was terribly unhappy when I first read accounts of German atrocities in books, such as Lord Russell's and in Sefton Delmer's grim articles in the *Daily Express*. People came to me and asked over and over again, how could you let it happen? They were Germans who committed these atrocities, weren't they?

Yes, they were Germans all right, and I don't know how to answer for them. Although it was only a minority who committed these crimes, and although it was kept secret from the ordinary German people, none of it can be explained away lightly. All I can do is to tell my own story, and try to show how our guilt came home to us in the end.

Today I have also to answer questions about the "miracle" of German recovery. Why have we recovered so quickly? Why are so many of our cities built up again and our factories thriving? Because we are great workers. There is, however, another side to the picture; the many widows who plod on in the background day by day, year by year, just scraping together a bare existence for themselves and their children. They too are Germans. You have only to visit some of the displaced people's camps in Germany to see the full aftermath of suffering from the war. All is not happiness by any means over there any more than it is anywhere in the world today.

I have told the story of Berlin and exposed my own tragedy in so doing. All I hope is that it will help in some small way to a better understanding between Mr. and Mrs. Schmitt on the one side and Mr. and Mrs. Smith on the other.